THE EAVES
OF
HEAVEN

by

Andrew X. Pham

on behalf of my father,

Thong Van Pham

THE EAVES
OF
HEAVEN

A Life
in
Three Wars

HARMONY BOOKS NEW YORK

All rights reserved.
Published in the United States by
Harmony Books, an imprint of the
Crown Publishing Group, a division of
Random House, Inc., New York.
www.crownpublishing.com

Harmony Books is a registered trademark
and the Harmony Books colophon is a
trademark of Random House, Inc.

Library of Congress Cataloging-in-
Publication Data
Pham, Andrew X., 1967–
    The eaves of heaven : a life in three
wars / by Andrew X. Pham on behalf of
my father, Thong Van Pham.—1st ed.
    1. Pham, Thong Van. 2. Vietnamese
Americans—Biography. 3. Refugees—
United States—Biography. 4. Vietnam—
History—20th century. I. Title.
E184.V53P4554   2008
973'.0495—dc22
   [B]   2007033894

ISBN 978-0-307-38120-0

Printed in the United States of America

DESIGN BY BARBARA STURMAN

10 9 8 7 6 5 4 3 2 1

First Edition

HUMBOLDT PARK

IN MEMORY OF MY MOTHER
WHO TAUGHT ME COMPASSION
    AND SACRIFICE
AND MY FATHER
WHO TAUGHT ME REASON AND
    JUSTICE

AND FOR MY WIFE
WHO SUPPORTED ME THROUGH
    ALL MY STRUGGLES
AND MY CHILDREN
WHO BROUGHT ME JOY

THONG VAN PHAM

If I could,

I would trade

a thousand

years to hear

my mother's

laughter.

TRAN TRUNG DAO

CONTENTS

AUTHOR'S NOTE

It seems that as memoirists, we are not historians, not even of our own lives. That is the job of biographers. Memoirs are our love letters and our letters of apologies, both. They hold our few gems, the noteworthy lessons of our journeys.

I did not set out to write my father's biography. I have not written my father's memoir. I have lent his life stories my words. The perspectives and sentiments within are his.

Except for the obvious and the famous, many names have been changed, primarily to make it easier for people who may not want to appear in his life story.

This work, the distillation of years of collaboration, has been my greatest pleasure and honor.

ANDREW X. PHAM

THE EAVES
OF
HEAVEN

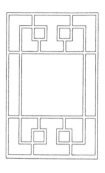

PROLOGUE

ANCESTORS

My family came from the Red River Delta, an alluvial plain of raven earth and limitless water. It was an exceptionally fertile country, though not a youthful land with treasures to be plundered. What riches it had, it yielded solely to sweat and toil. It had known centuries of peasant hands.

Generations beyond recall, my ancestors had tilled this soil where fortunes were made and reversed by countless successions of insurgencies, raids, and wars. The rise of our clan began with my great-great-great-grandfather Hao Pham, a noted officer in King Nguyen Anh's army. For his battlefield victories against rebellious warlords, he was awarded a vast tract of land after the king's unification of Viet Nam in 1802. As was customary in the feudal order for the richest man in the area, he won the privilege of lord proctorship over all the villages within a day's ride by horseback of his home. He assumed the post, raised a big family with three wives, and lived out his days in comfort. When he retired, his eldest son succeeded him, acquiring the same commission. Later, in the French colonial period, when the clan's property had grown even larger, his grandson became domain magistrate. So it went from generation to generation, both land and titles passed as birthrights from fathers to the firstborn sons. By the time of my grandfather and father, ours grew to be one of the two richest clans in the province, our holdings spreading out to the horizon.

Still, it was a realm of rice paddies, mud houses, and shoeless peasants. It was a world before the arrival of electricity, banks, and refrigeration. In the whole province, there were only two cars. My uncle Thuan owned one, but kept it merely as a modern marvel. He was more comfortable astride a horse. In our village of a thousand souls, there was a single firearm—a double-barreled shotgun Uncle used to hunt birds. For weaponry, there were swords, spears, and martial arts. The only other technological intrusions into our village were two mechanical clocks; my father owned one, and my uncle owned the other. Prized collectibles, neither was used to tell the hour. For that, there were the crows of the cock, the height of the sun, and the length of one's shadow. The average peasant owned three sets of clothes, brown or black pajamas, the same exact outfit in varying degrees of wear, with the newest reserved for holidays and temple visits. He rose before dawn and labored till dusk, and might expect to have a small amount of meat with his dinner. In the material sense, it was a simpler world. There was little, and yet everything, to be desired. Though perhaps as flatlanders we lacked imagination. Folks prayed for good health, good weather, and good crops. And that strange year, the last of the good years, all things were granted. Heaven laid the seal of prosperity upon our land. We were blessed with the most bountiful harvest in memory.

That summer, Uncle Thuan, the head of our clan, confessed to his third wife that he believed the wind of fortune was shifting, and that, at thirty-nine years of age, he felt disaster looming. Omens had shown themselves. First, the string of good years crowned by a historic crop signaled a grave imbalance in nature; another cycle was approaching. Second, a crow, that provincial harbinger of death, had alighted in his courtyard and stared into his audience hall. The scarecrows he had erected hadn't prevented the cursed bird from paying him another visit. Last, he dreamt that the bamboo hedge encircling our ancestral estate was filled with voices speaking a foreign tongue; an evil had laid siege to our home. Within days of this nightmare, talk of war was rampant throughout the countryside. Disturbing reports came through his intelligence channels. The underground worlds were gathering their forces. A great storm approached, so warned his Nationalist informants; so concurred his Communist agents. Then, the colonial French suppressed and denied the rumor, which naturally made it a fact. The shadow of war had fallen upon the world. Dark days would sweep down from China. Within weeks, World War II would reach the Red River Delta on the heels of the Japanese army and mark the downfall of our clan.

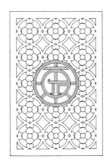

1. LEAVING HOME

Right after my high school graduation in 1956, I found myself on a bus headed north to a small coastal town where a summer teaching position awaited me. Outside the windows, the ratty fringe of Saigon slipped away— dirt lanes and sewage creeks banked by weathered shacks and smoldering fires. Women stooped with age swept smooth the bare ground in front of their homes. Naked toddlers stood in doorways, knuckling sleep from their eyes. Fresh incense on roadside altars sent tendrils of prayers heavenward. Above the mottled tin roofs, early sun flicked through the foliage. A breeze carried the grassy scent of paddy water. I was twenty-one and striking out on my own for the first time. I had a suitcase with two pairs of slacks, three white shirts, underwear, a toothbrush, a bar of soap, and a comb. My first week's wages would afford me another pair of trousers and a shirt. It wouldn't be appropriate for the students to notice their new teacher's meager wardrobe.

Passengers outnumbered seats on the bus, but the

driver kept on picking up more people along the way, the ticket-man happily pocketing their fares. The bag-man roped the luggage together in a great camel-hump on the roof: bamboo cages of ducks and chickens, wooden crates, boxes, rucksacks, bundles of fresh vegetables. A number of people spent their whole trip standing or sitting on their valises crammed in the aisle. Some used the bus as a local shuttle service to nearby villages.

It was a Friday, so there were plenty of travelers, too many toddlers for a peaceful journey. Somewhere up front, a baby wailed relentlessly. A ruckus broke out at the rear. A rooster had gotten loose and half the bus erupted into flurries of hands, feathers, and screams. The owner leaped over two rows of seats, caught his rooster by the neck, and landed in the lap of a merchant woman. She said, "Thank you, Buddha, but what's a granny like me to do with two roosters?" Trader-women hooted. A plump matron said, "I'll take the big one, he's not so bad looking." Another chortled and said, "The feathery one has more stud potential." They cackled, and the man, red-faced, crept back to his seat with his bird tucked safely in a sack. The women continued cajoling as though they were sitting at home. Their cheerful mood was infectious, and I felt rather buoyant, even though I was wedged between an old man, who squatted barefoot in his seat, and the window. But having the window was enough for me to consider this as a propitious beginning. Lightheaded with freedom, I felt as though I was flying on newly discovered wings.

It seemed so effortless, as if I had, by receiving a diploma, strolled through a magical portal, and left behind my whole family crowded in a shed of a house. The ease by which this job came to me made it seemed like destiny. Things had been difficult since we fled Hanoi two years ago, so I loved feeling that I was at last on the right path. All I did was answer the first ad I saw in the *Saigon Daily*. It was a math and science position at a private school. After a few letters, I was granted an interview.

The principal came to my family's noodle shop. Mr. Thinh Nguyen was a short, thick-bodied man in his late forties, with a small hump on his back, which he immediately explained was from a motorcycle accident. Despite this handicap, he was elegant in his movements and had the graceful glide-walk of a short-legged man. He smoked small French-style cigarettes made in Vietnam.

By our accents, we knew we were both northerners. As it turned out, he had studied in Hanoi and roomed not far from our old neighborhood. I told him my family were refugees, arriving two years ago under the Geneva Accord, which gave the Vietnamese Communists the northern half of the country. He said he had to leave his home a few years before then. Like most refugees, he didn't talk about why he fled or what he left behind, and that was fine with me. Everyone had lost something. No one willingly chose an impoverished exile, dislocated from his birth-village and the spirits of his ancestors. I respected his silence and he did not press me for details of our plight. I appreciated the courtesy. Looking around at the rancid hovel in which my entire family lived and worked—the crude tables, the dirt floor, the windowless loft—I thought it would sound vaunted or, perhaps, blatantly false if I tried to explain who we once were, or spoke of our lineage. It wasn't shame; we were beyond that.

As soon as we started talking about my academic records, he switched over to French. I liked it because I felt more comfortable in French when speaking with superiors and elders. French was more egalitarian than Viet. It was generous of him. Besides, it was natural for us to speak French, since it had been the official language of academia in Vietnam for longer than we had been alive. Generations of Vietnamese students spent lifetimes in classrooms speaking, writing, reading, and breathing French texts. So it did not seem ironic to me then that we sat there, two North Vietnamese exiles in a dark and greasy noodle shop on the edge of Saigon, conversing in French when neither one of us had ever set foot in France. We both had suits of Parisian cut and sported Western haircuts, and were more well-read in French poetry and European literature than most French soldiers. And yet, if we saw a Frenchman strolling toward us, we might, out of revulsion, cross the road to avoid him. The language had become a condition of our lives. It did not occur to us to scorn it or discard it from our tongues. It would have been impossible to try.

As the principal started talking about his school, his quaint town, and the fine French things he enjoyed, I thought of the manicured villas around our neighborhood in Hanoi; the fabulous bistros my father frequented with the whole family; the bouillabaisse, the croissants, and the ice cream. The best times of my life in Hanoi came flitting back into my head. Soon I was swimming in romanticism, drawing parallels between Hanoi and Phan Thiet, even though the most I'd seen of Phan Thiet until then had been little sketches on the labels of fish sauce bottles. As for the looks of the town or its people, I hadn't a clue, although I imagined it to be some idyllic fishing village of white beaches lined with coconut palms, maybe with an ice cream parlor where I could enjoy a peach melba after a swim.

"Most of my teachers are moonlighting from the public schools. You won't feel alone," he said after we had chatted amiably for about an hour. "I only have three teachers on my permanent staff, and this position is for the only full-time science-math teacher for the tenth, eleventh, and twelfth grades. It's only three morning classes and the job comes with room and board. Do you think you're ready to teach?"

"Yes, sir."

"Congratulations, you've got the job. With your father's permission, we'll start you in your own classroom next week."

My father was concerned, with good reason, that a job far from home might sidetrack me from my goal of a higher education. However, he disapproved of my recent involvement in students' political demonstrations, some of which had turned violent. He knew that a summer out of town would keep me out of trouble. On top of that, we needed the money. Our *pho* restaurant, my father's ill-conceived attempt to bring northern cooking to the southerners, was on the verge of collapse, taking with it the last bit of a mighty family fortune that went back many generations. We had lost everything in the fall of Hanoi. With financial catastrophe looming, he swallowed his protests and made me promise that I would write every week and return to attend Saigon University in the fall.

To escape, I would have promised him all the fish in the Saigon River.

On the 28th of July, two years ago, my family had fled Hanoi in a huge Dakota cargo plane. We were traveling with my stepmother's parents and their other daughter, who was my age. The cargo hold was packed with refugees sitting on the baseboard of the plane and clinging to straps and netting. We landed at Saigon's airport. Disoriented after a long and turbulent flight, we stumbled off the plane, anxious to get out of the cramped hold and put our feet on the ground again. Half the people were covered in vomit. We huddled in the shade of the plane, each toting a single allotted valise, and squinted at our new homeland. It felt like a foreign country.

The airport was three times larger than Gia Lam Airport in Hanoi. The tarmac sprawled in every direction. Buildings and gigantic hangars lined the long runway. Squadrons of warplanes and cargo carriers were parked in neat rows. The humid air was impregnated with the sting of fuel and engine exhaust. Convoys of trucks rumbled back and forth across the tarmac. Crews were unloading and refueling the cargo planes. They were flying nonstop around the clock, transporting refugees, French troops, and equipment out of the North. A somber mood of retreat permeated the scene.

A fat Chinese-Vietnamese man wearing a khaki colonial hat, a white short-sleeved shirt, khaki pants, and a pair of sandals took a list from the French sergeant, and then came forward to welcome us with open arms. He beamed a generous smile, which immediately put us North Vietnamese on guard.

"Welcome to Saigon, misses and children. My name is Mr. Fourth," he said.

It took us a moment to grasp his southern accent. Among other things, he got the "v" and "o" sounds mixed up with the "z" and "u."

His phrasing sounded very odd. Older people flinched, as North Vietnamese commonly addressed a group by saying "Dear ladies, dear gentlemen." I would later learn that "misses and children" was the southern way of saying "folks" and that South Vietnamese seldom called each other by their first names, but by the order of their birth. If a man was the firstborn, they called him "Second" because the title "First" belonged to the village headman. Accordingly, Mr. Fourth was the third-born in his family.

He had us board two buses to go to our temporary lodgings. Outside the airport, orchards and houses lined the busy, fume-choked road. Without rice fields, the land looked drier than in the North. We passed through a tin-shack slum. The air above the roofs wavered with heat. It was a sprawl of rust and decay. The streets were bare, unpaved. Mounds of putrid garbage stewed in the sun. There wasn't a single tree to shoulder the searing heat. Women wore pajama-like clothes and wrapped checkered scarves on their heads. Most men went shirtless and shoeless, covering themselves with only a pair of shorts or a sarong that came halfway down their thighs. There were small groceries, motorbike repair shops, and fruit vendors with strange bright-colored fruits piled high in baskets and bananas hanging under the awnings. Closer to Saigon proper, there were more two- and three-story buildings, dwellings mixed in with shops and warehouses. Every sidewalk was teeming with kiosk-diners filled with shirtless men drinking. People ate right on the street, their backs to the thrumming traffic, their heads swimming in engine exhaust. It was a sobering sight because in Hanoi only the expensive restaurants and bistros put tables on the sidewalk. The cheapest vendors would be the ones putting low benches on the side of the road for customers. In Hanoi everyone was fully clothed; even laborers didn't go outside shirtless, much less sit down to eat. Saigon seemed to me a very unruly, graceless city. It might have been uplifting to see the city center, but the bus took a meandering route, veering on the outskirts and turning onto one small street after another until we arrived in Saigon's Chinatown.

Compared to Hanoi's Chinatown, which spanned a few city blocks, Cho Lon was practically a city. It coexisted side by side with Saigon like an unattractive sibling; it was grimy, bustling, cacophonous. The buildings were crammed together, as if they grew on top of one another. Every door was a storefront with bins of goods, produce, and meats spilling onto the sidewalk. Upstairs were offices with placard billboards and living quarters with laundry hanging out the windows. The city generated its own breeze, a mixture of sewage, garbage, aromatic noodle soup, baked buns, dishwater, roast duck, and mildew.

It was, in fact, the powerhouse of South Vietnam. Cho Lon Chinese controlled the vast majority of trading houses, which also handled the shipping and warehousing of every conceivable commodity for domestic consumption and export.

The buses delivered us to a three-story hotel on a wide commercial street. Typical of the low-end Chinese establishments, it was a sad, dark, dingy place, manned by a humorless middle-age Chinese who couldn't summon a greeting or a smile. The lobby was an eight-by-eight-foot space with a wooden bench and a board painted with the hotel rules in Chinese and Viet. It was devoid of decoration—not a single painting, poster, or potted plant. The windowless rooms were small and hot, with clumps of cobwebs in the corners. The ceiling fans did nothing but draw out the reek of mildew and cigarettes from the peeling walls. Stuffy air from the hallway oozed into the rooms through wooden screens above the doors. There was a communal bathroom on each floor. Surprisingly, there was one redeeming feature in the building: the toilet. It was a squat affair with a cast-iron water tank mounted up near the ceiling. Back in Hanoi, where there was no sewage system, we only had pit toilets filled with calcium oxide powder, the compost collected periodically by municipal workers using ox-drawn carts. A flush toilet, I thought, was surely a sign of civilization.

But Saigon held little prospect for us to make a new life. The first week, Father roamed about town looking for work only to return well after dark empty-handed. With the Chinese manager patrolling the hall to keep people from cooking in the hotel, Stepmother made do with greasy Chinese fare and low-grade rice from street stalls. We gathered on the floor and ate the lukewarm food Stepmother laid on the straw mat.

Father didn't eat much. He sat slump-shouldered, shaking his head, talking in his quiet, defeated voice. "There's nothing. It's hopeless. They won't hire me because I'm not Chinese."

Stepmother said, "Can you look elsewhere?"

"The Chinese control everything; they own everything. Look around you; they even got the government contracts to house us northerners." Father sighed. He had handled a fair amount of government transactions in Hanoi and knew how profitable it could be.

But it was easy to forget our dire situation because the ultimate entertainment center in Saigon sat directly across the street from the hotel. It was an ugly, enigmatic compound the size of three city blocks enclosed by a tall, corrugated sheet-metal wall, looking very much like a giant construction site. There was not even a single billboard over the gate to hint at what was within. A policeman guarded the entrance and enforced a single rule: No shirt, no entry. Bare feet, body odor, and rags, however, were acceptable. Men, women, and children of all ages passed through at all hours. The place bustled during the day, but at night, it turned into a raging carnival.

It was owned by Mr. Vien the Seventh, the biggest mafia boss in South Vietnam, who had his own army based in a forest between Saigon and Vung Tau. The establishment originally started as a casino, but it grew to provide every service, material good, and entertainment imaginable. It grew until it became true to its name—The Great World. Beneath the great span of its interlacing roofs were jewelers, gold dealers, pawnshops, clothing stores, exotic-medicine purveyors, herbalists, massage parlors, theater stages, private rooms for hourly rental, opium lounges, teahouses with hostesses, nice restaurants, little noodle stands, food stalls, candy shops, bakeries, and an amusement park with, among other rides, two merry-go-round carousels and our favorite, the bumper-car arena. It even had its own climate, controlled by fans and vents.

Allowance in hands, we followed other refugees into the Great World. We lost ourselves in the crowd of gamblers, drinkers, opium users, whores, pimps, crooks, businessmen, and entertainers. While my brothers and I stayed close to the amusement park area, wasting most of our money on bumper cars, my cousin Tan ran off alone to the gambling tables.

Even Father could not resist the draw of the Great World. Within a week, he abandoned his job search and surrendered himself to the familiar comfort of the pipe. Day after day, he woke up, got dressed as though he were going to an interview, and strolled across the street directly to the opium lounge inside the Great World.

It had begun—his last, irrecoverable descent. At night, phantom ants crawled up his legs and kept him awake. We children took turns kneeling at his bedside to massage his limbs, kneading the atrophied flesh to ease his ruined nerves. Rigorous at first, then more softly in tiny, gradual increments. Slowly, gently. Slowly, gently. The addict's lullaby. It was like putting a child to sleep.

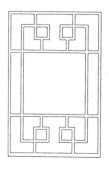

2. FATHER

When I was seven, Father heard from the nanny that, unlike my cousins, I couldn't swim. This was an acute sin for a child of the Red River Delta; after all, the entire province was practically submerged, the countryside riddled with rivers and creeks. The land was flat and low. People dug ponds for the earth needed to build the foundations of their homes. Our ancestral estate stood on dirt from four gigantic ponds, the largest of which was the size of a small lake.

Father took me out to the carp pond one afternoon. It was a hot day. My brothers and cousins followed uninvited. They were in a parade mood, giggling and skipping along behind me. A bundle of towels in hands, Chau, the buffalo boy whose main duty was taking care of the livestock, brought up the rear. We marched down the brick-paved path, hugging the shade of the longan trees, overhead birds rioting in the branches.

Father and I had just come back from one of our trips to Hanoi. My parents had a villa in the city where they often holidayed during the slow period between the planting and the harvest seasons. Father had brought me into Hanoi to enroll me in a prestigious French school. His plan to educate me in an urban setting was canceled when we, by chance, saw a Japanese sergeant draw his sword and chop off a boy's hand for stealing rice cakes at the local market. In Father's eyes, it was a clear sign of the cruelty to come, and he promptly took me back to Tong Xuyen. I was re-enrolled in our village's one-room school and was taught by my father's second cousin, Uncle Uc. I was ecstatic because I knew Father never stayed long in the countryside.

A city man, Father was never comfortable at the estate, though he did try his best to fit the part of a country nobleman. Here at the family home, he preferred the traditional gown, the dignified attire of the educated. In the humid weather, it also was far more comfortable than the Western suits that filled his wardrobe in the city. Father struck a handsome figure in either traditional or Western dress. Our relatives said he got his oval face, height, and fair skin from his mother, just as his older brother Thuan took after their father with his square jaw, stockiness, and darker complexion.

"Daddy, Daddy," cried Hong. He was four years old, Father's favorite. "I want to go on the boat."

"After your big brother learns how to swim." Father smiled and picked him up. He carried Hong the rest of the way.

"I want the big one!" Hong shouted, pointing at a rowboat the workers used to harvest water lilies. The carp pond was nearly a hundred yards wide.

Father walked me out onto the little pier. He put a hand on my shoulder and said, "Go on, son. Jump in and swim."

"Yes, Father," I said. "But I don't know how to swim."

He frowned at my lack of faith and turned to my cousins and said, "Nephew Tan, do you know how to swim?"

Tan quipped, "Of course, Uncle. I can swim all the way across the pond and back."

My cousin Tan was a natural athlete. He was precocious and bore a striking resemblance to his father. He was a month older than me, both of us born on the estate, delivered by the same doctor. Tan was Uncle Thuan's first son from his first wife, so he was heir apparent to the bulk of our ancestral fortune. He grew up with certain privileges and expectations. This made him very sure of himself, even though he had lost his mother when he was two years old. Since her death, Tan was closer to my mother than he was to his two stepmothers.

Father said, "Nephew Lang, can you swim?"

My cousin Lang just nodded and said, "Yes, Uncle."

Lang was a very good swimmer. It was the only thing he could do better than his half-brother Tan, but Lang wasn't the type to boast. In fact, it probably never occurred to him that he was better than Tan in anything. Lang was a quiet and lonesome boy, his mother's only child. Although he was technically Uncle Thuan's first son, he was relegated to a secondary status because his mother was Uncle's Thuan's second wife. Lang was older than Tan and me by a year, but he was always content to follow our lead. People said he was not normal because the doctor had to pull him out of his mother's womb with forceps, the marks still visible on his skull.

Father patted my brother Hung's head. "Even your little brother Hung can swim. Don't be afraid. Just get into the water. It'll come naturally."

"Yes, Father."

I took off my shirt and inched toward the edge, shaking because I had never jumped into deep water. Minnows darted under the shadow of the pier. The water looked cold and dark, the deep bottom thick with moss. All my cousins and younger brothers were watching me. I took a deep breath, pinched my nose, and jumped. The chilly pond swallowed me and then popped me back up.

"Stop splashing!" Father yelled. "Kick your legs back and forth. Paddle your hands like a dog."

I kicked and clawed, fighting furiously. It was no good. I kept going under. A flurry of churning limbs raised my head above the surface. Gasps of air and then under again. Tan and Lang hopped in and began treading water next to me.

"Don't touch him," Father said.

Lang shouted, "Kick your legs and paddle like this! Like this!"

I tried, but the water pushed me down. The harder I thrashed, the faster I sank. Water was drawn up my nose. I screamed and went under.

Chau, the buffalo boy, got into the water and pushed me up back onto the pier. I lay on the hot planks, coughing water out of my lungs, too scared to look at Father. He didn't say a word, his disappointment radiating in waves. My cousins were paddling about the ponds like ducks.

"Try again," Father said.

"Yes, Father." I jumped in.

I floundered, too exhausted to fight. Chau fished me out again. Ears ringing, I heaved water out of my stomach. The pond, the sky, Father had all gone woozy around me.

I understood Father must have expected a lot from me because I was his first son and someday I would inherit his fortune and carry on his line. Somehow, somewhere from my very beginning, I must have disappointed him. Since I could remember, I was always terrified of him. I was left-handed, and it annoyed him immensely. And I was naturally absentminded and clumsy. I often wore my shoes on the wrong feet. Mother regularly caught me going to school with my shirt on inside out. Food spontaneously spilled from my bowl. Things magically got knocked over whenever I came near. Every minor failure ignited Father's temper like a stick on a hornet's nest. I became so nervous in front of him, I moved like a wooden puppet, incapable of walking, talking, or eating like a normal boy.

"Try harder."

"Yes, Father."

I went in once more. The water had turned as ominous and dark as pitch. Against my limbs, it was as light as air. I flapped my arms, but fell into the depths. My lungs burned. Looking up from below, the sunlight was gentle, the sky luminous, forgiving. I felt Chau's hand on my arm. We were rising. Then I was flopped onto the pier, gasping, vomiting. I blinked the water from my eyes.

Father was already walking away. He couldn't bear to look in my direction.

3. PHAN THIET

My days in Phan Thiet had fallen into a comfortable rhythm. I lived alone in a second-floor flat as bare and simple as a fresh canvas. Nothing on the walls, no curtains on the windows; only a table, a small dresser, an oil lamp, two chairs, and a narrow divan with a straw mat for a bed. The plank floor was worn smooth, the plastered walls veined with cracks. My apartment was a studio of light: one window opened to the north, the front balcony faced west to the town center three blocks away, and the back balcony looked out to the sea and the sunrise. Two alleys of single-level houses lay between the rear balcony and the beach. From my vantage, most houses were hidden by fruit trees and coconut palms. It was like looking at the sea over a huge garden.

I taught mathematics and physics at three morning classes, four days a week. The subjects were easy, the students docile. I always left school before lunch, and I didn't socialize with the faculty because they were all much older and married. They knew I would be leaving at the end of the summer. On the home front, my land-lady and her two children, who lived below me on the first floor, were very nice but kept their distance, waiting to see if I had any bizarre habits. Suddenly I realized that I hadn't had so much free time since childhood. I found that I spoke very little outside of class since there was no one to talk to. I also discovered that I didn't need to talk. The quietness descended on me as a novelty.

With room and board included with the position, I didn't require much money and sent most of my salary home, keeping just enough pocket cash for small pleasures: fried seafood noodles at a kiosk near the park, an icy pickled lemonade on the beach, excellent dim sum by the movie theater in the town center. There was not much else to spend money on, nothing to buy, and that was the most pleasant thing about my new home. Phan Thiet was quaint, lush with coconut palms and fruit trees, drowsy with the drone of the sea. It had a lack-adaisical loveliness that I had never seen before. The whole town was steeped in idyllic lethargy; it could not be bothered to take interest in anything, certainly not in a young teacher wandering aimlessly.

Phan Thiet was a walking town. There were few bicycles. I saw no privately owned cars or motorcycles. There was no pedal-cyclo, only rickshaws. Most everyone walked, and so I developed a habit of strolling for hours from one end of town to the other, moseying down alley after alley, and combing the beach for shells that I never kept. Although I left my camera in Saigon, I couldn't help but search for good shots and imagine how I might have caught them on film. Down near the quay, sun-charred men packed fish into great wooden barrels to make fish sauce, the salt on their arms like snow. Above, a deep blue sky that would have translated into a three-quarter gray on black-and-white prints. By the salt flats, the air stung the nostrils. It was a little difficult to breathe. Small-boned women raked sea salt into gleaming white hills. They wore peasant palm hats with fabric chin-straps pulled up over their noses, looking like bandits, eyes glittering in the blinding glare. I always find my-self drawn to the water. I was enamored with the beach, its great scimitar sweep of sand sown with slender fishing boats, their war-like bowsprits to the trees.

I felt every part a stranger in this exotic land, and so took great pleasure in observing the locals. Phan Thiet people were poor, but they knew how to relax. Being fisher-folk, they also possessed the distracted ease of those who kept one eye on the ocean. They worked mostly during the cool morning, napped in the afternoon, and nibbled like birds all day long.

Their favorite snack was a rice dumpling called *banh cang*—a local specialty. Late in the afternoon, a few houses in each neighborhood set up tiny tea-tables at their front doors. For about an hour or so, at around 4:00 to 5:00 in the afternoon, they steam-baked round dumplings in clay molds over tabletop coal burners. The clam-shaped dumplings were slightly crusty on the outside and creamily gooey on the inside, garnished with a sprinkle of sautéed scallions. They were served with one of two sauces: a fiery garlic-lime-chili fish sauce or a dark gravy made from a pungent and mildly sweet sardine stew.

My neighbors, who had a mom-and-pop sundries store, weren't from Phan Thiet. They were real southerners from the Mekong Delta, even more genial than the local coastal people. Every evening after supper, they invited friends and neighbors to gather on a few wooden benches in front of their home to drink beer and nibble dried squid or fish with bits of pickled vegetables. The women didn't drink, but enjoyed the gathering all the same. It was always a casual affair, often with a guitar present. They took turns singing southern Vietnamese folks songs called *vong co*. The lyrics were composed in six lines that were both sang and read. In the middle, there was one word the singer emphasized by modulating the tone and dragging the syllable out as long as possible. The longer he held the note, the louder the applause. I had seen girls titter and swoon over singers with bottomless lungs.

I often wanted to go down and join them, but I was shy by nature. These were the only times when I felt lonely. It wasn't because I was alone, but rather because I missed Tan. Since we were kids, I had relied on him to befriend strangers. It was much easier for me to just follow his lead into any gathering. Sometimes it was still a shock to me that he left home so soon. I had always expected we would go to college together.

TAN first showed his unhappiness with our family situation two years ago, right after the government relocated us from the hotel in Chinatown to the refugee camp on the outskirts of Saigon. There was no casino to relieve his boredom. In fact, there were no restaurants, cafés, shops, or any other sort of comfort whatsoever at the refugee site. It was a bizarre settlement of canvas tents on a vast dirt field, set back a quarter of a mile from the interprovincial road between Cu Chi and Saigon. The surrounding scrubland was the most desolate country I had ever seen. It didn't appear to support anything more than a few sparrows and finches. The parched air was unusually bright. An errant cigarette would surely be enough for the arid landscape to burst into flames

We stayed with Stepmother's parents and her sister, ten people in a single army tent. There were roughly one hundred such tents in our site alone. With more than six hundred refugees, the camp quickly fell into disarray and filth. Children yelled and shouted, playing from morning to night. Babies cried all day long. People squabbled over space. Laundry lines were strung up between tents. Foot traffic kicked up a permanent dust fog.

Within a week, several other camps sprung up in the vicinity to accommodate the flood of people pouring in from the North. Folks rushed back and forth between the camps looking for friends and family. Later arrivals told harrowing tales of being evacuated by rail to the port city Hai Phong and going south by ships. The Communists had organized demonstrations and blockades to prevent people from leaving the North. Strangers pulled refugees from trains and buses. As more people tried to flee the North, the Communist government detained whole families on fraudulent charges.

Hearing their stories, Stepmother kept saying how lucky we were to be among the first wave to go south, and to have a decent tent at a camp with bus access into Saigon. Father smiled and quoted an old Viet adage, "Be the first to arrive at a feast, the second to cross a river."

But Saigon, from our sad perspective in the refugee camp, could hardly be called a feast. Among us boys, my cousin Tan was the most depressed. Although he hadn't said a word to the family, his grumpiness spoke volumes about his feelings. We were crammed into the tent so tightly that there was only a small aisle down the middle. At dusk, swarms of mosquitoes descended into the camp, and we spent most of the night sitting inside our nets. During the day, the tents were like ovens. I got dizzy if I stayed inside for longer than five minutes, but outside wasn't much better. There wasn't a single tree to provide relief from the heat. The best we could do was clear a patch of ground beneath some bushes and collapse beneath the paltry shade, panting like dogs through the midday hours.

Weeks went by, each day worse than the last. The few wooden latrines at the back of the camp began to reek so bad, no one could use the cooking and washing area nearby. It became a serious health issue. People had to resort to relieving themselves in the bushes, and it didn't take long before the entire area became a stinking mess. Sewage formed black pools of rot around the compound. People began to fall ill.

Tan bussed into Saigon daily, but couldn't find work. I tried enrolling in several schools in nearby towns without success. Baby Hoang and our little sister Huong fell sick. Father gave up looking for work. Stepmother did her best to keep things going, but we all knew that unless we left the camp soon, someone would become critically ill.

A month after arriving in the camp, Father rented a small shophouse with his brother-in-law Uncle Ty. Our two families of eleven people shared the two-room house, cooking and eating together for four months until Uncle Ty bought a modest house. The influx of northern refugees was forcing property prices up steadily, so Father finally had to buy a house while he could still afford one.

Our new home was a wooden shop-house, twenty feet wide and forty feet long. It had a clay-tile roof, a packed-dirt floor, and a small open loft at the center of the house. Being right on the market square, there was always the reek of rotten vegetables, fish, meats, and garbage. On a hot day, it was like living in the middle of a city dump, and even a light rain would leave the street muddy for a day or two. But once it was dry, vendors would wash their stalls and platforms, and the runoff would return the street to its normal muddy state. During the monsoon, it was a hopeless, knee-deep pond.

Father hired a drunken cook from Hai Phong and turned the front room of the house into a noodle shop. Business was poor at the start and worsened continually. Belatedly, he realized that the market was too small, servicing only the local neighborhoods. Father didn't dare close the shop because street vendors would claim the space in front of our house, blocking our door and making it difficult to sell the house or reopen another business. The street vendors paid gang protection money, so it would be impossible to evict them once they settled in. We could do nothing but continue to live in our smelly shack and watch our savings trickle away.

In Hanoi, even our servants had better living quarters. It seemed amazing to me, the distance we had fallen within the span of five short years, from living like princes to eking out a living in a mud hole serving noodles. Stepmother, who came from a wealthy family, endured the hardship courageously without a single complaint. I decided that if she could bear it, so could I. My little sister Huong was only five years old, and baby Hoang was two. My brothers Hung and Hong were in their early teens, too young to fully comprehend our predicament.

The person who fared most poorly was my cousin Tan.

"It's a spiraling descent," Tan told me when we were alone. "We will keep going down and down. It's time we look out for ourselves and find a way out of here."

Tan's refusal to work created an embarrassing and awkward situation for Father. While the whole family pitched in to make ends meet, Tan left to look for employment downtown. He came home only to eat and sleep, avoiding even the smallest task because he considered the noodle business beneath our station. Tan told me several times that he couldn't believe Father had put us in this dump while he had enough money for a decent house like Uncle Ty's. Tan talked about joining the armed forces like his half-brother Lang, who enlisted in the navy after arriving in Saigon with Aunt Thuan and her children.

"I can't leave my family," I said. "I want to finish high school and go to college."

"I'm going to look for work as a secretary or clerk."

I wished Tan luck, but I thought it was hopeless. He was still thinking like a rich kid. Tan would never stoop to restaurant, construction, or any other manual labor. But in a way, I was thinking like a rich kid as well; I was expecting that I would have the time and leisure to study.

"You still have hope because we haven't hit the bottom yet," Tan said and laughed with a sneer.

I had to turn away to hide the blood rising to my face. It was a controlled staccato laugh filled with disdain. Tan and I were closer than brothers, best friends since we were toddlers, but there were times I could barely keep my fist from smashing into his face.

Two months after we received our *Tu Tai 1* diplomas for graduating from the eleventh grade, a major achievement at the time, Tan successfully enlisted in the air force. He was following in the footsteps of his older half-brother Lang. Tan left immediately for basic training and vanished from our lives.

A LETTER came from Tan one afternoon. My landlady gave it to me when I returned from my classes. I took it down to the beach, where I now swam daily. The evening fishermen hadn't stirred from their naps to prepare their boats. A group of children played on a wrecked skiff far to the south. I sat on the sand and opened the letter. There was a photograph of Tan, grinning, the Eiffel Tower in the background. Tan said he wasn't tall enough to be a pilot so they transferred him to Morocco for aircraft mechanic training. It was the time of his life. A virgin when he left home, Tan was now drinking whisky, dancing in clubs, and sleeping with bar girls. Women were fantastic, he wrote; not all of them were like the working girls we had seen up north. He urged me to start dating. He said life was passing me by. It made me chuckle to imagine Tan carousing in the bars, wrist-deep in cards, a girl on his arm, behaving like one of the drunken French soldiers we had had to deal with at our inn in Hanoi.

I often thought of him when I came down to the beach. Before coming to Phan Thiet, I had seen the sea only once. Tan and I were fifteen then and had ridden a bus all the way from Hanoi to Do Son on the shore of Ha Long Bay. A gray, blustery day of needling rain, we stood on the wind-teased beach and compared the churning, frothing ocean before us against what we had read in *Moby-Dick* and we were deeply impressed.

"There is much ugliness, but there is also much beauty in this world," my mother had once said, she who spent most of her days in her garden reading poetry written worlds away.

Mother had taught me that the eaves of heaven had a way of turning in cycles, of dealing both blows and recompenses. For every devastating flood, there followed a bountiful crop. For every long stretch of flawless days, there waited a mighty storm just below the horizon. For every great sorrow, there was a great happiness to come.

I stripped down to my shorts and walked into the tickling surf. Floating in the calm sea, a vast blue above me, I was filled with a cozy, billowy warmth. It was the same sensation I had as a boy whenever Mother looked at me. She had smiling eyes; it was a pleasure to be within her sight. It seemed like only last week. It had been seven years since she passed away after childbirth.

She was still watching over me. This I knew. I had the feeling that I hadn't stumbled upon this place and this peace at all, but rather it was something Mother had guided me to, something good to help me hold the course against what would come; like giving a traveler a drink of water before a long, difficult passage.

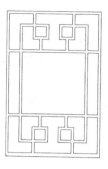

4. MOTHER

My mother was born one province over to the west. She came from a more prestigious and even wealthier line than my father. Her uncle was a county chief. Her cousin was a senator, and her parents were both scholars. She had a mandarin upbringing, but she was uniquely modern in a time when most girls were limited to a primary education. She was fluent in French and the classic Vietnamese Nom script. Her passions were Vietnamese and French literature, poetry, and theater. When she came of age, her parents were certain that she needed to marry a modern, educated nobleman who wasn't a political fanatic—it could have meant disaster and death in even that relatively peaceful colonial period.

In his early dashing days, Father was very much a man of the city, fluent in French and passionate about French poetry, French cuisine, French wine, Western theaters, Charlie Chaplin movies, and motorcycles. He was a devoted enthusiast of various European pleasures the colonial French made accessible to their supporters and the rich Vietnamese ruling class. His parents hoped that a wife and family would force their youngest son into maturity and wean him from the city's seductive pleasures. When they told him firmly that it was time for him to marry or have his allowance curtailed, he yielded, but vowed that he would never marry a girl with blackened teeth. It was the one modicum of modernity he required of a wife. His father looked to his mother, who, like most women of her generation, had lacquered her teeth at fifteen with calcium oxide—black onyx-like teeth had long been a vanity of the local women. His mother simply nodded and said, "If he prefers a white rotting smile, so be it."

They were introduced by a professional matchmaker and blessed by monks. The initial contacts between the families went well, and when they actually met, neither found the other repulsive. In fact, they found each other to be intelligent and pleasant. They weren't in love, but as the popular wisdom said, love would come in time. After a few auspicious meetings, they wedded. A year later, I was born. My two brothers followed a few years behind. Having fulfilled his filial obligations of marriage and siring male heirs, Father strayed back to Hanoi and the high life he had enjoyed as a bachelor. Mother was left to raise three boys and manage the estate alone.

For years, Father divided his time between Hanoi and the country estate. Every time he left, Mother was very sad. His return was always an occasion to celebrate. Father always brought gifts for everyone, Mother, aunts, and cousins included. There were French biscuits, cloth, chocolates, and magazines for the women. Father gave my brothers and cousins toys, but he gave me three books that turned me into an avid reader: *Gulliver's Travels*, *20,000 Leagues Under the Sea*, and *Voyage to the Moon*.

Once he brought Mother a beautiful phonograph. It was a compact, well-crafted machine, housed in a polished wooden box. The lid was embossed with golden letters and had a picture of a dog sitting in front of a phonograph, head canted to the flaring flower-shaped speaker. Inside, the hand-cranked turntable was covered with dark blue felt. It had a chrome-plated arm with a diamond-tipped needle.

The first day he brought it home, Mother invited all the Aunties, nieces, nephews, and staff to the house for after-dinner tea. Father and Uncle Thuan were considered too serious for such fun. Mother didn't invite them, so everyone else could relax and enjoy the party. We sat on mats on the porch and in the garden. Gardener Cam lit some paper lanterns and hung them on the trees. We stuffed ourselves with cookies, candies, and cakes, and listened to the phonograph. Mother played Vietnamese ballads and French songs one after another. It was one of the finest nights because I remembered Mother smiling and laughing a lot.

Mother was happy whenever Father came home, and she tried her best to make his stay pleasant, hoping that it might keep him there longer. During one of his visits, I overheard them talking in the sitting room. It was right after supper, when Father liked to have his tea.

Mother said, "Things are chaotic all over the country. You should be home helping your big brother."

"He has been governing the domain fine without my help."

"It's not the same anymore. There are robberies everywhere. The roads have become very dangerous since the Japanese invasion. When the soldiers come, it's to requisition our rice and conscript men for the Japanese. Law and order are the least of their concerns. They only care about conquering Asia."

"I know, but Big Brother Thuan hasn't asked for my help."

"He expects you to volunteer. Don't you know the villagers sound the temple bell in the middle of the night, once or twice a week? Big Brother Thuan has to take his gun and guards into the villages to chase off the robbers. Some days, he gets so exhausted he has to cancel half the arbitration cases."

"He should teach the villagers how to fight for themselves."

"They're farmers. They're peaceful people. It's not in them to fight, and Big Brother Thuan can't hold off all the bad elements alone. It would be good to have you here to assist him."

"Why should I? He always treats me as though I'm incompetent."

"He's ten years older than you. You shouldn't feel offended about it."

"I don't like working under him."

"You could stay home and help me manage our own estate."

"What will I do here? You're managing very well, and everybody likes you. You don't need my help."

"Just having a husband at home makes all the difference," she said softly. "It's very hard seeing you only once every other month. The highway is getting more dangerous too. I get very worried thinking about you traveling back and forth like this."

"As you said, this is a time of turmoil. I think it's better if I stayed in the city where I can blend in with the crowd. Here I stand out like a big fish in a small pond. If things turn bad, the big fish will be the first target. Besides, it's not good to leave our villa in Hanoi empty in this unsettled time."

"Cousin Chinh is there; he can look after our villa for us."

"I can't trust that playboy to manage anything."

"Then the children and I will come live with you in the city. We had some good times there, didn't we? Remember our dinner parties?"

"Yes, yes, but it's not a good idea now. You're the manager of our estate. Your sisters-in-law need you."

"Not as much as I need you."

"Let's not talk about this anymore. I want to look into some businesses in Hanoi in case things become too unstable in the countryside. There are many opportunities in Hanoi now that the Germans control the French in Europe, and the Japanese control the French here."

"You prefer the city. There's nothing at home to amuse you."

Father did not reply. He left the following day. There were rumors, of course, that he had a mistress in Hanoi.

5. DALAT DAYS

Morning mist smothered the trees. The sky was overcast, threatening rain. I came to bid her farewell at the Dalat train station. It was perched on a wooded hillside at the edge of town—a two-room brick cottage with a concrete platform. Higher up the slope, the stationmaster's shack listed to one side like a doting guard. At the far end of the landing, a pair of traders unloaded burlap sacks from an oxen-drawn wagon. The train was nowhere in sight, its empty track stretching off into the still, white haze.

Anh waited for me at the long bench under the eaves of the station house. In her hands, the ticket that would take her back to school in Saigon. She sat on a handkerchief, the rear hem of her lavender *ao dai* folded over her lap. When I stepped onto the platform, she rose and extended both her hands. Anh was slender, quite tall for a Vietnamese girl, and had sharp cat-eyes. She didn't say hello, or ask how I was—she never did. Instead, Anh took my hands in greeting, dipped a little

curtsy, and smiled the smile that won me from the first moment. It was the sort of smile that glittered as if she had something precious to share, that coming upon me was a well-anticipated encounter, the most pleasant part of her day. It was entirely unguarded. I couldn't remember ever seeing a smile like that. Perhaps, I thought, it was because I was a northerner, and I knew northerners were incapable of such unrestrained expressions.

"Your dress fits you beautifully," I said, careful not to compliment her directly. That would have been too forward. I didn't know how she managed to wear a different dress every time we met.

"Thank you," she said. "And you look good in your uniform."

Last year, after my summer in Phan Thiet, I had returned to Saigon and enrolled in the Institute of Administration. Students who passed their freshman exams were sent to the military academy in Dalat for basic training. It was a simple summer program aimed at providing future graduates of the Institute of Administration an excuse from military service.

"I just came from the morning session. I don't think I'll have time to change when I get back this afternoon. Sergeant doesn't like us summer-cadets running around town in uniform. People might credit the *real* cadets with our bad behaviors." I grinned and reached for her waist.

She hugged me, giggling.

"Where's your valise?"

"I left it with the stationmaster."

"Is that safe?"

"Of course. Why wouldn't it be?"

I shrugged. She was far more trusting than I.

It seemed tragic that this was only our seventh date. There was so much I didn't know about her, though what I had fathomed fascinated me immensely. She was a romantic girl who knew poems by heart and could reconstruct whole movie scenes with manic gestures and a breathless voice. A mystic, she read palms, interpreted dreams, and traveled fearlessly when the stars were favorable. We had one

thing in common. She had grown up without a father, I without a mother. We were matched by our needs. I came from a rigid world of order, form, class division, nobility, and peasantry. My parents did not marry for love. It was an act of obedience and filial obligation, one that they honored their whole lives. And here before me was this wild child of sand and sea, a fatherless girl who did not know how to mask herself. She lived on her instincts, willfully and zealously; beneath sun or rain, it mattered not.

I had asked her for this early rendezvous. The station, I knew, would be deserted. I took a camera out of its case and she twirled into a playful pose. Life was still a game to her. This, I would learn, was one state of happiness.

"What's that perfume you're wearing?" I framed her against the tracks.

"Carven by Elizabeth Arden." She knew to look away from the lens.

"French?" In my viewfinder, her long hair was as dark as steel.

"From Paris." She turned her face, suddenly mysterious.

"It's lovely."

At the time, most college girls hadn't considered accentuating their beauty, but Anh knew enough to choose one of the most expensive and subtle fragrances on the market. It seemed amazing to me that she came from Phan Thiet, the same backwater fishing town where I had spent last summer teaching.

"Why do you ask?"

"I might buy a bottle for myself since I'll miss the scent."

She gave an un-ladylike snort and pinched me.

I never told her it was this perfume that had first caught my attention.

It was a Sunday, three weeks prior. I had a day's leave from the army camp. My barracks buddies tramped around town on their usual weekend routine, looking for girls to escort to their afternoon coffee by the lake and, hopefully, an evening dance at the clubs as well. I

begged off to go hiking with plans of taking a series of photographs of Dalat's waterfalls. I was fiddling with my camera on the side of the trail when I caught the scent of her as she walked past with a little girl. They held hands and hummed a folksy tune. What happened next was an impulsive move, quite out of character for me. I trotted back down the trail, oddly compelled by a need to see her face. *Pardon me, Miss. Could you tell me the way to Cam Ly Waterfall?* I used my friendliest tone. But then she smiled her smile, the smile that bloomed like wonder itself. It was as simple and elegant as that. It rendered me speechless. Before she uttered a word, I was already consumed with a singular desire, a wanton need, to win this girl for myself.

THERE was time for an early lunch, so we caught a ride with an army truck back toward town. It left us on the shore of the Lake of the Fragrance of Spring. We walked as we had for all our outings. We leaned close, held hands, pecked each other on the cheek, allowing ourselves, as tourists, small public displays of affection. Bend after bend, the road was hazy and quiet, save for housewives walking to market with woven satchels tucked under their arms. Bicyclists pedaled sleepily down the center of the unmarked road, undisturbed by the occasional three-wheeled Lambretta taxis grunting past, crammed with up to eight passengers. Once in a long while, a local bus, a truck with benches, came through on its rounds. When a real car came down the road, people turned to look.

Dalat was still a quaint resort town, tucked high in the cool mountains at the end of the rail line, surrounded by conifer forests, trout streams, waterfalls, and lakes. Earlier, it had been a retreat for the French, who regularly fled the stifling heat of the lowlands. These days it was a vacation destination for rich Vietnamese and top-level government officials. European-style villas dotted the hills, and tiny bungalows hid in the woods, joined by meandering gravel paths. Three asphalt streets flanked with little shops and two-story buildings coiled around two hills, forming the town's business district. It was small and rustic enough to permit visitors a proprietary sense of belonging.

We paused and took a picture beneath the big pine tree by the ice cream parlor where we had spent the entire afternoon of our first date. I took another photo of her standing at the trailhead where we had embarked three times to a creekside clearing where we picnicked on roasted chicken, baguettes, fruits, and lotus-scented tea. Then another snapshot at the cozy alcove of rocks that sheltered us from a storm. I clicked through the entire roll, feeling helpless that I couldn't possibly capture her in all the places that needed to be preserved—the tree-lined walks that seduced us away into the hills, the park benches, the mimosa trees, the moonlit lanes on which I had walked her home, the long good-night kisses by the hedge. She was leaving, and I was afraid.

I wondered if she would forget the intimate, nameless places where we had talked through the lazy hours. I wondered if, like me, she felt as if we had lived a whole, though tiny, life here.

We paused at a few boutiques and peered through the glass storefronts, but she wouldn't let me buy her anything. She knew I was poor. We strolled through our usual window-shopping circuit, down the one avenue then up the other, weaving back and forth around vendors crowding the brick sidewalk. The streets curved and sloped in such a way that the town appeared laid out like an old-fashioned vertical painting, buildings and trees in the distance rising to the sky or falling off toward the valley. Climbing the hill to the town center, you saw the narrow, cranky buildings edged against mountain and sky. Turning around, you saw rooftops layered against the lake and the dale below. I was fond of Dalat for its crooked intersections, its uneven buildings, its sweeps and jags that made the light changes captivating.

Anh wanted a baguette and bananas for her trip, so we stopped at the main market. It clung halfway up the hill, a quilt-work of multicolored tarps strung up at different angles, overlapping and flapping in the wind. Beneath, aglow in the filtered light, was a congested world of colors, aromas, odors, and noise, all ruled by women. Sellers sat snugly behind their counters, arranging and rearranging their wares. Shoppers stomped about on thick clogs, holding their hems away from the mush of trampled banana leaves and mud. They haggled, gossiped, laughed, yelled, napped, cackled, and sang over baskets of fruits, bins of produce, sides of raw meat, coils of sausage ropes, silvery fish laid out like steel blades, great bags of spices, barrels of rice in a dozen varieties, toy-like plastic wares, and every conceivable household item, short of furniture.

I waited for her on the market fringe amid peanut roasters, pork-bun steamers, fruit-women with baskets of tiny peaches and blood-dark plums, flower-maids with packs of incense sticks and altar bundles of carnations and daffodils. Wrapped in sweaters and scarves, schoolgirls with rosy cheeks gathered around a vendor who sold fried dough fritters, hot from a bubbling oil vat. People bantered, rattling off quick words with a lilt that reminded me of the central highlanders.

When we topped the hill, it began to drizzle. Anh steered me to a kiosk tucked in an alley barely three paces wide, next to Thien Nhien Bookstore. It was one of those foldable tin-and-wood assemblies that at the end of the day could be carted home. The cook, a woman in her mid-forties, sat like a barrel of flesh behind the counter, flanked on three sides by six woks, each set on a coal stove no bigger than a flowerpot. Despite the chill, she sweated through her white peasant blouse, her face flushed and jovial. Equally good-humored, the thin husband, a chain-smoking man with huge hands, made coffee and served the customers while their teenage daughter prepped the food and washed dishes at the back end of the alley. It was a bustling operation of six tables sheltered under a green army tarp.

"This is my favorite place. They make the best *banh xeo* in Dalat," she announced and waited for my reply as was proper.

"Then I insist we eat here before you leave." I grinned.

Anh gossiped with the woman, touched her forearm, laughed, talked about catching the afternoon train, and somewhere in between special-ordered our *banh xeo* with all her favorite fillings. She had a way with common folks that was beyond me. Even though my family had become miserably poor, our lot no better than any cyclo driver's, a big part of me was still rooted within my family ancestral estate, in its orders and values. I always felt more at ease going to the market or to new eateries with Anh. Everywhere we went, folks welcomed her like kin. She had a natural confidence entirely different from any girl I had met. The way she moved, how her long-fingered hands danced when she talked. I never got tired of looking at her. I especially liked the way she smiled whenever she caught my eyes.

We shared a tiny wooden bench, our backs to the mildewed wall. The man brought us a pot of tea and two tin espresso presses set atop small glasses with a finger's worth of condensed milk.

Anh said, "I know you don't usually drink coffee, but it's a real treat in this weather. Try it, for me."

Caffeine made my heart race. "It'll probably give me a heart attack, but, for you, why not?"

She smiled, the whole of her canted toward me, a bundle of warmth in the dancing wind, in her hair a scent of lily.

She said, "You won't forget my address in Saigon, will you?"

"Didn't I tell you I've got a photographic memory?"

Anh looked dubious. "Then tell me again, how you'd get to my uncle's house."

We had made no promises to each other. It would have been improper to speak of our feelings. Before any of that, I must tell her about my family, our history, and my father, who spent most of his days sprawled on the floor with his opium pipes, smoking away the final vestiges of our ancestral rice fortune. I must tell her of the squalor of our lives, of my crushing study loads at two schools, of my struggle to help support my family on a meager tutoring salary. There was another whole troublesome world out there that I did not want to let invade this moment. I wanted our hours encapsulated until the sweetness of these days had become an unimpeachable part of the past.

I repeated her precise directions from the Main Post Office at the center of Saigon to her uncle's house in a middle-class neighborhood on the opposite side of the city from mine. Then I said that on my first day back in Saigon, I would get a haircut and a shave. I would put on my best shirt, buy the prettiest bouquet of flowers, then take a cyclo to her house because, after all, the man she'd met in Dalat was a handsome cadet and I didn't want to look like a disheveled, sweaty bum who had walked across the city.

Anh giggled, squeezed my hand, and showed her pleasure by preparing my coffee. She lifted the lid of the espresso press, turned it upside down on the table, placed the press on top, and stirred the condensed milk at the bottom of the glass until all of it had turned into a caramel swirl. She presented the glass with both hands, then waited for me to taste it before preparing hers. These were traditional gestures of affection, and for the first time in my life, I allowed myself to revel in them.

I was twenty-four and had never been with a woman. I knew nothing about love, and everything I knew about sex I had seen while managing our inn in Hanoi. For a young lad who hadn't so much as held a girl's hand or even seen adults kissing, the sight of peasant girls rendered homeless by war and desperate by hunger prostituting themselves to the French soldiers was shocking. They were no different from the girls I had grown up with in the countryside. The experience tainted not only my idea of sex, but also my general view of women. Since then I resisted the advances of girls. I feared I was ruined.

I had thought I would never marry.

It was a miracle to meet Anh and feel my insides flip-flopping about. I was desperate to hang onto her, if only to make these emotions last a little longer. I liked the way I felt when I was near her.

I gave her the thin package I kept under my coat. It was a silk scarf I had seen her admire. She gave a sharp cry of delight that made everyone turn around. She bound her long black hair in it—which somehow made me immensely pleased.

Holding hands underneath the table, we huddled like conspirators over our chicory coffee. The man brought us a platter of fresh vegetables, herbs, and pickled radishes, and two plates with big, fat crepes made from a batter of rice flour, turmeric, and coconut milk. They were crunchy on the outside, moist and slightly chewy in the middle, coddling a steamy center of bean sprouts, mung beans, and a mix of sautéed pork, shrimp, and scallion. We broke the crepes, dipped pieces in a delicate lime-chili fish sauce, and ate them with sprigs of cilantro, fresh lettuce, basil, and *la chua*, sour leaves that tasted like green apples. The scallion oil in the crepe glistened on the fresh herbs like a light salad dressing. Anh fed me perfect morsels wrapped in crisp lettuce. And, as she had promised, the milk-coffee was a fabulous accompaniment. Small, unforgettable decadence. I enjoyed being here with her so much, I couldn't stop smiling. I had never felt this way. I stole a kiss and tasted tangy sugared lime on her lips.

We ate, oblivious to the crowd, the bustling shops, the humming traffic, the jostling pedestrians, the chanting hawkers. Rainwater ran green in the gutter. A lavender hue fell over the town, softening the cries of babies, the bells of donkey carts, errant laughter. Even the pale moss-washed buildings lost their edges. The world went all crumbly, and I was keen only on the red curves of her lips, the way she gasped after a bite of chili, the unbelievably delicious warmth of her thigh against mine.

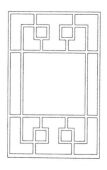

6. THE MID-AUTUMN FESTIVAL

Under the looming shadow of war, Uncle Thuan performed one of the wisest acts in his life. It would mark
the pinnacle of our clan's ascendancy, and also the dawn
of our quick dissolution. He opened his personal treasury, instructed the servants to ready his ancestral estate,
summoned the fireworks-maker from Hanoi, and be-
stowed upon the village an extravagant Mid-Autumn
Festival—an event that would be well remembered
among those who lived to see the next millennium.

I was seven years old that year and remembered
the great swell of excitement and activities that over-
took the estate. At the time, I had two younger brothers
and four cousins, all Uncle Thuan's children from three
wives, living at our ancestral estate. My father had decided not to come home for the festival, so I had a wonderful time. It was thrilling for my cousins and me to
watch all the carpenters and craftsmen prepare for the
celebration. We tailed them everywhere and got under-
foot at every opportunity.

The preparation began immediately after the Rituals of Forgiveness in mid-July, a full month in advance. Walls received fresh coats of paint. Roofs were mended, squeaky doors oiled. Three bedrooms were added to the guests' wing to accommodate relatives coming from distant provinces. New sleeping mats were laid in all quarters. Moon-gazing divans were built, flower gardens expanded, strolling paths cleared, courtyards repaired. Workers installed additional stoves in the main kitchen. In the garden next to the carp pond and the existing cow-roasting pit, bricklayers constructed earth kilns with unbaked clay bricks for roasting piglets and chickens. A thousand moon cakes were ordered from renowned Chinese bakeries in Hanoi. Gifts of livestock, silk, porcelain wares, and jewelry were purchased and sent out with the invitations to the honored guests.

Our stockman fattened the piglets to ensure that there would be thick layers of fat on every cut of meat roasted. The resident artist, who was also our tutor, painted many poems in classic Nom characters on long cuts of red banner cloth. The guards spent days polishing the arrays of altar brassworks, serving trays, ornamental relics, giant candleholders of six-foot-tall brass storks, and the whole decorative brass armory. And every night after supper, all the staff and the adult residents of the estate, including the magistrate and his wife, sat down with piles of bamboo sticks, colored papers, paint, glue, and twine. Over tea, sweets, and tall tales told beneath a waxing moon, they practiced the traditional art of lantern making. On Mid-Autumn Night, every child would have a beautiful lantern for the moonlight parade.

On Mid-Autumn Day, important guests started arriving for the festival in the afternoon. My cousin Tan and I came out to the Ancestral Gate to watch them. It was a fine sight. We had never seen so many new faces. The wealthiest came in horse-drawn carriages. High-ranked officials from the old warlord lines rode horses and wore mandarin robes and slacks. Each had a retinue of two to four guards and banner bearers. Local visitors, often of more moderate wealth, traveled in wood palanquins with silk canopies carried by liveried men. Distinguished scholars and elders of modest means came in man-pulled rickshaws. None of stature passed through the Ancestral Gate on foot.

Villagers arrived in droves, coming through the rear gate. They found their way to the courtyard, sat on mats laid on the paved bricks, and helped themselves to tea and sweets from the kitchen. In the grand hall, people congregated to play Chinese chess and cards—the men with men, the women with women. Men stood around, chatting and swaggering with the confidence of farmers after a good harvest and a new promising crop already in the fields. Mid-autumn was the season of indolence; all the hard work of planting was long finished and there was nothing to do except watch the seedlings grow.

People sorted themselves into parties befitting their stations. Folks of equal wealth sat on the same straw mat. Even then, families of similar status stayed near each other. It was a world where titles, however minor, mattered. A man's social station determined everything, from whom he may wed to which school his children may attend. It determined where a person sat, when he spoke, the manner in which he addressed others, and even how large a share of a public feast he took home. It was a harsh world where people relied on the rigid order of the centuries.

A hush rolled across the dining hall as the magistrate and his wife made their entrance. Uncle Thuan was a stocky man of average height with a dark, broad face, a boxy jaw, and a prominent forehead. He was built in the image of his line—men who knew both the plow and the sword; wide-beamed shoulders, meaty hands, and nut-brown skin, though his bearing was of someone born into wealth, who knew from his earliest youth that he was destined to rule. He eschewed Western trappings, displayed no pocket watches or rings, and refused to wear European suits even when he went to the Province Seat on official business. He kept his hair long in the traditional topknot tucked inside a formal headdress. His attire rarely varied from what he wore today: sandals, white trousers beneath a mandarin robe of black silk, the ivory insignia of his office pinned on his chest.

Aunt Thuan, the mistress of the estate, was in her late twenties. The well-bred daughter of a wealthy merchant family, she was tall and her slimness made her seem even taller when she stood next to her stocky husband. She wore black slacks beneath the traditional *ao tu than*—a modest silk gown of four colors, cinched by a sash around the waist. Her glossy black hair was wrapped in a tight coil and piled above her head, encircled by a velvet headdress. She was a classic beauty in that she had all the prized features: pearly white skin, oval face, full red lips, and slanted almond eyes. Men said she was the most beautiful woman in the province. Women were envious. They claimed that her full lips were a sign of wanton sexual desire; that the slant of her eyes indicated a mean spirit; and that her high cheekbones were a bad sign for her husband's longevity.

None of this touched her, for she was a supremely confident woman. Although she was the third wife, wedded after the death of the magistrate's first wife, she had proven to be a very efficient and sharp-minded administrator, so capable that she immediately stepped over the second wife and assumed the role of mistress of the estate.

She accompanied her husband as he made the rounds to greet their extended families and then she quickly retreated to oversee the festivities while he continued through the hall from one group to another, and then out to the courtyard to greet his guests. The whole village had turned out for the festival. People sipped tea and sat patiently, waiting for the magistrate to complete his rounds. The meal would not commence until all were properly received.

Concluding the welcoming ceremony, Uncle climbed to the top step of the Ancestral Temple and looked down at the courtyard packed with diners sitting on mats, children darting about, folks circulating, greeting and congratulating each other. Council elders, dignitaries, and honored guests, more than a hundred strong, quietly rose from their tea-mats and aligned themselves in suitable rank behind him, the highest standing in the front row closest to the magistrate. People simply knew the proper thing to do; the gestures of ritual were instinctive.

Hands clasped behind his back, Uncle waited for the crowd to hush. He did not need to be announced; after all, the entire village revolved around him. Its entire population worked, had commerce with the estate, or served others who did. In one capacity or another, he was the judge, jury, sheriff, moneylender, landlord, and patron for all present, and this endowed him with a sort of compelling gravity, more so because he took pleasure in the drama of having people wait on him. In moments, the din subsided and all eyes turned to him.

"Honored guests, family, and friends, it gives me great pleasure to see you all here to celebrate this most auspicious Mid-Autumn Festival with us. We thank you for honoring our house with your company. We wish you all good health and good fortune. Let us feast."

While the foods served to the commoners were not as glamorous as those served at the magistrate's wedding banquet, the board was well laid with popular country dishes: roasted chickens, rice noodles brushed with scallion oil, poached fish, sweetmeat dumplings, cured hams, spring rolls, bean curd stuffed with minced pork, stir-fried vegetables, shrimp cakes, fresh herbs, pickled radishes, and dipping sauces. One of the favorite entrees was the crunchy-skin piglets, roasted and rubbed with five spices. But the most anticipated course was *bo thui,* an appetizer of cold cuts of veal served with a thick brown sauce of fermented soybean and mashed sweet rice. It was a delicacy most folks enjoyed perhaps only once a year at a major village banquet. The calf had to be slow-roasted whole over an open wood flame so that the hide turned a yellowish gold and the shoulder, when cut, revealed a thin layer of rare meat at the bone, a thick band of pink meat, and a slender well-done strip near the hide. Finely sliced, the meat's tenderness was heightened by a single chewy, smoky strand of hide.

Within the Ancestral Temple, servants provided the same meal to fifty of the most powerful and wealthy men in the province. The men spread themselves out according to status among the five dining mats. In the adjacent room, their wives took similar positions beside the magistrate's wife in accordance with the rank of their husbands.

Diners sat in the lotus position with the rear hems of their robes draped over their laps, and ate from the communal tray using chopsticks and small bowls.

For these guests, the magistrate had prepared an additional delicacy, the house's stork stew, a recipe refined over four generations since his great-grandfather planted the bamboo hedge around the estate. Strong winds often dashed storks into the hedge, breaking their wings and crippling them. At first, the birds were killed as acts of mercy and eaten so as not be wasteful. Over the years, the cooks discovered that young stork meat was exceptionally appetizing when first pit-roasted and then slow-cooked in clay crocks with wild mushrooms, lotus seeds, rice wine, soy sauce, and the tender noodle-like baby bamboo shoots grown in inverted pots. It was served only at special occasions because storks were graceful creatures. The claypot stork, as it was called, became the famed heirloom dish reserved for honored guests.

After the feast, Mother and Aunties went into the kitchen to supervise the cooks in the massive task of wrapping hundreds of quartered sections of pork, meat cakes, fruits, and sweet rice in banana leaves. Every guest would receive a proper share of the feast at the end of the night. The most important guests would receive a whole piglet head, a tail, and slices of the neck meat. The next group would receive half a pig's head and half a tail. The middle tier would have a slice of the piglet's neck meat, and so on down the hierarchy. The list would be checked and re-checked. A mix-up with the bamboo baskets would be disastrous. People bought titles and positions mainly for these honors and privileges, so the gifts were tokens of a person's public stature.

In the courtyard, Aunt Thao, my father's younger sister, who was in her twenties and unmarried, gathered us children to watch the theater troupe perform the dragon dance. Above, the sun was slipping behind the bamboo hedge, leaving a pink moon to climb a honeyed sky. In the evening glow, the courtyard looked reddish and warm like freshly baked bricks. A breeze sighed from the wetland.

A thicket of sparrows swooped, whipping, and diving dizzily in the lowering dusk. The gardeners began lighting the estate's vast array of shadow lanterns, each the size of a barrel. As if by a silent agreement, guests took flames from the incense braziers and began lighting the hundreds of lanterns strung throughout the grounds. The glow spread outward from the main courtyard like a breath, illuminating the buildings, the rosebushes, the hedges, the picnic lawn, the pond, the swimming pier, the winding footpaths leading to the four corners of the estate.

At once little boys and girls scattered like fireflies, each carrying a special paper lantern shaped like a star, sailing ship, snail, globe, horse, deer, or rabbit. There were fat carps with gaping mouths, eagles with flapping wings, and stars with spinning arms. We ran, skipped, and paraded our gorgeous, glowing ornaments until the candles burned out. Then, suddenly, over the pond by the rose garden, fireworks exploded, drawing multicolored blooms of sizzling sparks. Curly tails, starbursts, and poppy comets zipped, screamed, and buzzed across the night sky, and then mushroomed into pure rainbow light, blotting out the stars.

Honored guests gathered on divans and gazed at the moon. Servants brought out hot jasmine tea and trays of moon cakes. There were two types: chewy lotus cakes and flaky-crust cakes, both palm-size squares stuffed with a marvelous variety of fillings. People cut them into small morsels for sharing and spent the evening sipping tea and sampling the medley of fillings: sweetmeats, salted eggs, nuts, lotus seed paste, red bean, mung bean pudding, and candied fruits.

Mother gathered her three boys around her on the divan and let us eat our fill. We gorged ourselves until our bellies hurt. Two-year-old Hong and four-year-old Hung groaned and fell asleep in her lap. She smiled at me. My mother had the full round face of the alluvial-plain women. When she smiled, her whole face beamed. I liked the way she coiled her long black hair around the crown of her head. I leaned my head against her arm, in my belly a fat, warm, bright feeling. I was so very happy that Father had decided not to come home for the festival. I looked up at Cuoi, the mythological boy in the moon. He showed himself clearly tonight, fishing and playing his flute beneath the *da* tree.

A gentle calm settled over the garden. People sat on straw mats and watched the silver orb as if it were a moving-picture show. Moonlight fell like fairy dust on the earth, the dark trees, the paddy-sea, on the upturned faces of the rich and the poor alike. Ever so slowly, the moon drew away, higher and higher, its features blurring in the distance.

Night snuggled around the waning party, and at last, it was time for *Quan Ho,* the lovers' serenade. Folks drifted into the garden and seated themselves before the moonlit pond. Two choirs of nervous teenagers aligned themselves, boys to one side, girls on the other. Gangly lads tugged at their tunics, elbowing rivals. Panicky coughs. Abruptly they belted out the first chorus, crackling voices going in several directions at once. Line by line, they sorted themselves and found their momentum. Older boys crowed in their newly found baritones, singing for the audience, but trying to catch the girls' eyes. As slight as spring vines, the girls, soon to be women, listened intently to the riddle posed, then huddled together, whispering, searching for a witty reply to be sung in equal rhymes. Hand in hand, they gathered themselves and released their winsome voices. They soared, trilling and spinning on threads of meanings. Back and forth, the village youths declared their adoration, flirting with wit, with improvised poetry, with ancient verses. Tradition led them with the lyrics of love, fidelity, obedience, and obligations. Grandparents and wizened elders smiled, for they too remembered wooing and being wooed beneath the Mid-Autumn Moon.

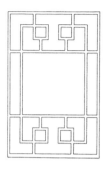

7. SEA GRUBS

I remembered there was a fortnight after the Autumn Harvest Moon when the edges of the sea thickened. That brief season saw many boats moored or hauled up for repairs. Fisher-folk rose in the violet night. The sea was hatching its lemon-hued grubs, roui, by the billions. Centipedes with tan lines running their inch-long backs churned the sandy bay. At the first light of dawn, folks waded into the soupy tidal marsh and simply scooped up roui in bamboo baskets. It was a crop that perished by noon.

Harvests, plantings, and seasonal delicacies marked country life and so it often seemed as if we had waited the whole year for the roui vendors to arrive at our door. The women had sat on buses all morning to rush their catch to us by midday. In the baskets, the top layer of grubs had died, their fragile casings spilling custard-like cream that congealed into a gooey brown sheet. Vendors dug beneath the surface for the live grubs. Roui was sold by the bowlful, thick as oatmeal.

Mother always came down into the kitchen to prepare her special roui patties. In a great bowl big enough to feed everyone in the estate, she beat eggs together with roui, grated mandarin orange peels, chopped shallots, and strips of black wood mushrooms, seasoned it with salt and pepper, and added clear noodles to hold the mixture together.

The moment she ladled the batter into the hot oil pan, everyone abandoned their chores and ambled to the kitchen. The scent of fried roui patties was irresistible. It woke the little ones from their naps and drew all us children, young and old, from our games. We crowded around the hot pan, jostling, begging, whining like pups and threatening to overturn the hot pan until we were fed.

There was no waiting for mealtime; folks devoured cha roui the instant it was ready. Such was its precious urgency. The men savored cha roui with pickles and rice wine. Mother and the Aunties ate cha roui rolled inside lettuce leaves and dipped in a mild lime-chili fish sauce. I loved mine hot and crunchy right from the pan. Crispy outside, soft and moist within, these were our custard pastries, our peasant's seafood puffs.

It was incomparable, a singular taste that encapsulated my child-hood in its entirety. Somewhere between the tangy mandarin and the sweetly caramelized shallots lay the essence of our misty, dark Ha Long Sea, a flavor I have not found anywhere else in the world.

8. SAIGON NIGHT

Cho Lon, Saigon's Chinatown, was also its nightlife hub. Although the Great World was no longer in business, peace and the influx of foreign investments had brought a profusion of bars, clubs, inexpensive eateries, dim sum shops, and cafés into this part of the city. There were hundreds of places to have a good time on a student budget.

The Saturday after the exams midway through my sophomore year in college, I took Anh out with my three best buddies and their girlfriends. Anh and I had been dating six months since I came back from Dalat. She knew all my friends' girlfriends.

We went to our favorite nightclub on the seventh floor of the Dong Khanh Hotel.

Thu, Ha, Tat, and I had been friends since our high school in Saigon. Thu was a pudgy joker and fantastic dancer whose presence was required at every outing. Ha was the nice guy, pole-thin and at six-foot ridiculously tall for a Vietnamese. Tat was Mr. Handsome.

The girls were crazy for his round, deep-set eyes, high-bridged nose, and curly hair. I was the bookish one.

The club was packed because there was no cover charge and the drinks were cheap. The girls wore both traditional and European dress while the boys were in the standard dark slacks and white long sleeves. We danced the waltz, rumba, tango, cha-cha, and even did the twist for hours.

While the girls ran off to freshen their makeup, the guys sipped beers around a table at the back of the club. As usual, the conversation was about the future. There was no need to talk about the past because we were all northerners from well-to-do families—and because it was depressing.

Before the Japanese invasion, Tat's father was an official in the administration under the French. After the French were removed, the whole administrative system came under the Tran Trong Kim regime, a puppet government set up by the Japanese. Tat's father quickly rose in rank. In the South, he was retained, as were many former Tran officials, by the Diem administration. He became a department manager in the Ministry of Justice and earned a comfortable living.

Ha and Thu were both from the upper merchant class. While Thu's father was able to salvage part of his wealth before leaving Hanoi, Ha's father lost everything. Thu's family restarted a moderate life in the South. Ha's family lived off their meager savings. Having lost his will to live along with his fortune, Ha's father spent his remaining days reading novels in bed.

But we were young and did not see ourselves as poor. Tat, Ha, and I were in our second year at Saigon University, pursuing our degrees in pedagogy. I was also attending the government's Institute of Administration with Thu, who was my study partner at the college. He knew I wanted to pursue a teaching career and was trying to convince me to stay with the administration program.

"You've passed basic training in Dalat. The rest is easy," Thu said. "All you have to do is finish the program and you'll be exempted from military service."

Tat snorted. "The country is fine. Besides, if he becomes a teacher, he'd be exempted as well."

"I'd drop one program if I were you," Ha said. "You know what happens when you try catching two fish with two hands."

Tat, Ha, and I thought that there was no prestige in being a paper pusher in the government's bureaucracy. We were stuck in the old mindset that saw honor in pursuing the difficult paths, and one of those was teaching. I was doing very well in both schools and was intoxicated by my own abilities. I could not see beyond my success.

The girls returned from the WC and ordered a round of iced teas. Ha's girlfriend, Loan, was gregarious and always tried to please others with her compliments.

"You're very handsome, Tat! I think you would look fabulous in photos," Loan gushed, trying to flatter him. She turned to the other girls. "Don't you think he could be a French movie star?"

They giggled, nodding with Loan, but Tat flinched, his features hardening.

"I wish I had your nose," Loan crooned, mistaking his reaction for shyness. "I could be a famous singer, even with my voice!"

Tat snapped, "Shut up! You're just a peasant. What do you know about anything!"

He brushed her off his arm. I could see he was on the verge of striking her. Tat stomped across the crowded dance floor and out the door without saying good-bye, leaving his date, Bich, without a word. Loan gasped, looking at us. Ha shook his head, telling her never mind. Loan burst into tears. The girls gathered around her. Thu, Ha, and I glanced at each other; none of us wanted to explain it to the girls. Ha offered to take Loan and Bich home. Thu put his arm around Lien, shrugged, and said it was getting late.

It was past 1:00 in the morning when Anh and I took a cyclo back to her uncle's house. It was a modest single-level home in the residential maze of a middle-class neighborhood. There was a brick courtyard and garden behind the picket fence. I had never seen the inside of the house. Her uncle was a high school counselor and didn't approve of premarital relations between boys and girls.

The moon beamed from high overhead. Anh fumbled with her purse. She had forgotten her keys and was afraid of waking her uncle. I couldn't take her back to my house. This was not the proper way to treat a girl. Besides, my father already expressed his disapproval of Anh and me dating. I was in a quandary. There was no all-night diner, and taking her to a hotel would have compromised her reputation.

We lingered indecisively at the gate under the arch trellis with blue ivy blooms draping over us, the pale moon on her arm. A sense of fullness welled within me, a sort of engulfing warmth. I wanted to share this feeling with her. I wanted absolutely to be with her. I gathered her into me. She was supple within the circle of my arms.

"I have an idea," I whispered. "Are you feeling adventurous?"

Anh nodded, grinning. Her trust was empowering.

I took her hand and we fled down the moonlit alley, her heels a flurry of clacks. A dog barked. We could have been the last souls left in the city. She giggled into my ear. I inhaled the scent of her.

A cyclo driver was waiting on the main street. I told him our situation and made a proposition: an all-night tour of Saigon in his cyclo for the price of a hotel room—three times what he would have normally earned. He smiled and dismounted to tilt down the cab for Anh.

Entrusting ourselves to a stranger, we floated deeper into the night, delighted. In ponderously slow strokes, he pedaled toward the city center, and then looped around the grand cathedral, the government buildings, and the commercial avenues. Saigon was flat, lush with tall trees; the night air fragrant with blooms. It was like going through an immense tropical park, the asphalt streets, fluid in their emptiness, like canals. We sailed through the city unimpeded. It was strange to know there was no French gendarme to stop and question our movement—a liberty I never knew in Hanoi. Saigon was at peace, without fears. We did not even own the privacy of four walls, but there was an impression of wealth as if the city was truly ours.

Down by Ben Thanh Market, merchants were preparing for the coming day. We ate coconut tapioca pudding and sipped hot soy milk among laborers at a roadside stand near the market. He brought us down to the quay where a dozen cyclos had gathered by the river. Slouched in their cabs, exhausted drivers slumbered. One young man strummed a guitar, his cohorts drowsily humming along. A bottle of rice wine was being passed among them. We dallied, watching them for a few songs, then moved onward. Our chain-smoking cyclo-man enjoyed rolling in the night breeze.

Anh asked me why Tat was so upset. I said he didn't like being reminded of his family's secret. He would never admit that he had foreign blood.

"It's not a big thing," Anh whispered.

"It is for people of our parents' generation," I said.

She frowned. "I don't understand."

"When I first met Tat through Ha in high school, I asked Tat why his hair was so curly. We were riding our bicycles. Tat kicked my bike so hard I fell over. I would have punched him right then, but Ha stepped in and calmed us down. We almost became enemies from the start." I took a deep breath, still not sure if Tat had forgiven me for that unintentional slight. "I didn't know Tat's mother had given up a half-French son for adoption."

"Tat's younger brother is very handsome. The first time I met him, I thought he was European."

"We are free now, but the older generations had to live under colonial rule. It was common for French bosses to have affairs with the wives of their Vietnamese subordinates. Sometimes, it was coerced. Sometimes, men offered their wives or even their daughters to their bosses to advance their careers."

Talking about it made me sad for our country and our people. It stirred up a slew of old feelings and made me feel dirty. How had generations of colonialism reduced us? How had we reduced our-selves? Are we doing that still?

Anh fell silent. She curled into me, drawing her legs over mine. The hems of her *ao dai* draped us like a blanket. The cyclo lurched over a small pothole. The night felt tender, fragile. I couldn't help but hope for a better future.

She rested her head on my shoulder, eyes lulled closed by the cyclo's gentle rocking. I was intensely aware of the warmth of her body. I wondered what she saw in me. Anh had many suitors more wealthy and accomplished than me, but she chose to wait patiently throughout our long courtship, six months of ice cream parlors, cafés, and dance halls. It was not customary for a woman to initiate talk of commitment or of a future together. To venture beyond cud-dles and kisses was to enter the realm of matrimony—something unimaginably irresponsible for a college student, so far from success, working several jobs to help support his family.

I held her hands. She had long fingers, the palms coarse, hands unafraid of work. Anh opened her eyes and smiled the same smile that won me from the first moment. I knew then I would not give her up, that when the time was right I would ask for her hand. With the decision came a liberating sensation, that of falling.

The sky was dark, but you could feel the shift toward dawn even before the eastern horizon changed. Downwind from the *pho* shop, the cool air was laced with the reassuring aroma of beef soup.

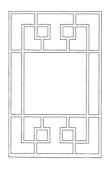

9. CRICKET FIGHT

From the time of the Japanese invasion to the onset of the Great Famine, the country reeled through a period of escalating turmoil. A pervading lawlessness spread across the land. Opportunists thrived in the cities, availing themselves of monopolies and commissions—the largess that once was the sole purview of the French. Bandits plagued the highways. Peasant uprisings were common in the countryside. Underground, Communists and Nationalists were vying for power. The former gained popularity among the commoners. The latter had promoted the Japanese promise of liberating Vietnam, but the Japanese proved themselves even crueler masters than the French. The populace staggered under new taxes and outrageous rice requisitions. Young men found themselves conscripted and taken away to work as coolies. In its drive to conquer Asia, the Japanese army was quickly draining the country's resources and setting the stage for a famine that would decimate a fifth of the population.

It was the grand prelude to disaster and, for me, the happiest years of my life.

I had the blessings of a privileged childhood, though, naturally, I was not oblivious to war. I'd seen guns and soldiers and heard of battles—it was all the adults ever talked about. But these things served as mere passing curiosities and random facts, because I was at that early age of boyhood ruled by binary simplicities: daylight and nightfall, school hours and free time, boredom and fun. It was that age where clouds had animal shapes and the seam of heaven and earth appeared as real and solid as the stitching on my shirt. Time had a spacious quality in which life unrolled as a series of unconnected events. I looked at soldiers marching through our village and saw only their impressive guns and uniforms, not the suffering they brought. I looked at a poorly seeded paddy and saw only the tadpoles to be caught, not the season of hunger to come.

My cousin Tan and I reveled in this intermediate age of uselessness and early independence, too young to be harnessed for chores, too big to be confined to the playgrounds. We had escaped adult supervision. The days were ours to squander. We roamed and played in the sea of rice paddies. We had the occasional guidance of the buffalo boys, who were essentially older versions of ourselves, stretched out and filled up though still shirtless, barefoot, and sunned as brown as syrup.

Our favorite buffalo boy was Chau, the widow cook's only son. He was thirteen, which was effectively an eon older than us. For a few brief months, he went to school and sat with us in our village's single classroom taught by my once-removed Uncle Uc. Soon after Chau learned how to write his name, he thanked our mothers for giving him the opportunity to learn and asked for their permission to quit. His mother kept his white short-sleeved shirt, sandals, and writing tablet with hopes that Chau would come to his senses. The moon-faced boy with the lotus grin had given up the classroom for the bright sky and naps on the back of a buffalo. Oh, how we envied him. He had chosen to be a lord of the fields, whose days were freedom itself; whose head was rich with outdoor intrigues; whose hands were capable of crafting kites, slingshots, fishing poles, bird traps, toy kilns, bamboo flutes, and countless small marvels. He knew where the tart berries grew and could find spicy wild onions on any river-bank. He gave us the secret of honey-grass: A fragrant fistful of it stuffed in the pillow kept the nightmare away. He was the finest of our childhood tutors.

Armed with slingshots and fishing lines, we barefooted across the summer days with the village children. We built tiny earthen ovens and baked catfish and snakehead fish encased in clay or wrapped in banana leaves. We had everything we needed: giant hay bales for hide-and-seek; cool, slimy ponds for splashing; and wind for our kites. We climbed trees and, perching like birds, gorged our-selves on longans, tangerines, and guavas plucked from branches. We lived to wage valiant battles on the lakeshore. Magic wands and en-chanted swords. Bamboo popguns and watermelon rinds. We were bandits, legionnaires, French commanders. We were the native he-roes who expelled the invaders.

Of all the boyhood diversions, cricket fighting stood out as the singularly superlative game that captured our imagination and en-dured fondly in our memories even when we had long outgrown it. It was a game that consigned boys and girls alike to countless hours scouring gardens and fields for crickets. At any time of day, we could be seen tiptoeing in the grass, ears cocked to the cricket songs. We flooded them out of their burrows, the large unpredictable browns, the ferocious reds, the swift blacks. We kept them like jewels in ex-quisitely crafted matchboxes, equipped with cellophane windows for viewing. We lived, ate, slept, and went to school with our beloved pets. It drove Teacher Uc crazy, the chorus of crickets that rang out suddenly in the middle of his lessons.

There was a spot between the village and the estate where we gathered to play. I only remembered it as a timeless place infused with a tender, silky light; an island in the silvery sheen of paddy water, speckled with fluorescent green rice shoots. There was a fishpond and an old, sleepy tamarind tree on a rocky patch of soil near where the village road joined the provincial highway that led to the city and the world beyond.

We met there, a rabble of boys and girls, to barter and trade crickets, marbles, cellophane papers, empty cookie tins, sweets, and playing cards. Someone was always gnawing on a length of sugarcane, and we passed it around like a communal lollipop. We showed off our pets and traded the ones we didn't want.

My best friend Hoi gave me a tiny chestnut-brown cricket. It had a peculiar keening song. I gave him a coconut candy and a sheet of cellophane paper. Hoi's grin grew until his eyes squinted shut.

"Oy, Thong! Come look at Binh's cricket," Tan shouted. "It's the sorriest looking bug I've ever seen. Its mother must have been a cockroach."

It was a pretty cricket with a reddish coloring on the belly and wings like lacquered rosewood. Binh didn't respond to the insult, a sign that he was not eager to risk his cricket.

"Look at his limp feelers. He's scared," Tan said to the group. This was a rite of cricket fights, open to players and spectators alike— the trading of slurs and insults until a challenge materialized. "He's scared just like his owner."

It was the cue for the audience chorus: "Just like his owner! Just like his owner!"

"Thong's cricket will eat yours like peanut brittle," Tan mocked.

"Ha!" Binh had taken the bait. He puffed up to his full height. "Mine will snap yours in half first!"

I leaned into him. "Oh, your mouth is so big, I bet your mother keeps chickens in there!"

The crowd shrieked in delight: "Chickenshit mouth! Chickenshit mouth!"

They laughed and quickly divided into two bands, each giving allegiance for one boy and his cricket. Volleys of taunts and jeers slung round and round, and there was no way either Binh or I could back down without being called a coward or a sissy.

"What's the bet?" I yelled, holding up my hands for silence.

"Ear boxing," Binh said.

Pig-bellied Chung, the class clown, squeaked and scurried around, fingers fluttering like a timid sand crab. Everybody laughed. The prize for winning a cricket fight had always been the pleasure of inflicting pain on the loser in one of several creative methods. Binh had made a cheap bet.

"Kick," I said.

Hoi shouted, "He'll never pay up!"

A cackle ran through the group. Binh blushed. We all remembered the time Binh lost and refused to be kicked by a boy half his size. After that, no one, not even the girls, would accept his challenges. Being ostracized from the game proved unbearable, and a mere week later, Binh apologized and took the little boy's foot to his bottom like a good loser.

"Kick! Kick! Kick!" chanted the merciless choir. Everyone, except the boy getting a hard foot in the rear, was a winner.

"Five kicks," Tan suggested.

"Ten kicks!" cried another, splaying digits to a roar of laughter.

Binh ignored them. "Same as before then: one kick."

"One kick!" Chung quieted the rabble, playing the part of the ringmaster. "Reds from the stable of Binh against Blackie from the stable of Thong."

Chung placed a large glass pickling jar on the ground, and the kids quickly gathered around the miniature stadium, packing four-deep, squatting, crouching, piling on top of each other, vying for a good view. Binh carefully opened his matchbox, shook the cricket into his cupped palm, and then placed it in the jar. I put mine in. They were the same size, as evenly matched as one could hope for.

Binh tapped the jar to agitate the crickets. They squared off, hesitating. Left on their own, crickets rarely fought. In most encounters, the hierarchy was immediately established with the weaker cricket submitting to the dominant one by turning away, baring his flank, and fleeing.

I could feel my face reddening. If my cricket was a coward, they'd mock me too. I wished I had kept my cricket safe in his box. Chung dropped a small brown female cricket into the jar and guaranteed a fight.

The moment Reds and Blackie noticed the female, they lunged at each other and grappled. They used their front legs like arms and kicked with their large hind legs. The dagger-like spurs on the hind legs were sharp enough to cut through their armor. The female cricket stayed clear of the combatants. Blackie mounted Reds from behind and bit off a feeler. Reds jumped, launching the both of them across the jar. They struck the glass and tumbled apart. A detached limb twitched on the floor. It was one of Reds's forelegs. Blackie came forward and took a kick that spun him sideways. Then they engaged in the deadly clinch, clawing away at each other.

We crowded around the mini-stadium, yelling, cheering, locked in the momentary eternity of mortal combat. The crickets separated and, as abruptly as it began, it was over. Reds had his belly slashed open, yellowish entrails showing. He was also missing a feeler and both front legs. Blackie fluttered his wings in a feeble victory dance. He had lost a foreleg. He would not fight again.

The crowd sighed with satisfaction. I scooped my cricket back into the matchbox to be released back to the garden where I'd caught him. Chung reclaimed the female and chucked the red cricket and the broken pieces into the pond for the fish.

The children giggled and moved back to form a circle for us. Binh knew the strategy: Every time you win, you must kick the other boy with all your strength because next time, his cricket might win and he might kick you even harder. Binh had done exactly that to me three times in a row, so he knew he had it coming. Bending over, he braced himself, hands on knees. He didn't see that I had taken a few steps back. I bounded forward and, in a running kick, unleashed the blow with all my weight behind it. Binh grunted and pitched forward onto the ground, red-faced, eyes in the back of his head, hands clenched between his thighs.

In my eagerness, I had missed and kicked him in the groin.

All the boys and girls laughed so hard they forgot whose turn was next.

In the irrigation ditches, small silvery fish darted, tadpoles lingering along the edges. Way off, a cock crowed. On the breeze rode the scents of a countryside childhood, paddy water, black earth, and honey-grass. Across the fields, the buffalo boys flew their singing kites. Butterfly-shaped wings of red and yellow swooped and climbed, making wistful looping melodies in a bright blue sky.

Some joys were so simple as to be incorruptible in memory, untouchable, neither by distance nor by tragedy. It remained unfathomable to me throughout the bridging decades, how things could abruptly change within a brief span of seasons, not enough time for a child to become a man, or for an orchard to take root. Laughing children of the rice paddies, many of us would not live out our teenage years. None came through unscathed.

We all would fight battles not of our choosing. We would be fierce crickets.

10. The Recruiter

The stage was set for war. Within months of splitting the country into North and South, it became apparent that the U.S. would renege on the most important stipulation of the Geneva Accord: It would not allow a free and democratic election to reunite Vietnam. In a single stroke, millions of displaced people, northerners who had migrated south and southerners who had followed the Communists north, would never see their homes again.

On July 7, 1954, the Americans selected Ngo Dinh Diem, a former mandarin and a Catholic, as their choice for prime minister of a Buddhist country. U.S. President Eisenhower gave aid directly to Vietnam, bypassing the French and sending a clear message that France's time in Vietnam was over. Without hope of regaining control, the French withdrew their remaining troops in South Vietnam and stopped supporting the Vietnamese factions that had sided with them.

Guided by American advisors, Diem overthrew his own emperor in a referendum and seized power for himself—the vilest of treasons that would have, in the previous generation, warranted the beheadings of Diem and his entire family. While the U.S. continued to provide Diem with generous military, financial, and organizational support, it placed no requirement on Diem to allow democratic development through freedom of speech and a multi-party system. Empowered and unfettered, Diem quickly eliminated his political rivals, silenced critics, and initiated a ruthless campaign to rid the South of opposition by branding all dissenters as Communists and imprisoning thousands regardless of political affiliation. Within five years, Diem became the dictator of a police state.

The peasantry grew deeply resentful of Diem's corrupt policies and cronyism. Persecuted for voicing their complaints, many farmers became Communist sympathizers, which, consequently, facilitated guerillas' operations in the countryside. Insurgent activities grew more violent and frequent in the South. Even Diem's own men turned against him, staging a coup that nearly toppled his regime.

In December of 1960, Ho Chi Minh formed the National Liberation Front (NLF), which had its own armed forces called the People's Armed Forces of Liberation (PAFL), which the Diem government and the Americans called Viet Cong. Although the South Vietnam government controlled the countryside during the daylight hours, at night the PAFL controlled vast areas of the Mekong Delta and parts of the Central Highlands. Throughout 1961, the Viet Cong launched large-scale assaults against the Army of the Republic of South Vietnam (ARVN). As the conflict developed, the South became critically divided between the pro-Diem faction headed by the Nhan Vi party and the anti-Diem factions, which included suppressed religious and political groups as well as the Viet Cong.

In 1962, I was living and teaching in Ben Tre, a reputed hotbed of Viet Cong insurgency. I had decided to drop out of the Institute of Administration and continue pursuing my degree in teaching. Anh and I were in love, but we couldn't get married because of my father's disapproval. A wedding without his blessing was unimaginable, so we simply moved in together.

In Ben Tre, Anh and I rented a one-bedroom duplex in a government-worker complex. It was a modest unit without a kitchen, but it was the best home we had in four years of living together. The backyard had a guava tree with fruit big and sweet enough to sell at the market. Two large fish-egg trees with juicy pinkish-yellow berries shaded the front yard. Our next-door neighbor was a friendly widow who lived alone and took it upon herself to teach Anh the art of homemaking.

Ben Tre was the best post I could find, given the recent glut of teachers. Even with good recommendations and experience, I had to commute half a day by bus and ferry for part-time work at two different places, a public school in Ben Tre and a private high school in Saigon. The situation had worsened with each passing year. With the intense competition for a limited number of jobs, it was inevitable that politics entered the workplace.

At Ben Tre High School, many faculty members joined Diem's Nhan Vi party; the more ambitious ones went as far as converting to Catholicism to advance their careers. The school principal had no qualms about showing his favoritism for Diem supporters. Despite my two-year seniority at the school, I was assigned the least desirable courses. The classes that I had been teaching for two years were given to new instructors, all Nhan Vi party members. I dared not lodge my grievances for fear of being branded a dissident, but I couldn't keep my opinions to myself when my students asked about current events and the political situation.

One evening after school, I had a visit from Khoa, one of my students who had helped me find our apartment two years prior. I enjoyed talking to Khoa and didn't mind helping him with his studies. He often dropped by my house for visits during the weekends, bringing small gifts of fresh fruit from his family's garden. This was the first time he showed up without notice. I was surprised to see Khoa looking rather nervous.

Khoa greeted Anh and me, then promptly said, "Teacher, can we talk on the patio?"

I agreed and Anh brought us tea and chilled sugarcane batons on the patio. It was unusual for Khoa to ask to speak in private. I waited for him to sip his tea before asking if he had problems at school.

"No, Teacher. My classes are fine." He paused and then looked directly at me. "I heard you were going to a meeting tonight."

"I'm meeting Tra later after dinner. I think he needs some help with his studies."

"Teacher, did you know Tra is a Communist recruiter?"

I shook my head, stunned. Tra was one of my favorite students, diligent and very bright. Although Tra was shy and quiet in class, he often sought me out during lunch and recess breaks to talk about the fighting in the countryside. Many students were very worried about being drafted into the army, and it seemed normal to me that Tra was concerned about the brewing war. When I was his age in school, politics was all my friends and I could think about.

"Tra and I are from the same village. His uncle was killed in a land dispute with the government, and Tra's family lost the land the Viet Minh gave them. Tra has been a party member since he was thirteen," he said. The way Khoa met my eyes squarely told me he was putting himself in danger by this revelation.

"Tra is planning to introduce you to his superiors so they can judge your political affiliation."

"Are you serious? I've never shown any indication that I might want to join the Viet Cong."

"But when students asked you about the government's policies and the country's stability, you said the leaders were creating a privileged class for their party members. You were very pessimistic about the government pacification program. You said it would fail."

"Yes, but that doesn't mean I'm a Communist sympathizer."

"It's enough to make Tra think that you might be. But he's not sure—that's why he's bringing you to his superiors. If they think you're sympathetic to the Communist cause, they'll try to recruit you. By doing that, they will expose themselves. So you must join. Otherwise they will consider you a danger to their organization. They'll find a way to eliminate you."

I was shocked. All this time I thought I was safe in Ben Tre by keeping a low profile and focusing on my work. I never took part in teachers' rallies and I was very careful of saying anything critical of the government to any of the faculty.

"Teacher, from now on, please be careful about what you say to the students. Half of them are Communist sympathizers and party members."

"Why aren't you a member?"

Looking at the lines in his palms, Khoa sighed. "My father was a devout Buddhist. Before he died, he made me promise to remain neutral as long as I could. Besides, who would take care of my mother and sister if I got killed in this war?"

I asked him, "Did your family lose land?"

"My father was a carpenter. The Viet Minh only gave land to farmers and sharecroppers, so we gained nothing from the Viet Minh and lost nothing in the government's reparation program."

I KNEW about the land reforms and remembered the troubles the government had with the peasants, but I had no idea how entrenched the problem had become in the southern countryside. During the first few years in the South, my family was engrossed in our own struggles in Saigon. We didn't pay much attention to what was happening in the provinces.

Khoa said many of his classmates had seen their fathers jailed and their lands confiscated.

During the war, the Viet Minh had decreed a land reform in the South, where the majority of the land was owned by a small number of plantation families who had prospered under French rule. The Viet Minh redistributed the land to sharecroppers and small-plot farmers. The French could not control the countryside, so the reform went smoothly. For nearly ten years until the French's surrender, the peasants owned, tilled, and invested in their land. Following the conditions of the Geneva Accord, the Communist forces, including Viet Minh soldiers from South Vietnam, were regrouped to the North and left the South to a government newly formed and backed by the Americans. In 1955, the South Vietnam government invalidated the Viet Minh's land reform and restored the land to the original owners. The peasants staged violent protests and refused to vacate their homes. The rich landlords reclaimed their properties with the help of the government, the newly formed Army of the Republic of Viet Nam (ARVN), and the police. In the chaos that ensued, there were accusations of land grabbing and abuse of power. Farmers were killed during the riots. Others were murdered in their homes. Tens of thousands of peasants were branded as Communists, jailed, or sent to reeducation camps.

AFTER Khoa left, Anh came out and sat down next to me. Dinner was ready, laid out on a mat in the front room. I could smell the claypot catfish and sour cabbage soup with pork short ribs. Under our neighbor's tutelage, Anh was developing into a marvelous cook. She could make a feast from market scraps.

Anh put her head on my shoulder. "Is something wrong?"

"What makes you think that?"

"You're scowling at the air."

I chuckled, adoring her in every way. At times like this, when she knew me so well, I didn't care one bit that my father did not approve of her or of our living together. He had said having a girlfriend would distract me from my studies. I was still young enough to fool myself that it was possible to hold two jobs and still pursue my degree at Saigon University.

Anh said, "If you don't join the Nhan Vi party, you might not have your job next term. And you can't avoid the Communist recruiters for long. This is Ben Tre. You can't straddle the fence. If one side doesn't shoot you, the other will."

"It is never wise to choose the lesser of two evils."

Suddenly, I felt very sad. I thought of my friend Hoi, my cousin Quyen, Uncle Uc, and so many people from my childhood. We had gone nowhere. These were the same choices my friends had had to make a decade ago between the Resistance and the French.

Anh said, "Then we must find a new home."

I looked at her to see if she understood the import of that decision. After two years of moving from one hovel to another, this was the first apartment where we had our own toilet. Our home sat beside a lake. We had enough money to live. We were happy here. We had been saving prodigiously so that someday we could afford a proper wedding. Anh was pregnant. Moving house would use up everything we had.

"Are you sure?"

Anh smiled, placed my hand on her belly, and said, "I think it's a girl. We're going to be a family. I'll follow you wherever."

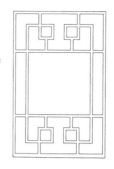

11. Hoi and I

Hoi whispered, "Look! A *muong* grasshopper to your left."

It was a big one, light green, the exact shade of young rice leaves, with black sesame seed eyes. Clinging to the underside of the leaf, it had its wings folded back, hind legs cranked high, poised to spring.

I hushed him and tiptoed around the plant. *Muong* grasshoppers were very skittish. You had to come at them from their blind side. I cupped my palms and clapped my hands over the grasshopper.

It jumped.

Hoi wailed, "Oh, you let it escape!"

"I didn't let it escape! It's just too fast." I was as disappointed as he was. *Muong* were the prettiest and the tastiest of all grasshoppers. They were also the hardest to catch.

It fluttered a short way on white wings and settled back into the field. Hoi slunk past me, eyes fixed at the point where the grasshopper had vanished into the

71

green. He took slow, careful steps, one hand steadying the bamboo basket slung at his waist.

I was hot and tired, and I wanted to quit. There wasn't a single cloud in the sky or a shade tree in sight. We had prowled the fields the whole blistering afternoon and all we found was grasshoppers. Hoi carried his crab basket, even though neither of us had seen a single crab in weeks. We had our lines with us, but the Walkers' camps crowded the riverbanks at every fishing hole. Folks said Walkers ate babies and small kids, and blamed them for missing vegetables, poultry, and pets. Although we were too old to believe that, we knew Walkers were very thorough scavengers and would eat just about anything they could get their hands on. We wouldn't find anything on the land they had covered.

They started arriving after the last harvest, when the Japanese forces imposed a massive rice requisition to feed their armies. At first the men came, alone or in small groups, mostly sharecroppers and tradesmen. They all walked, too poor for any other means of travel. You could tell they were either related or at least from the same village by the way they stayed close to each other, shared food, and let the eldest ones speak for the rest. They carried bedding, cooking pots, and the tools of their trade. Clearly, they were not beggars. Even though they worked for food, there wasn't enough rice in the village to feed them all, and eventually they moved on to the larger towns.

The next wave brought women, and now there were children as well. Our village was overrun with strangers. The stronger ones still made their way toward Hanoi, but those too famished to continue camped down by our creek. They begged at the market and came to my family's estate for the free soup Uncle Thuan offered twice daily.

At first, I didn't understand the turmoil around me. I disliked these strangers invading our village. When I refused to help serve in the soup line, my mother said it was the responsibility of the rich to care for the poor. Heaven would not look kindly on us if we turned our backs on these people. She said that with the Japanese army's relentless rice requisitions, most villagers did not even have enough food for their own families. We should not be afraid of these transients; they were only farmers who lost their rice stocks as well as their seeds. They took to the road because there was no hope in waiting for the next season when they had nothing to sow into the land.

Hoi halted and stood completely still, his eyes roving about. He didn't move for a long while. I almost told him to give up when he raised a hand to warn me. Hoi crouched down and snaked his right arm slowly between the rice plants. His hand shot out and grabbed the top bud of one plant.

"Did you catch it?"

"Of course." He giggled with a squinty-eyed grin. He had the fastest hands of any boy I knew. Hoi was half a head shorter than me. I was better than he was at studying, flying kites, and running, but he was better at things important to nine-year-old boys: fishing, hunting crickets, making flutes, and throwing rocks. Hoi showed me the grasshopper. It was as big as a thumb.

"Hey, kids!" A woman shouted from the dike separating the fields.

She wore faded black clothes, pants rolled high up her pale, bony legs. The afternoon sun clawed through her tattered peasant hat of palm leaves, making tiger-stripes on her face. She was as weathered and thin as the scarecrow in our garden. I thought she was a Walker.

She shook a long pair of bamboo tongs at us. "Don't step on the rice plants!"

We stood in the middle of the field. Like many paddies that season, it was so sparsely seeded that we hadn't stepped on a single plant.

Hoi waved. "Oh, hello, Mrs. Cau. Did you find a lot of feces today?"

"Not a lot, not a lot at all. Not enough food to eat, not enough feces to find," she replied in a sing-song tone. "Not enough feces to find, not enough fertilizer for the crop. Not enough fertilizer for the crop: Not enough food to eat!"

"Don't worry, we won't step on rice plants."

"You'd better not. It's bad enough with the Japanese devils

stealing rice right out of our mouths, we don't need kids trampling the crop as well . . . ," she said, her words trailing off. Abruptly, she turned and walked away with the basket on her hip, her tongs moving side to side, skimming the top of the grass, searching.

"Poor Mrs. Cau," said Hoi. "She's a widow with no children. She has to collect shit every day to make a living."

"That's enough to make a living?" I asked.

Hoi shrugged. "Lots of village people go out to the fields to shit. We are not like rich people with outhouses."

"So? At least you don't have to put up with the smell of the latrine! Don't complain."

"I'm not, I just said she got enough."

"She trades it with someone for rice?"

"No, she mixes it with ashes from burnt straw and grass and sells it as fertilizer. She goes out twice every day: once very early in the morning when the dogs haven't already run out, otherwise they would eat most of the shits, and once in the afternoon after lunch."

"Where does she live?"

"Her place is at the end of the village. My mom makes me go there to buy fertilizer."

"I want to go there with you next time." I had a rich kid's curiosity about poverty.

"Why? Her shed smelled so bad, I thought I'd fallen into a giant pile of shit whenever I went there!"

We laughed, but I still wanted to go. Besides, there wasn't much else to do. We used to play games, but ever since the last harvest, all Hoi wanted to do was fish or hunt for edible critters. It had been weeks since we were in school. Teacher Uc had not been paid in months and only half of the students made it to class. The older kids had already dropped out to help their families in the fields. Most of our friends had fathers or brothers who had been conscripted as coolies for the Japanese army. Those who came to school couldn't hear the teacher over their own growling stomachs. It wasn't long before Teacher Uc, who happened to be my father's second cousin, decided to disband the classes.

Hoi asked me, "When do you think we'll have classes again?"

I shrugged. I knew his parents were very proud that Hoi was the first in the family to attend school. Hoi was the family's only son, and his parents treated him like a prince, the family's treasure and salvation. Regardless of a man's prestige and fortune, not having a son to carry on the family line was the biggest failure of a man's life, an unforgivable sin against his ancestors.

"I'll ask my mother to let you come and study with us," I said and clapped him on the shoulder. Teacher Uc tutored us twice a week at home. Every Friday afternoon, he stopped by for tea and cakes with my mother.

Hoi glanced up and smiled as if he knew something that I didn't and wasn't about to tell. He turned and headed off toward his house. Hoi was the poorest student in the class. His family didn't have a single rice plot. I knew he wasn't comfortable being inside the estate. Whenever my cousins were around, Hoi got very quiet and refused to eat anything I gave him, always saying he wasn't hungry.

Hoi's family lived at the edge of the village, in a two-room bamboo cottage. The yard had been turned into a vegetable garden full of beans, yams, maniocs, and eggplants. When we got there, Mr. Bui was on his knees, working on the hibiscus shrubs that fenced around the family's property.

I bowed. Hoi grinned and shook his basket.

"Did you boys catch any field crabs today?"

"No, Father, but we've got plenty of grasshoppers." Hoi's family was fond of crab soup. It was very good with *banh da*.

"What are you doing, Mr. Bui?"

"I'm mending this hole. We lost a lot of vegetables from our garden last night."

"Walkers," Hoi mumbled and led me inside. His family didn't have a big guard dog; they couldn't afford to feed another mouth.

Small dogs were worthless because they were often lured outside, killed, and eaten by the Walkers.

The house was smoky and cramped. The whole family slept in the back room and used the front room for making *banh da*. Mrs. Bui and Hoi's sister, Lan, were hovering over the cooking fire built in the middle of the floor. Even though I was from the wealthiest clan in the village, Hoi's family was always nice to me, especially his mother.

"Mrs. Bui, I brought you some guavas from our garden." I had access to our whole family orchard so it wasn't hard to bring them something whenever I visited. We had all sorts of fruit trees, so something was always in season.

Mrs. Bui thanked me. Lan looked up, grinning. I knew she liked green guavas with chili-salt. Small and even more frail than her mother, Lan rarely talked, the size and manner of her smiles saying most of what she wanted. She was fourteen and pretty in a wan, wispy way. She spent most of her days with her mother in the kitchen.

They squatted in front of four steaming cauldrons of boiling water, each kettle with a cloth stretched taut over it like a drum skin. They poured a ladle of rice batter onto the cloth, swirled it into a thin round layer, and placed a tin lid over the cauldron to let it steam, working fast to conserve firewood. In a few moments, they removed the thin *banh da* with a bamboo stick and laid it out on a rack to dry. It was simple but exhausting work.

"Mrs. Bui, you're making a lot of *banh da* today," I said, pointing to the racks filled with wax paper packages. "You must have many orders."

Mrs. Bui opened her mouth to speak, but stopped herself. She took a deep breath, then smiled. "Would you like some *banh da?*"

"No, thank you, Mrs. Bui. We're going to roast some grasshoppers," I said.

If food weren't so scarce for them, I would have accepted. Since Hoi and I became friends, *banh da* had become one of my favorite snacks. There were many ways to eat them. You could toast them and eat them plain like crackers or with dips. You could serve them with meat or salad, or add them to soup, or deep-fry them like chips. You could also soak and cut them into strips to make noodles. But none of these dishes were the sort of food people ate during the famine. It seemed odd that they were grinding up rice to make *banh da* while people were stretching their rice stocks by making thin soup. This was almost wasteful, because rice satisfied the stomach far better than *banh da.*

I would learn much later that foot soldiers often soaked *banh da* in water, rolled them up with a bit of brown sugar, and ate them on marches, during ambushes or fire-fights when they could not light a cooking fire.

WE sat under the eaves and killed the grasshoppers by pinching their heads. Hoi buried them in the embers of the cooking fire. I was salivating by the time he brought them back on a hard square of dried palm leaf. The toasted grasshoppers were very hot. Their burned wings had turned into thin layers of ash clinging against their bodies. I snatched the biggest grasshopper, plucked off its head, and stripped away its legs. Rubbing the steamy little nugget between my palms, I blew away the ashen wings and burnt bits. When it was cool enough, I popped it in my mouth. It was flaky and crunchy like a butter pastry with a nutty-meaty cream center, and faintly salty like tofu skin.

I didn't know why, but the first one always tasted the best.

But they were all so good, we gobbled them up as quickly as we could. I didn't care that Hoi had less to eat at home than me. We raced through the whole batch, not bothering to count out our shares.

I smacked my lips, looking at the final pile of grasshopper heads. "We were lucky to catch so many. I thought the Walkers got most of them already."

"They can barely move. To catch a grasshopper, you have to be fast."

I took out two peanut candies from my pocket and gave him

one. Hoi had expected it all along. I always brought some sweets and they would be the last things we ate.

Hoi bit a small piece from his candy and sucked on it to make it last longer. "You are my best friend."

"You are my best friend too," I said.

He grinned broadly. "Hey, look at all those dragonflies on the hedge. You want to catch some and catch frogs with them?"

"Yes, but it's late. I'd better get home before my mother sends someone looking for me."

"I'll go with you to your gate."

It was part of our routine, the fifteen-minute walk along the inner village road that took the better part of an hour. We were of an age without a notion of time. We picked up sticks, rattled fences, beat hedges, chased cats, and threw stones at birds.

"Here it comes . . . ," Hoi whispered, gesturing with his eyes to a shadow creeping behind the hedge.

I realized with a jolt that we were crossing the territory of the Beast, the biggest and meanest dog in the village. I heard branches snapping. Without a single warning bark, Beast shot out of the bush, punching a hole through the foliage.

We sprinted. Beast closed the distance in a flash.

Hoi shouted, "Now!"

We spun around. The monster was right behind us. I flung the first stone without aiming and missed. Hoi struck Beast smack on the head and made it wobble. I whizzed another one into its flank. Hoi threw so fast his arm blurred. He didn't miss once. Snarling insanely, the dog circled and tried lunging at us from the side. Hoi hurled another stone into its jaws. Beast stumbled, yelped once, retreating. We kept pelting until it bolted back to the safety of the hedge. Beast vented blood-chilling barks, challenging us to come closer.

I was tingly from head to toe, flushed with fear. We jogged to a safe distance before cheering. Hoi and I slapped each other on the back, congratulating and puffing ourselves up like heroes. Grinning, we skipped down the street.

"It's going to get us one of these days."

"I hope the Walkers get him first," said Hoi.

"He's too strong for them. Besides, any dog that mean must taste terrible."

Hoi laughed. "I bet he'd be tasty. His owner must have fed him well for him to get that big."

Neither of us had ever eaten dog meat, but that didn't stop us from speculating what it might taste like. The discussion lasted us the rest of the way to my family's estate. We stopped at the side gate. It was still open. The sentry was expecting me. Farther down the road, a huge crowd queued up at the main entrance. It was nearing time for the evening soup.

I asked Hoi, "You're going to take the long way back?"

"Yes. I don't think I can hold off Beast on my own."

I wished I could walk him back to his house. "Here, take some more stones, just in case."

Hoi touched my arm and loped away. I watched him from my gate. He always looked back right before disappearing behind the first turn in the road.

Hoi shouted at the top of his lungs, "I'll bring some dragonflies, and we'll catch lots of frogs tomorrow!"

It was my lasting image of him, my best friend, unalterable by all that was to come. I could not remember him as a leader of Uncle Ho's Youth Brigade or a hero in the Resistance. But I remembered the distance between us; our symmetry. I remembered him, a shirtless, barefooted boy standing in the thickening dusk, just a purple silhouette at the far bend of the road, inky branches curving over him, those arms of darkness, those crashing waves.

12. THE DRAFT

The bad news came over the radio after dinner. Anh was crouching over the tin basin on the floor, washing the dishes, and I was grading my students' papers. It was our usual routine. The announcer called my age group and then read the list of canceled draft exemptions. A pot clattered on the cement slab. Anh hugged her knees, her eyes closed. My exemption as a teacher had been rescinded. The music came back on the radio. I turned it off. Anh came to the table and sat quietly next to me, hands folded in her lap.

There were no words to comfort her. We couldn't look at each other; that would confirm the looming disaster. We stared at the wooden tabletop. It was second-hand, banged up and full of scratches, but it was ours. We earned this tiny two-room alley house with years of hard work. Anh saved and skimped, never spending anything on herself. She did the neighbors' laundry. I taught full course-loads at two different schools at opposite ends of the city, commuting on buses four hours daily, six days a week. We had just moved into Saigon from Ben Tre to avoid the Viet Cong recruiters. All our bright plans were shattered.

We put the baby to sleep in her crib across the room from our bed. Anh turned down the oil lamp, unrolled the mosquito netting, and curled into my arms. She was usually bubbling with gossip and stories about her day and the neighborhood, whispering us both to sleep. Tonight she was still, her hands clutching mine.

I was more afraid of being away from my wife and child than I was of being sent to fight. This was all the love and happiness I had built for myself. I wondered how Anh would manage. She had never held a job. I knew with shameful and terrifying certainty that the day would come when she would have to pawn her single piece of jewelry, a jade bracelet, to feed our child. The thought was devastating. My precious little world was crumbling. I was twenty-seven.

We held each other through the sinking hours. Midnight passed, then she whispered the most amazing thing: "None of this matters. I had a dream that we grew old together."

DRAFT Monday arrived quickly. The wonderful aroma of pork-and-mushroom dumplings filled our home. Anh smiled at me from the kitchen. She was making a special breakfast of *banh cuon* and a luxurious cup of hot cocoa with condensed milk. It was a delicious farewell treat—much better than my usual breakfast of one fried egg and bread. Her cooking skills had developed considerably since we first lived together. I teased her that if I weren't drafted, I'd open a restaurant and put her to work while I relaxed and counted the money. Anh giggled and pinched me. I was trying not to think that our savings would only last her a month or two. My soldier's wages would come late, and they would be a pittance.

"I want to see you to staging camp," she said for the fourth time.

"It will be hard for me to say good-bye there. Stay here; try to think of it as a long teaching stint out of town. In a few weeks, they'll transfer me to the training camp or the military school. We can see each other then."

Friends who had been drafted told me what to expect. They gave me a list of what to bring: a mosquito net, a pair of pants, two shirts, boxers, toothbrush, toothpaste, and a comb—certainly nothing of value. I bundled everything inside a brown paper bag and tied it with a length of twine. Bring money if you want to eat, they said, but keep your wallet and your wits about you; we're all educated and slated to become officers, but there are thieves among us.

I waited for half an hour, but no one from my big family came to send me off. I had thought that at least one of my brothers would come with good wishes. Father was still disappointed with my marriage. No doubt he considered this draft was part of the bad luck that came with Anh. It was just as well. Our family was never good at showing our feelings.

Anh walked me down the alley, carrying the baby. She was silent in a distracted way that I had learned was her expression of sorrow. She knew how to hold her tears, and I was grateful for it. On the main street, the sun had climbed above the buildings and the sidewalk was bustling with pedestrians and vendors. We stopped at the curb. I put my bundle on the ground. I kissed the baby and gathered the three of us into a big long embrace, not caring that strangers were looking. I hugged them until the knot in my throat was about to undo me completely.

We looked at each other and sighed. She smiled, squeezing my forearm. I hailed a taxi. Anh hung on to the door and wouldn't let go. I pried her fingers loose. I looked through the rear window. She kept waving until the taxi turned the corner.

QUANG Trung was a training camp for non-commissioned officers, half an hour from Saigon, sitting on a thousand acres of bush land suitable for staging counter-guerilla training. Near the front gate, they had fenced off a large barren area from the rest of the camp. Within the enclosure, there was a handful of wooden structures and military tents housing several hundred men. This was the staging ground for draftees.

Dozens of young men arrived at the same time as I did—some by taxis, others by motorbikes, most attended by family and friends. It was a somber gathering, women sobbing, their men trying to put up brave faces. I took a deep breath and went directly to the gate. The bored guard waved me through without glancing at my ID card.

At the administration cabin, a hundred new draftees milled about the dirt yard in various states of dejection. It took three hours for the two typists to peck out our names and personal information while chatting, smoking, and taking breaks every half hour. Three soldiers lounged about, reading newspapers, trading jokes while waiting for the typists. They shuffled us from one line to another for no apparent reason, and finally assigned us bunks in tents housing twenty men each.

We went to the kitchen tent for lunch. A handful of men sat at the tables staring morosely into their tins. The moment I saw the scraps the cook ladled into my plate, I knew why. Hungry, I tried a spoonful of rice and spat it out. It was foul, mildewed rice. I picked out a couple of rice worms and laid them on the table. The salty soup had a faint smell of chicken and lumps of fat, but neither vegetables nor meat. We looked at each other and shook our heads in dismay. Our reactions didn't surprise the cook. He pointed us to a diner in the middle of the compound.

It was a big, flimsy wooden house with a tin roof and packed-dirt floor. A canvas awning extended the dining area around the house, sheltering a knickknack collection of chairs, benches, and tables. The structure was open on all sides, except for the back where the kitchen and storerooms were located. Service girls took orders from behind a long glass case counter displaying stationery, snacks, beverages, toiletries, and other sundries. They had four rice plates, grilled pork, beef, fish, and fried eggs, all served with white rice and boiled vegetables. I would come to learn that besides food, the three most popular items were beer to numb a draftee's mind, cigarettes to soothe his anxiety, and lottery tickets to give him hope. I became a chain-smoker in the staging camp.

Per diem cost for feeding each draftee was predetermined by the army, so the cheaper the food the camp commander fed us, the more money he skimmed from the budget. And the longer we were kept at the staging camp, the bigger the profit he pocketed. As if that wasn't enough, he permitted the diner to overcharge for meals and sundries, at three times market price, for more than seven hundred men daily, year round. Naturally, he reaped a healthy kickback percentage from the operator.

The diner became the center of our existence in the staging camp. Every single draftee spent money there. In my three weeks at the staging camp, I would end up spending the equivalent of my wife's grocery budget for three months. Day after day, there was nothing to do except wait for our names to be called for a physical exam or for transfer to training camps. When the sun was overhead, we crawled beneath bushes because there were no big trees in the camp. Sooner or later we crawled back to the diner to buy lemonades just for the privilege of sitting for an hour under the tin roof.

For me, within a few days, the scope of the whole staging camp passed from the realm of inefficiency to stupidity and then to the ludicrous. It made me furious. There was nothing I could do but sit in the hot dirt fuming. We were expected to fight for our country, and yet here we were, exactly where they put us, squatting under the searing sun, thirsty and hungry, crazy with insect bites, out of our minds with boredom, simply so our own superiors—the men to whom we were to entrust our lives—could steal from us repeatedly, day after day, for weeks on end. It was the sort of abuse that leached away whatever patriotic sense of duty a draftee might have had in the first place. It sowed a festering seed of doubt in the soldier's mind about his leaders, and it taught him from the very beginning to fend for himself. And it made him certain that the enemy had worthier leaders.

I had no idea at the time, but it would be no different at Thu Duc Academy, the officer training school, my next destination. Entrenched corruption, outrageous inefficiency, and plain apathy permeated the upper ranks of the South Vietnamese army. Even before I picked up a gun, I had already lost faith and respect for our leaders. No one around me actually harbored any hope of winning this war.

For the next seven years, the only things that gave me heart and held me steady in the face of danger would be the heroism and sacrifices of the soldiers, the noncommissioned officers, and the low-ranked officers in the South Vietnam army—these men who fought to defend their fellowmen and homeland even when they knew our leaders were lazy and corrupt. Their courage would inspire me to rise above self-pity and perform my duties to the best of my capabilities so as not to betray their effort, their blood, their lives.

ONE of my close friends from college, Hanh Vu, arrived at the camp a few days after me. Hanh was a lanky northerner from a lower-middle-class merchant family. He was an easygoing cynic. We spent most of our time smoking, drinking beer, and musing about the mistakes that had landed us in this bad situation. I told him that if they hadn't drafted me, I would have received tenure at the school by the end of this year and would have had a draft exemption.

Hanh shrugged. "Maybe you'd have had a few months of freedom and then they'd cancel that exemption too. The way the war is escalating, they'll eventually cancel all the exemptions."

"It's impossible to plan your life when they keep changing the rules."

"You should have stayed in the Institute of Administration. You probably would have been one of the big guys handing out these exemptions instead of one of us." He grinned. "Remember Thu?"

"He was a fun guy. We were study partners. I heard he graduated from the Institute of Administration," I said, smiling at the hilarious times we shared.

"Thu is a first-level manager in the Customs Office. They're all exempted from the draft over there."

I sighed, pleased for my old friend, pitying myself.

Hanh pounded me on the shoulder and chuckled. "Scoring high on your exams was probably the worst thing you could have done to yourself. Funny, isn't it? I barely passed, but here we are in the exact same lousy place."

Hubris brought me down the difficult path while wisdom would have led me toward comfort and wealth. How did I miss it? I had come of age in a time of opportunity. They were trying to form a new government under the guidance of the American advisors. New colleges and universities sprang up to educate those who would one day run the country. Admission into any program was easy. Education was inexpensive and accessible for those who wanted it. Ministries were handed out like rewards to college graduates. Students ranking in the top percentiles had the posts of their choosing. It seemed impossible for someone in my position to lose, and yet I had managed to do precisely that.

I FIRST saw Thien sitting beneath the trees with a stack of novels and chain-smoking his way through a pack of cigarettes, another unopened pack in his breast pocket. I showed him my book. "You want to trade?" Without glancing at it, he grinned a mouthful of rotted teeth, shoved his whole pile at me, and said, "Take whatever you want."

Thien was a warehouse manager with a salary four times an army lieutenant's. His desk job had plenty of perks, including time to indulge in books and sideline deals for extra income. Thien was one of the medical postponement aspirants who starved themselves to make their bodies unfit for service. His determination was profound. For breakfast, he took a cup of black coffee. Lunch, his only true meal, consisted of one small bowl of steamed rice. At night, he drank one beer to dull the hunger pangs. This was his third time in the camp. It was a long, tortuous road: three to four weeks in the staging camp waiting for the physical, which he must fail, and then another two weeks waiting for the army's medical board to review and grant a service exemption. With two medical deferments already on his record, Thien was aiming for a third, which would qualify him for a permanent discharge. Thien was hopeful because he had learned how to emaciate himself and had the proper contacts, as well as some money to bribe the doctors. But, he confided to me, he would need to take his body to the very edge this time.

I asked him if the postponements were worth abusing his body over and over without any guarantee of success.

"Have you ever been in a hospital?" he asked.

"Yes, and that's why I didn't study medicine."

When we first arrived in Saigon, my cousin Lang contracted typhoid. Lang had gone south with his stepmother, Aunt Thuan, and her children. Lang's own mother had stayed behind at the estate in Tong Xuyen, hoping to safeguard the ancestral land. For three weeks, my cousin Tan and I took turns sleeping on the floor next to Lang's bed in the general infirmary of a public hospital, feeding, sponge-bathing, and medicating him. The depressing experience put off any dreams I ever had of a career in the medical field.

I shook my head.

He said, "I mean the veterans' hospital. Until you've seen maimed and wounded men laid up in the convalescent ward, moaning and crying, you don't know what war is. Whatever I put my body through now, it'll recover, but there's no recovery from losing an arm or a leg. Death would be better than that."

"If there were a sure way out of the draft, I would try it."

"Without trying, you never know which way is sure." He wheezed out a laugh. He opened his wallet and showed me a picture of himself—unrecognizable as a robust young man—standing next to a slim, gorgeous woman.

"She is the other reason why I can't be in the army. We're engaged. She'll marry me if I get a permanent exemption."

I watched him deteriorate day after day. I wasn't certain if he would make it. A week later, he stopped eating rice. Before his medical examination, Thien lost consciousness and they carried him on a stretcher to the infirmary. I never found out if he got the girl, the army, or the grave.

THERE was a small group of men in my situation. We were older, married, and resigned to our fate, knowing that we wouldn't qualify for postponements. We didn't want to be drafted, didn't want to harm ourselves for a physical exemption, and didn't have enough money to drink ourselves into a stupor. We paired off in small groups and spent those long infernal days pacing like inmates around a broiling pen. We talked about our life at home as if it were another world—and after talking awhile, we realized that it was. We just wanted this part to be over quickly and start soldiering so we could send money home to our wives and children. A day in this hot dirt field was a day's wages lost.

ON my fifteenth day, I was called with twenty other draftees for medical examination. Two army trucks took us to a place on the edge of Saigon. Going through the outer suburbs, I felt as though an old film reel was playing in my head—flashes of the time when my family had just migrated from Hanoi. We had traveled on these roads from the refugee camp to the city. Although eight years had passed, the scenery was much the same, just more houses than before. I felt as though my refugee life had happened only yesterday. Then, thinking of what had occurred to us since, I knew a lifetime had passed and I had failed to seize the right opportunities.

The hospital campus was one of the most impressive institutions I'd seen. An iron fence went around the perimeter of the compound. All the buildings, even the guardhouse at the gate, were built with brick and roof tiles. The roads and walkways were paved, the gardens trimmed. A circular flowerbed with a flagpole fronted the main building.

The trucks left us at the side of one of the small buildings. The sergeant told us to line up by the door. An orderly came out, took four men inside, and told the rest of us to wait our turn. The queue broke apart as everyone sought the shade. Some stretched out beneath the trees and napped; others sat against the wall and smoked. The sergeant ground his teeth and shook his head. I could tell he wanted to order us back in line, but we weren't soldiers yet. After a few weeks in the camp, not a single man cared how he looked. Unshaven, unkempt, and filthy, we sprawled haphazardly around the grounds, looking like a work detail on break. The officers walked by smiling, laughing as if they were having a grand time, their eyes slipping easily over us. They knew who we were.

The examination was cursory, but it took two doctors, several nurses, and orderlies five hours to examine the fifty men in our group. They called us inside, four men at a time. When it was my turn, I was surprised that it took them less than ten minutes to take my name, weight, height, blood pressure, and urine sample.

The doctor was around my age, although his chubby face made him look much younger. He came in without glancing at me, a captain's insignia on his shirt collar. He didn't return my greeting and began by listening to my chest with his stethoscope.

"Turn your head left and cough," he said. "Do you have hearing or vision problems?"

"No, Doctor."

"Pull up your pants," he grunted. He was behaving as though he was a member of the elite class and I was a commoner.

I wasn't surprised to see him carrying that superior air. He must have felt godlike with his power to determine the fate of so many lives. Standing in front of him half naked and obeying his order to turn around this side and that, I thought of my high school friend Duc, whom I had tutored. He had surpassed me. Duc had become an army doctor working in this very hospital. All of a sudden, it dawned on me that my life up to that point had been a failure. I didn't feel ashamed or humiliated. I felt utterly beaten. I desperately needed a cigarette.

He barked out a code to the nurse who was filling out my form. Realizing he hadn't dismissed me, he said in an irritated tone, "You can go."

I grabbed my shirt and rushed out. My chest tightened, a constriction in my throat. I couldn't breathe. I couldn't sit down. I paced the hot pavement, blood pounding in my ears. All the choices I made since the day I set foot in Saigon replayed themselves in my head. The hard work and sacrifices had amounted to nothing. My best efforts had been defeated. My mind was hammered blank. I was dizzy.

My hands shook as I lit a cigarette. I burned up a knuckle-length in two pulls, but for the first time since I started smoking, it tasted like medicine. I pulverized the cigarette under my shoe. I never had the urge to smoke again.

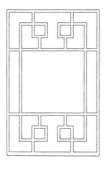

THE NORTH

1944

13. THE ORPHAN

Uncle Thuan and the village elders had foreseen the disaster, but not its magnitude. They had expected hard times from the very beginning of the occupation when the Japanese conscripted coolies and imposed heavy crop requisitions at two to three times the rates of the French. In the quest to conquer all of Southeast Asia, the Japanese were ruthlessly sapping the countryside of manpower and resources. As one season passed into the next, hungry peasants ate deeper into their seed stocks. Each new planting saw fewer seeds going into the fields and fewer hands to tend the crops. While rice yields spiraled downward, the Japanese quotas rose as the war went against them. The unsustainable drain on the peasantry was culminating in the country's most devastating famine, one that would decimate more than two million people.

That year, when the Japanese levied another large requisition on the October harvest, the poorest peasants realized that they did not have enough rice to last the winter and certainly not enough for the spring planting. Entire families abandoned their homes and took to the road. It was the first time we saw old folks, women, and children among the migrants, arriving daily by the dozens from distant domains.

I was nine years old the winter of the Great Famine. One afternoon, when Tan and I were playing hide-and-seek, we found a boy bundled in a blanket beneath a pile of hay at the back corner of the barn. Shriveled and bloated with starvation, he looked like some sort of bug, all head and belly, big-eyed and heaving ribs, almost hairless, semiconscious and possibly mute. He was past talking. It appeared he had crawled into the stable to die. From the first moment, I knew there was something very unusual about him.

"You're not supposed to be in here," Tan said, hunching down over him. "What's your name?"

The boy stared back at us, expressionless, watchful. His lips were cracked and dried with sores. He didn't flinch when Tan poked his swollen gut.

"Maybe he doesn't have a tongue, like Old Man Ngu," Tan said.

I pried open his mouth. "He's got one."

The boy was unperturbed at our prodding.

"You can talk, can't you?" Tan shook the boy's shoulder. "How did you get in here?"

"Hey, don't you know it's polite to answer when you're spoken to?"

The boy blinked at me. His eyes looked sad and alert, though oddly lifeless. They seemed too big for his head, and his head seemed too big for his body. Neither Tan nor I recognized the boy. We knew he wasn't from our village. Starvation hadn't yet set into Uncle Thuan's domain.

I said, "There's no food here. You might find some eggs in the henhouse, but there's nothing here except hay for the horses."

"Don't try to eat hay. It'll make you sick."

The hog trough was empty. Uncle Thuan had ordered most of

the pigs butchered and salted, saying that it was a sin to waste food on pigs. In fact, there wasn't much food anywhere on the estate. Dried fish, spices, pickles, and rice, foods that were usually left in jars and bins around the kitchens and courtyards, had been locked up in the storerooms. Fruits were picked green from the trees, for fear of the scavenging birds, and the vegetable gardens were guarded.

"We have to tell our mothers."

"No, we don't. They won't let us keep him," said Tan. Since his mother died when Tan was two years old, his father and stepmothers allowed Tan plenty of freedom. Tan didn't share my fears of adults.

"You want to keep him? Like a pet?" I didn't like the idea, and I wasn't sure if I liked the boy. There was something very strange and mysterious about him. A mole the size of a housefly perched in the middle of his forehead like an ominous marking, a sort of dark third eye. I said, "I have to tell my mom."

Tan threw up his hands. "She'll tell my father! And Father will send him to the temple like he did with all the other kids!"

Four boys had been left at our gate, but Uncle Thuan sent them all to the temple, each accompanied by a donation of rice to help the monks run their orphanage. During the famine, it was common for the poor to leave their babies or children at the doors of the rich in hopes that they would be adopted. People who thought they might come back someday to reclaim their children often left them at the Buddhist temples.

When I hesitated, Tan reached into his pocket and pulled out a pair of dice. "You win, we tell. I win, we keep him."

I nodded, and he rolled a nine in the dirt. The boy's eyes darted back and forth between us. He understood the wager.

I shook the dice in my palm. "What if I roll a nine?"

"Then we roll again!" Tan grumbled.

The dice tumbled on the ground and came up with a six and a five.

"I'll give you my best cricket," Tan offered.

It was a good deal, and I sealed the orphan's fate with a nod.

We went to the kitchen and brought back a bowl of rice porridge and salted fish to feed the boy. I knelt on the ground to raise the boy's head while Tan tried to spoon some food into his mouth. We got about a spoonful into his mouth when we heard someone rushing into the barn.

"Stop! Stop that!" the gardener cried, flapping his arms above his head. The old man grabbed the bowl and spoon from Tan and told me to put the boy down.

Gardener Cam said, "What are you trying to do?"

"We didn't do anything! We didn't bring him in here!" I said.

The old man guffawed, taking a moment to collect himself, and then said, "I know that. I found him in the hog pen yesterday. I gave him some sugar water."

"He's very hungry. Shouldn't we give him some rice?" Tan said.

"You can not feed starving people like him any solid food, not even that thick rice porridge. When they get to this stage, their stomachs and intestines can no longer digest normal food. Many have died of indigestion because they ate too much or ate solid foods that their systems can not process," the old man replied, glaring at us. "You could have killed him."

"We're sorry. We didn't know," I said. "I guess we should tell Uncle Thuan about him."

"No, no. Let's keep this a secret between only us," said Cam. "If we tell your uncle and aunts, they'll send him to the orphanage at the temple. There are too many kids there. In his condition, he'll die for sure."

Tan and I had been to the temple several times with the staff when they took food donations to the monks. The place was filled with sickly children. We looked at the gardener and nodded.

The old man breathed a big sigh of relief. A lifelong bachelor without any child of his own, he had taken a liking to the orphan.

□ □ □

□   □   □

TAKING care of the orphan in secret was an exciting game. We clothed the boy with our old shirts and shorts. When he could process food again, tidbits of dinner meats found their way into our pockets, and we sneaked into the barn to feed him before we went to bed. We gave him a black cricket in a matchbox to keep him company. Day after day of mothering the boy, we knew no more about him than we did the first time we laid eyes on him. Whenever we asked him a question about his family, he would just stare blankly at us. He was as helpless as a baby. He never told us his name or even thanked us when we fed him. He made almost no noise, as if he knew the delicacy of his situation.

It wasn't long before Aunt Thuan discovered our orphan. She scolded Cam and ordered him to take the boy to the village monks, but the wily old man convinced her that the orphan could be a sign from heaven. Bad fortune could befall the estate if she turned her back to a helpless child. Suitably worried, Aunt Thuan agreed to let the boy stay until he regained his strength.

With the mistress's permission, the estate staff gladly helped Cam nurse the boy back to health, taking him under their wing as a member of their extended family, even though no one was any wiser about his real name or origin. Such a profound silence, they speculated, could only have been brought on by terrible trauma. Soon he was well enough to help around the kitchen and the gardens. The staff taught him to endear himself to Aunt Thuan. When Aunt Thuan, Aunt Thao, and my mother sent messages between their households, the orphan would be on hand to run them, a chore that naturally earned him favor among the decision makers in the estate. Slowly but surely, the staff integrated him into their world. The gardener was very happy because the boy quickly became the son the old man had always wanted.

Two months passed and Aunt Thuan still didn't send the boy to the monastery. The boy's transformation back to health was miraculous. His swollen belly shrank and his limbs fleshed out. It was quickly apparent that he was older than Tan and me by at least three or four years. His face rounded out with pudgy cheeks, making his previously bulging eyes look narrow and small. The younger kids started calling him Dumpling-Face-Boy, a nickname he bore stoically.

As it became clear the boy would have a place in the estate, the gardener decided that it was time to give him a name. One day the old man came to the kitchen and announced to everyone that he had named the boy Vi—*the reason*. Granny Tu, who was the head of the estate staff, exploded into a furious tirade. She berated Cam right back out to the garden, calling him a foolish old coot with a wine jug for a head. She ranted for days that he had saddled the boy with an ill-fitting name that would bring bad luck upon our house. But the name had been given. It could not be undone.

It was a bad omen, but no one, not even Granny, could have predicted that Vi would grow up to be a killer who brought death to our house.

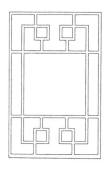

14. FAMINE

From that dark swath of sun-drunken days, I remembered
the naked trees by the dried ponds, their barks eaten; the
roadside cadavers with blackened mouths; and the Walkers, those wind-withered women, breasts like empty sacs,
those beaten men, their shame-rotted eyes, and the spider
children of bloated bellies and spindly limbs. The moans
of hunger, the wails of grief besieging our walls that the
decades could not drown.

I remembered kicking a skull. There were many. My
friends and I picked one that was detached from a body.
It was round enough to roll like the grapefruits we once
used. Bouncing across the dirt, it had no human feature.
Ravens had picked the eye sockets clean.

Shouts and shrieks of laughter. We played barefoot
soccer in the cracked, dusty paddies among the dancing
flies and the cawing crows as the sky spun round a hot
dangling sun.

This was a bone yard, here to the horizon. There was nothing to fear. Death was not found on a corpse—nothing left but a shell. Its reflection came to the faces of the doomed. Death had a sour spoor. It had a vibration. It revealed itself during the crossover.

How many grains of rice separated us from the dying?

These were the bitter seeds of indignity.

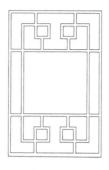

15. The Famine Soup

There were roughly a dozen mouthfuls of rice in a bowl of famine soup, give or take a spoon. The broth was watery and faintly seasoned with salt. At the best of times, it contained a few beans or peanuts.

Before things became truly scarce, the estate cooks added yam to the soup, making it more nutritious. Eventually, when the supply of yam ran short, they substituted manioc, which made people dizzy; some vomited. And then they used bran, the livestock feed, to supplement the soup. Though at the very end when the number of refugees had grown tenfold, when the soup could no longer be given twice a day, there was nothing left to go into the pot but rice, water, and salt.

A single bowl a day. Who could be sustained by so little?

When Tet came that year, there was no celebration. The harvest had been poor for several seasons. Still, the Japanese army forced farmers to grow jute on fertile land for its war efforts, and then requisitioned what little rice the fields yielded. People resorted to eating their seed stock and so had nothing to sow for the next planting. Many abandoned their homes in search of food, but by mid-spring it was too late. Word came that starvation had also descended upon the cities. Refugees lost hope and stopped walking. There was no point in walking to more hunger; nor were there rewards in scouring the fields and streams for food. No amount of work, scavenging, or begging could fill their bellies.

Everything had suddenly become scarce. It was the famine's strangest phenomenon. Fruits, vegetables, edible roots, and critters simply vanished. Refugees razed the land, eating grass, vines, wild fungi, leaves, and tree bark. Any creature they caught, they devoured: insects, reptiles, rodents, and birds. People dragged the creeks and ponds with fine nets, straining the waterways of even tiny fish, frogs, crabs, and snails. The populace's hunger disrupted the food chain at every level. Without the small creatures, the larger creatures starved. Save the carrion eaters, nearly every animal under the heavens went hungry.

The village market mirrored what was happening in the fields and streams. Vendors had fewer and fewer things to sell. Fresh fish and meat disappeared first, followed by staples, such as salted fish, pickled goods, and rice. Half a year after the initial signs of famine, there was nothing left to sell. The market was deserted. Villagers hoarded food. They had become infected with the fear of hunger.

So, poor as it was, our rice soup still drew so many from distant domains that all available hands at the estate were required to manage the throng during feeding time. When the crowd grew too large and uncontrollable, Uncle Thuan devised a way to feed them in three separate groups. The strongest and most aggressive always pushed themselves to the front to form the first group to be allowed into the outer courtyard where the soup cauldron was kept. They yelled and bickered, men shoving aside women and children to get ahead. Thin and filthy from weeks without bathing, they came as a thick, roiling mass of jostling bodies and arms, mobbing the cauldron. The cooks could merely ladle soup into the bowls thrust at them as fast as they could. Fights broke out, and the guards had to cane the brawlers as though they were animals.

Once this group received their food, the guards ushered them into the next courtyard, where they were allowed to eat. The second group entered and was fed in the outer courtyard. These two groups were not allowed outside until the last group was fed, because they were strong enough to take food from those too weak to defend themselves.

While the men of our estate watched the Walkers in the court-yards and made sure none sneaked into another part of the estate, the women and the older children went outside to feed the ones too weak to go inside for the soup. There were dozens. Many were prob-ably beyond help, but no one could bear to see them go without food. They lay on the ground with only a small basket or earthen bowl. They were too weak to carry their luggage, having dropped their last belongings somewhere along their journeys. They were ghastly thin and many had open sores on their bodies. Their limbs had atrophied to the point where they could no longer stand or even hold on to a bowl of soup. Their breathing was shallow and irregular. They shiv-ered in the hot afternoon.

They had a terrifying scent. It wasn't the smell of putrefying living flesh or that of a decomposing cadaver one might find on the side of the road. It was a very distinct odor, one I had found only on those caught deep in the long course of starvation. This was the very scent of death. It emanated dampness and decay, and it was everywhere.

UNCLE Thuan summoned our relatives and the rich families in the domain to assist him in feeding the refugees. Many responded. Those who could not donate food sent men to help with the soup kitchen, and those who could not afford either came them-selves. The most dedicated among these were Uncle Uc and my cousin Quyen.

Uncle Uc was one of my father's second cousins. He was thirty-eight years old, thin, and athletic, and had been the headmaster at our school for as long as I could remember. Uncle Uc lived with his wife, two daughters, and parents in the next village. Gregarious, humorous, and kind, he was usually the favorite guest at my mother's Friday afternoon tea parties. It was fun to be around him because he knew how to talk to children. He owned a French bicycle. It was black and had big wheels with thin rubber tires, mudguards, chrome-plated handlebars, and a little bell.

Cousin Quyen came by the estate twice a week after he had made the rounds to our relatives to collect food donations for the soup kitchen. He was twenty-four, tall, and—according to the servant girls in our estate—very handsome. A competitive tennis player and college graduate, Quyen was one of those idealistic young men who thought they could change the world. He was like an older brother to Tan and me.

I was very close to both of them and learned a great deal from their conversations. They brought news about the world beyond our little village. They said that the South was, in fact, largely untouched by the famine. It seemed incredible to me that there was a surplus of food in the South, but somehow through ineptitude, cruelty, or apathy, the Japanese army did not provide their Vietnamese puppet government the means to transport rice to the starving north and central regions. It also did not allow the Red Cross to help. Quyen talked about railroads being put under the exclusive use of the Japanese army and filled granaries rotting away while our people were dying throughout the northern countryside.

During one of his visits, Quyen brought a man from our village to help with the soup kitchen. His name was Trung. He was a part-time teacher and colleague of Uncle Uc. As usual, being Quyen's favorite cousin, I was allowed to eat lunch with them in the garden after closing the soup kitchen. I remembered it because this was the very last time I saw Quyen.

After the meal, Uncle Uc mentioned that he was surprised to see his colleague helping at the soup kitchen.

Quyen hesitated and looked at me, but then he made a little shrug and replied to Uncle Uc, "I asked him to come. Trung is a new member of Viet Nam Quoc Dan Dang."

Uncle Uc was clearly not pleased with what he heard. He said, "First of all, I don't think it's right to have this kind of meeting here at Brother Thuan's estate without his permission."

"Oh, no, we wouldn't want to put Uncle Thuan in a difficult position of having to approve or disapprove of our meeting. It's better if he doesn't know about it. And even if he does, he would pretend he doesn't because he wants to appear neutral."

Trung said, "Besides, this is more like a casual conversation between acquaintances who happen to meet at the soup kitchen."

Uncle Uc shook his head. "Well, people won't see it that way."

"This is just between the three of us," Trung said.

"Uncle, we're not asking you to recruit people. We're only asking you to say a few good words about our cause whenever you talk with the local folks. Maybe you can share our ideas with your students and their parents. You're the headmaster. People respect your views."

"I like your Nationalist party, but I am sorry. You know I have a family. The Communists have eyes and ears in every village. Both of you must be very careful."

"Don't worry. I'm always very careful." Trung seemed irritated.

"Can't you do anything in your class to help?" Quyen insisted.

Uncle Uc shook his head. "The Communists probably have children reporting on us. Most of the students in my class are from poor families. Their parents are more likely to listen to Communist propaganda than to your Nationalist ideology."

"We need a way to convince them. We have a strong base in the cities, but we need to create a movement here in the countryside," Quyen said.

"Well, then you have a very difficult task ahead of you."

"Once people know what communism is, they won't be interested," Quyen said.

"It's impossible to get the message out in the middle of this disaster. At the beginning of the famine, you might have had a chance to recruit and train the young Walkers who came looking for work. Now, people are starving; all they can think about is food. If I were you, I wouldn't try to recruit the ones who came for the soup. You don't know how many of them are already hardcore Communists."

"You're being very pessimistic," Trung grumbled.

Ignoring his younger colleague, Uncle Uc said to Quyen, "I'm trying to keep you from endangering the whole clan."

But it was already too late. The political parties had begun aggressively maneuvering against each other. It was common knowledge that many groups, including the Nationalists and the Communists, were using kidnapping, torture, and murder to eliminate their political rivals. We were not aware of it then, but Quyen was already targeted for assassination. It was the last time we saw him. Days later, he vanished on his way to Hanoi. The police found his body among several other Nationalists floating in Seven Hectare Lake on the outskirts of Hanoi.

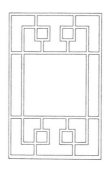

16. The Flood

The cries of hunger outside our walls had fallen silent. The soil reclaimed the weakest by the thousands. Those who had not found refuge had perished. The surviving hearts hardened. From the close of that long year of slow death, I remembered the Heavens grieving.

The black clouds of retribution boiled up from the horizon, billowing mountains impossibly high over the plains. A penance of darkness pressed down upon the land. In the paddies, peasants cowered. Lightning lashed the earth and released that infinite well of sky.

In the village, monks sounded the temple gong. Peasants, young and old, rushed to repair the dikes. All through the night, drums alarmed the length of the river. Rocks and sand flowed like loose detritus. The ground melted beneath their feet. The impenetrable night had turned liquid. The rain did not relent. The river overran its bank, crashing over the levees in torrents. In the murky light of dawn, they fled before the floodwater, racing to salvage their food stores.

The creek beside our estate poured into the hedge, then into the courtyards. Water rose waist-high. It filled the Ancestral Temple. We abandoned the first floor of our house for the second, water lapping at our heels up the stairs.

One by one, the gardens, the shacks, the low houses, the silkworm hatchery, the granaries, the barns, the orchards were swallowed. Live-stock drowned. Rodents sought refuge in the tree branches. The carp, the catfish, the trout were liberated from their ponds. The rain turned cold, the light steely.

At last, when there was so little left, the Heavens took yet more, as if to remind us of something essential we had forgotten. The deluge lasted three days.

We were washed innocent, naked beneath the open sky.

A long-drawn sigh, and the wind quieted with the coming dawn. From our rooftop perch, the new day brought an iridescent world of blue firmament and silver water. Not a strand of breeze or a whisper of memory. Our realm had become borderless, an inland sea.

There was more hunger to come, but every flood carried with it a promise of life; a rich alluvium-nourished harvest would follow in the next season.

All rebirths were brutal. Every loss must be mourned, every tragedy cleansed for a new beginning.

17. THE AMBUSH

It was 1963, the day after Christmas. The lowering sun glowed, a blighted smear on the marshy sky, a hand's length above the horizon. The rice fields lay empty, abandoned as still as night, not a bird in sight. A chill was in the air.

My mind was already focusing on the dinner my wife had waiting for me. Afterward, she wanted to take the baby to the park in the new stroller I gave her yesterday. Anh loved having strawberry ice cream by the town square.

The day's work was done. We felt accomplished as we drove out the gates of An Binh, the last hamlet on our payroll delivery route. There were four of us in a Ford Bronco: the driver, two armed escorts, and me. The car smelled faintly of the sweet rice wine and peppery boar jerky that Tinh and Truc, the escorts, had bought from the villagers. I had just finished disbursing over forty thousand Vietnamese dong to the last three units under my command.

After the military training at Thu Duc Academy, I was a lieutenant in the Army of the Republic of Vietnam. My first commission was as the new commander of the Rural Development Task Force (RD), a paramilitary organization aimed at winning over the people in the countryside. I was chosen based on my college education, because RD commanders must also work with advisors from the U.S. Agency for International Development (USAID). Fortunately for me, the RD office was in Phan Thiet, and I was able to move Anh and the baby there, where she could be closer to her mother. And I was able to see my wife and child almost every day.

It was as safe a post as I could have dared dream for. The most dangerous part of my job was the payroll trips in the countryside. While I usually stayed overnight on my visits with the troops to boost morale, I never lingered longer than necessary on these trips for fear that a rogue group from the Regional Force or the Civil Defense Force might stage a fake Viet Cong attack to hijack the payroll.

Along the side of the road, the troops walked in single file. With money to celebrate the New Year, all were in a payday mood, cheering, waving as we drove past. Except for the old World War II carbine rifles on their shoulders, they looked like villagers in their black cotton peasant smocks—thirty-five cadres, including six women. They faced a long march, at the end of which were drinks and games at the camp with the regular regional army. Many salaries would be drunk and gambled away by dawn tomorrow.

About a third of a mile from the hamlet, we approached a creek running at an angle to the road. Its shrubby banks skirted within forty yards at the closest point. The moment my eyes strayed into the trees by the creek, I felt a distinct sense of unease as if the sky itself was askew. My escorts had gone quiet in the backseat. I glanced at the driver. Chan had a puzzled look on his face.

The first shot came with a dull metal puncturing sound. I turned and glanced at Tinh, who sat behind me. His mouth was agape in disbelief, blood blossoming on his shirt. A deafening barrage of machine-gun fire rang out. The Bronco shuddered under the onslaught of bullets. Windows exploded, spraying glass shards.

"Ambush!" Truc yelled.

Chan stomped on the accelerator, swerving away from the woods. The windshield shattered. A tire blew. The vehicle fishtailed across the road. Then we were weightless as the Bronco plunged off the dirt road. First I saw the sky, like a fractured mirror; then the rushing ground. The car slammed into a ditch, hurling me into the dashboard. Everything went black.

When I opened my eyes, my hands were bloody, as was my face. I was sprawled across the front seats, half jammed into the foot well. The embankment canted the truck at an odd angle, exposing part of its undercarriage to shots fired from the trees across the road. Bullets punched through the passenger-side doors and floorboard. Truc and the driver were already out of the car. I scrambled across the seat after him, sliding out headfirst.

Chan was saying something. I couldn't hear him over the blizzard of slugs shredding the car at hundreds of rounds per minute. He shouted into my ear, asking if I had been hit. He wiped away the blood pouring from a gash in my forehead.

"Oh, God. Aahhh . . . I'm hit. Help!" Tinh cried from inside the car.

Truc sprang to his feet and reached for his friend. A wet, popping fleshy sound. Truc jerked up as if straightening to stand at attention. His blood splattered all over me. The bullet went straight through his head. He toppled backward and splashed into the rice paddy, boots sticking out of the water not two feet from me. Murky red water closed over his pulpy, mangled face.

A jolt went through me; my mind was seized. Every part of me rejected what I saw. I couldn't breathe. I had seen countless corpses, but I had never seen a man shot dead in front of me.

I hadn't noticed the gunshots tapering off. Chan and I remained on our backs, half submerged in the paddy. I felt ill, nauseous. Above, a mottled, gray heaven. Time seemed bizarrely out of phase, the air fragrant with rice wine and musty earth.

Reports of gunshots came from another direction. Down the road our men were coming to the rescue. Sergeant Viet led a charge with half of his men. The others retreated back into the hamlet.

"Help me! Aahhh . . . I can't move," Tinh moaned.

With Viet's men drawing the machine gun away from the Bronco, Chan pulled Tinh's arm from the outside while I climbed into the cab and untangled Tinh's feet, which were caught under the seat. Light shone through ragged holes in the doors. The first bullet, the one that got him, was meant for me—the highest-ranking officer who invariably sat next to the driver. Had we been going a fraction of a second slower, the sniper would have found his mark.

Tinh mumbled. No, he was sobbing. There was blood in his teeth. "Oh, God. Oh, God. I don't want to die."

Chan and I could only look at each other. The bullet was still lodged in his upper right chest. Neither of us had tended a gunshot wound before.

Remembering my rank, I forced myself to wiggle three feet up the shallow embankment to assess our situation. I thought I could pick off a few if I sighted them in the shrubs. I loaded Truc's carbine and peeked over the road. The light was against us. A hail of bullets raked the ground in front of my face, clumps of soil popping like firecrackers.

"I can't see them."

"If they charge, we're dead," he said, clearly as frightened as I was.

We fired a few rounds toward the creek to let them know we were armed. The quick return volleys nearly got us. We wiggled back down the embankment with our faces firmly pressed to the ground. I could feel bullets hammering into the earth.

Down the road, Viet's men entered the sniper's range. Immediately, the three leading cadres crumpled to the ground as if they had run into an invisible fence. The rest dove over the side of the road. Our rescue squad could not come closer.

"Lieutenant!" Viet shouted to me, his word barely audible between the bursts of machine guns.

"I'm fine. We've got one injured and one dead."

"They've got us pinned, Lieutenant. Can you make it to our position?"

There was nothing else to do. I shouted, "We're going to try."

We gathered the two escorts' rifles and ammo belts. I put my Colt .45 into my rucksack along with the payroll ledger, to keep it from getting in the mud. We began crawling across the paddy, our faces in the rice stalks, chests skimming the water, arms and legs deep in water and gooey mud. We dragged Tinh between us by his armpits. Every time we pulled, Tinh groaned in pain. Chan paused and looked to me. I shook my head. More than a hundred yards and three footpath dikes separated us and our men.

Choking with pain, Tinh yelled for us to stop, but we kept dragging him. He jerked away, gasping, "Leave me. I can't make it. Leave me."

"You'll make it," I said.

"Leave me!"

Chan snapped, "Shut up! We're not leaving you here!"

Tinh started cursing, then begging. We ignored him. A few more yards, he shrieked and went abruptly limp.

"He passed out." Chan sighed.

Although there was half a foot of paddy-water, most of Tinh's body was caught in the deep muddy bottom. We struggled to keep his face above the water and our heads below the level of the road. Bullets whizzed scant inches over our heads. Limbs laden with mud, we crawled a few paces, paused shaking with fatigue, and then started forward again. When we came to the end of the field, we heaved Tinh onto the dike, rolled him over to the next paddy, and scrambled after him as a hail of bullets strafed the ground and water all around us. Foot by agonizing foot, we wormed through the sludge.

It took us an agonizing hour to rejoin our troops. Viet and I organized an orderly retreat with sharpshooters covering the rear while the main group crawled back to the hamlet. The Viet Cong moved their guns and hounded us the whole way. Every time we tried to stand up, they raked us with bullets. It was sunset by the time the whole group retreated into the hamlet. I collapsed on the ground with the rest of the men, too tired to move or think of what to do next.

"Khanh, Cung, Thien, Binh, each of you go to one corner of the hamlet. If you see anything, shoot to alert us!" Viet stomped about, shaking up the men. "It's going to get dark soon. We must set up our defenses before they attack."

He turned to his radioman. "Radio! Call headquarters!"

The team had a PRC-7 handheld radio roughly the size of a small loaf of bread with a single preset channel linked to headquarters, which, in our case, was a small room back in Phan Thiet manned by one veteran. I sighed with relief when his voice came over the radio. Hearing Viet reporting our situation at full volume startled me into realizing I should gather my wits quickly and set a plan to defend the hamlet.

"You're hurt, Lieutenant," said one of the team's nurses, examining the gash in my forehead.

I waved her away and told Nhan, Viet's second in command, to take the three women cadres ahead and set up a triage. I took the radio from Viet and talked to Lieutenant Lan, my assistant at headquarters. Our radio man had reported the attack two hours ago and asked for support, but Lan said Captain Trieu, the Province Military Chief of Staff in Phan Thiet, was waiting my for report. I said we desperately needed reinforcement. If the Regional platoon camping in the hills marched immediately, they could be here before nightfall. Lan said he would go and talk to Captain Trieu personally.

We carried the wounded to the community center in the middle of the hamlet. Villagers watched from a distance. Someone must have known about the ambush or seen guerrilla movements in the fields, but we hadn't received a single signal, not even the usual vague whispers: *You had better leave now,* or *That road is bad.* Still, I couldn't blame them. If anyone had tipped us off, he would be murdered before the week was over.

Our team had worked here for more than a month and was on friendly terms with the locals. Children came for a closer look at the wounded and ran back to tell their parents. A little girl slipped her hand into Nurse Nhung's hand and walked along, smiling. The village head came and asked if we needed anything. I told him to have people stay in their houses in case of an attack. I didn't want to get the villagers involved. I took the lead and tried my best to look confident for the men.

Since early last year, more than two thousand strategic hamlets had sprung up throughout the South in an attempt to insulate villagers from communist propaganda and prevent Viet Cong (VC) infiltration into the populace. People were forced to move either into the hamlets or further out toward the VC-controlled areas. Naturally, everyone, including the VC underground, moved inside, and in spite of all the government promotions and American subsidies, strategic hamlets became ready shelters for the VC sympathizers and a severe hardship for the peasants. They had to live in these squalid settlements and were allowed outside to work at dawn and expected back at dusk. Villagers walked miles each day to work in their own paddies. Their gardens lay neglected; productivity suffered.

An Binh was a typical hamlet built like a rectangular fort with its back to the river. Though its construction was sound, the design was medieval. Except for the waterfront, which was strung with barbed wire, the hamlet was enclosed by a three-foot dike topped with a sturdy six-foot fence of dried indigo branches as thick as a man's forearm. Just behind the fence was a four-foot-deep trench to stand in for defending the perimeter. The main avenue ran down the middle of the hamlet, straight from the front gate to the river. Two smaller streets, going east and west, intersected perpendicularly with the main. The hamlet had a community center, a playground, and some thirty-odd bungalows, closely packed and cheaply built.

The center of the hamlet was a two-room community house

with a packed-dirt floor. The nurses had set up a triage in the meeting room, so Nhan, Viet, and I withdrew to the classroom. I sketched the hamlet's layout and its surroundings on the chalkboard. We sat on little benches around a knee-high children's table and planned our defenses.

A devout Catholic from the North, Viet was forty-two, a small man, dark and wiry, with disproportionately large forearms. He had migrated to the South with his family in 1954. Viet had been fighting Communists since he was a teenager, first as a member of his village civil defense, later as a soldier in the French indigenous force. His native village, Bui Chu, was a Catholic bastion that had suffered and fought bitterly against the Viet Minh until the very last days before the Geneva Accord.

Viet's second in command was a tall, lanky southern farmer with mild, easy manners. Already in his mid-fifties, Nhan was still as fit and alert as a man half his age. Unlike Viet, who fought on religious grounds, Nhan had a vendetta. His eldest brother, a village chief, had been murdered by the Communists ten years ago while Nhan was fighting under the French. His brother's death brought hardship on the entire clan. Nhan retired after the French withdrew in 1954, but several consecutive crop failures set him back into working for the government.

We debated over why the VC attacked our truck prematurely instead of waiting to ambush the whole team. It also seemed bizarre that they did not try to enter the hamlet while we were pinned down outside. We were certain about two things. First, the ambush didn't make sense. Second, our twenty-seven men could not hold the hamlet without prompt military reinforcement.

"How many rounds of ammunition do we have left?" I asked Nhan.

He smiled as though I had asked him how many guests we were expecting for dinner. It was one of those all-encompassing smiles that could be a response or an expression for a dozen different emotions.

"Just under fifteen hundred rounds left."

"Order the men to shoot sparingly," I said. "Make every bullet count."

Viet shook his head. "It'll be tough since we're up against AK-47s. Our green recruits were pretty shaken up by them. Half of my men ran back to the hamlet at the first shot. They didn't stay around long enough to hear my orders."

I chuckled. "I was pretty shaken up too."

Viet said, "The local guerrillas don't have these kinds of armaments. We're definitely up against the National Liberation Front's regional force."

"In that case . . ." Nhan sighed. "It could be a whole NLF company. A whole company will overrun us in no time."

"Then we all die," Viet said.

"Maybe our Regional Force will reinforce us soon enough," Nhan replied.

"Don't count on it. We're bastards to the big military brass in Phan Thiet. Besides, those cowards at headquarters never stick their heads out unless they absolutely have to." Viet snickered. He was a hardcore crusader, one of the very few people I'd met who wasn't afraid to die.

I radioed Lan. Our strategy depended on whether or not we could count on reinforcement. Lan said Captain Trieu, the Province Military Chief of Staff, refused to send troops unless we were actually attacked. I said if we were under heavy attack, it would be a funeral march because by the time they got here, we would be dead. It wasn't good enough. I told Lan he would need to do better and signed off.

"Too bad there's a half-moon tonight; otherwise we could try to sneak out of this hamlet and run to the hills," said Nhan.

Viet dismissed that notion with a flip of his hand. "Even if we're lucky enough to have cloud cover tonight, they'd still hear us sloshing through the paddies."

"We will just have to figure out a way to last as long as we can," I said.

□   □   □

WE called the team into the classroom. Heads hung low, they shuffled inside and squatted on the ground. Like all RD teams, this one was a mix of draft-dodgers and retired soldiers, some too young to shave, some too old to fight. They had enlisted for the back-breaking work of building bridges, roads, houses, and schools; teaching children; and providing basic health care. They had to be paramilitary propagandists for the government and good Samaritans for the villagers. The ARVN looked down on them as draft-dodgers and the Americans' peons. USAID secretly used them as decoys to provide cover for the American intelligence operatives—a fact I had recently learned.

For their troubles, RD teams were favorite targets for the guerrillas. It was much easier to take potshots at men working in the fields than it was to attack a well-armed platoon. And when they died, their families received almost no compensation.

Seeing the fear in their faces, the way they turned to me for direction, I felt the full burden of leadership for the first time. A few hours ago, I had handed them the wages of an unwanted war, like poison in their pockets, the money some would soon repay with their lives. Anxiety for my own safety vanished, and I felt strangely composed.

"Brothers, you all know our situation is precarious. I just want to give you my thoughts. You know our job is to help improve people's lives, but the Viet Cong believe we're traitors and spies for the Americans, so they hate us. They hate us more than they hate the soldiers.

"Now, I know you did not join RD to fight. And you know I didn't volunteer to be in the army, so like you, I don't want to be in a battle."

The seven older cadres didn't need a pep talk, but I could tell by the way their faces softened that they appreciated the honesty. Veterans didn't follow bravado. It was a trait in leaders who led men to their death. And at the same time, I couldn't tell them the whole truth. How could I explain to them that their own Regional Force, less than an hour's march away, wouldn't come to their rescue?

"But tonight we must fight because they've got us surrounded and outgunned. And they will kill us if we don't fight with everything we have. If we stand together, we might get through this and see our families again. All we have to do is to hold out long enough for the Regional Force to get here. It's our only chance of survival."

In the next room, an injured man moaned. A shiver went through the gathering. Nhan cleared his throat and said he agreed completely with me. Viet added that he would rather get killed than captured by the VC. The veterans nodded. Pale-faced, the draft-dodgers sat in silence. I turned the briefing over to Viet, who set about explaining our defensive plan.

I TOOK the radio outside and sat on a bench beneath a lime tree in the playground. I felt as though I should say a prayer, and I wanted to say one, but I didn't know how. I wasn't very religious. Not many people of my generation believed in anything. True faith was rare when you saw how true believers suffered and died just as easily as anyone else. I had seen a full twenty years of war. So for a few minutes, I thought about my mother. I believed her spirit protected me.

Dusk deepened into night. A northern wind cleared the sky for a scattering of stars and a half-moon. I radioed my assistant, Lieutenant Lan, at headquarters. Lan was very apologetic, saying that he had pleaded with Trieu for every sort of concession. I was angry, but I couldn't blame Lan. I knew Trieu was no hero. His decision was not surprising: Why should he get his soldiers killed for a bunch of paramilitary guys working for the Americans.

There was one option left: An Binh hamlet was within range of the pair of howitzers at Phan Thiet Airport. I didn't want to mention it earlier. In the ARVN, if an officer in the field called his superior at

HQ and requested one of two things, he invariably got the lesser of the two, or nothing at all.

"Ask Captain Trieu to support us with his artillery tonight when they attack. We won't have a chance without it."

"Good idea. I wonder why he hadn't thought of it."

"Of course, he did. He just didn't bother mentioning it."

"Then I'm sure he doesn't want to do it."

"Damn it! I don't care if you're sure or not. Just ask him!"

"OK, sorry, Lieutenant. I'll go talk to him again."

Even though shelling the creek amounted to little more than a gunnery exercise for his men, Trieu would most likely decline because it was his privilege. If I wanted his help, I would have to promise him a favor in return, effectively placing myself in his pocket.

"Wait! I changed my mind."

"I'm still here."

"Go see Mr. Richardson yourself and ask him to make that request for us. If you can't convince Mr. Richardson, get him on the radio for me."

Ben Richardson was the head of USAID in Phan Thiet. On the record, he was an advisor, but in reality he was our boss from both the objective and financial perspectives. Trieu wouldn't dare refuse Richardson's request—not unless he wanted to risk a transfer to some unsavory post.

"Good idea, sir. Anything else?"

"No, that's all."

"Roger that, sir."

"Over and out."

Putting down the radio, I chuckled. Why should I bother worrying about what that arrogant fool will do to me? Before Trieu could take his revenge on me, I would have to survive tonight first.

The hamlet had become eerily silent and deserted, the streets empty, ghostlike with bluish-gray shadows, the corners and crannies filled with night. Cooking fires had been extinguished. Even the dogs had gone into hiding. Houses darkened, their doors locked, windows shuttered. The entire populace cringed, coiling tightly into itself. People knew they couldn't leave the hamlet. The VC would not bother distinguishing them from RD cadres trying to escape. They did what trapped peasants had done through the ages: They barricaded themselves inside their homes and waited out the night, whatever the outcome.

A déjà vu. I had been here, in a place like this. I remembered those long nights hiding in bushes, hay bales, field shacks, waiting for dawn as the legionnaires swept through the village and scoured our ancestral home like malevolent demons. That was fifteen years ago. It made me immensely sad.

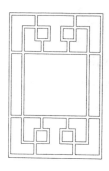

18. THE LAST MAGISTRATE

The raven came to see him for the third and final time, the day before his death. It alighted in the brazen afternoon, dropping like a blot of ink onto the broiling courtyard. It peered into the audience hall and, spreading dark wings, cawed at him. He accepted the harbinger with equanimity. Six years he had been waiting.

Pham Van Thuan was the last magistrate of his line to preside in Tong Xuyen Domain. Forty-five years old, he had few regrets. He had fathered four sons and four daughters among his three wives. His accomplishments and social status were adequate for a man who knew what he wanted from life. Two things mattered to him: the prosperity of his domain and the impeccable quality of his service as magistrate. He took pride in executing his office faithfully and wisely. Of the hundreds of cases he had judged during his two-decade tenure, only a handful of his rulings had been overturned by the district court. This was a well-known fact, as his name had been mentioned in the upper halls for promotions. If he so wished, he could have risen all the way to the Senate, but like his father and his grandfather, he was a simple man who cherished the country life. Hunting birds in his orchards, strolling in his gardens, and raising pigeons were his passions. For him, the greatest pleasure was seeing Heaven reward the peasants for their hard labor with righteous rain for the planting season and sultry sun for the harvesting days.

When he told his wife about the raven, she begged him not to go to the council meeting the next day in the district town. The Three Temple Lunar Calendar listed the day's base-nature as Fire. His was Metal. Incompatible, as one melted the other. It would be a bad day for travel. Terrified, she rushed to the Ancestral Temple and lit three incense sticks for the Lady Buddha. She knelt at the altar and prayed as she had never prayed before, making desperate pledges for her husband's safety.

She knew it was a time of great political upheaval. World War II was ending, and the various factions were maneuvering against one another. Vietnamese were killing Vietnamese to gain advantage. Days before, their nephew Quyen, an active Nationalist, had been kidnapped and murdered by the Viet Minh. Quyen was among the first victims in the Viet Minh's drive to eliminate key members of the wealthy class that formed the core of the Nationalists.

That evening, a pensive spell descended on the magistrate, and he asked for the traditional mat nha service. His wife protested that the Lunar New Year was months away; there were no blossoming narcissus available for the centerpiece. He smiled and said any bloom from his garden would do. So she cut roses from his prized bushes and put them in a bowl of water. She placed the arrangement on a platter full of white riverbed pebbles coated with mat nha—a honey-like extract made from the tiny sprouts of sweet rice grains. She served it to him with a pot of black tea. They sat in the gazebo, looking out on the carp pond. He held a pebble in his mouth, the essence of rice slowly dissolving on his tongue. A mild sweetness, the flavor of freshly steamed jasmine rice.

Above the darkening bamboo hedge, the sky turned coral pink. Shoals of finches danced, racing over the fields. He was deeply in love with the land.

She would later recall that he was not himself when he woke the next morning. He seemed distracted. Moreover, he was in a good mood, which in itself was very unusual. Even the servants who helped him dress noted that he seemed happy, almost carefree. He put on his trousers and dark blue silk robe without much fuss about the quality of the ironing or the proper starchiness in the fabric. He pinned the magistrate ivory emblem on his chest and donned the ceremonial headdress of coiled cloth. A servant polished his leather boots while he talked to his wife about the dinner he wanted that night.

He ate his usual breakfast of glutinous rice patties with slices of meat cake and hot tea on the veranda, where he could watch his pigeons stirring in their roosts. His wife sat and pleaded with him to take the car, but he refused. Various political factions were inciting riots and there were demonstrations daily at the district town. Driving his luxurious automobile—there were only two in the entire province—through crowds of famine-stricken peasants would bring only trouble. He knew people instinctively feared and respected an official mounted on a horse.

He rode out the gates with Canh and Khi, his two most trusted guards, jogging at his side. He was in high spirit, full of plans for improving the security of the district and his own domain. He told his men that he would buy horses for them so they could travel faster. It would help them catch highway bandits. He also told them that he would seek permission from the district chief to arm his bodyguards with guns. Heaven knew all the political factions had access to plenty of firearms.

They traveled comfortably, the men at a jog to match the horse's slow canter. It was an easy pace for the dawn hours, the air still cool and pleasant, the sky whitish and overcast. Tendrils of mist hugged the newly sown paddies.

They rounded a bend in the road where a tall ancient tree brooded by the river. There was a moment of stillness. A gunshot rang out, startling birds from the bushes.

The bullet slammed into his chest and pitched him backward off his horse. Canh and Khi closed around the magistrate, sheltering him with their bodies, but no more shots came. Blood gushed from his mouth. He shook briefly, eyes fixated at the sky. There was a hole in his chest the size of a sour berry. His ivory badge gleamed red with blood.

His life—the important parts—was blessed with peace and prosperity. He would be survived by many loved ones. He had sired eight children: three with his first wife, one with his second wife, and four with his third wife. He had fulfilled his filial obligations, cherished his wives, and left his children a greater estate than the one he had inherited. He had lived his own life and had been privileged to judge the deeds of others. He had presided over more than his share of hearings on robberies, rapes, domestic violence, land disputes, drunken brawls, smugglings, and sundries of minor crimes. It was enough humanity to last a lifetime twice as long as what he had been given. He had been fortunate to guide his domain through the Great Famine and to savor the imminent fall of the Japanese, who had brought so much death and suffering. It was as much as a man of his era could hope for. And so ended the feudal age for the line of Pham of Tong Xuyen.

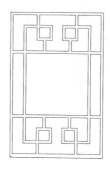

1945–1946

19. The Democratic Republic of Vietnam

In the closing months of World War II, Vietnam saw its first significant opportunity for independence in eight decades. The French, beleaguered in Europe, had not returned, and the ruling Japanese faced defeat on several fronts. In March of 1945, the Japanese foresaw the end of their empire and abruptly disarmed the entire French governing force in Vietnam. They dismantled the Vichy French colonial administration and imprisoned French troops and civilians, and then coerced Emperor Bao Dai to declare Vietnam's independence from France and its membership in Japan's "Greater East Asia Co-prosperity Sphere."

The country quickly plunged into a period of lawlessness and turmoil. The Vietnamese Nationalists, the Communists, and several other religious and political factions vied for power. Throughout the country, these parties engaged in attacks, ambushes, and assassinations against one another. Widespread unrest, riots, demonstrations, and sabotage disrupted the country. Governmental services fell into disarray. The Japanese army continued to commandeer transportation channels for military purposes, depriving the famine-stricken North of the rice surplus in the South. More than a million starved to death; millions more suffered from hunger and disease.

On August 6, 1945, the U.S. annihilated Hiroshima with an atomic bomb. Nagasaki suffered the same fate on August 9. On August 14, Japan surrendered. Ho Chi Minh immediately gathered more than sixty delegates from numerous ethnic minorities and political groups to form the People's National Congress. Despite earlier conflicts, on August 16, they formed the National Liberation Committee of Viet Nam and selected Ho as the president. This was the provisional government of the Democratic Republic of Viet Nam. Ho declared a general insurrection to establish control before the French returned from Europe.

Mobs swelled the streets of Hanoi as demonstrations shook the city for three days. On August 19, the Viet Minh took over Hanoi without a fight. The historic string of events came to be known as the August Revolution.

On September 2, half a million people, impassioned with patriotism, swarmed into Hanoi's Ba Dinh Square to witness the provisional government of the Democratic Republic of Viet Nam formally assume office. General Vo Nguyen Giap thanked the U.S. for its help and acknowledged America as a friend of Vietnam. Flanked by American military officers from the Office of Strategic Services, Ho Chi Minh read the Vietnamese Declaration of Independence: "All men are created equal. They are endowed by their Creator with certain inalienable rights; among these are Life, Liberty, and the pursuit of Happiness . . ."

IN accordance with the Allied agreements in Potsdam, the Chinese army moved into Vietnam to disarm the Japanese in the North and to serve as a temporary occupying force. General Luu Han led a rabble of 200,000 Chinese troops, many barefoot, with wives and children in tow. Underpaid, undernourished, and undisciplined, they came without provisions and plundered villages in their path, dragging a caravan of stolen goods, produce, and livestock all the way into Hanoi. Once inside the city, they seized the luxuries that once belonged to the Japanese and the French. Soldiers ransacked warehouses, mansions, and public buildings, carrying off furniture, chandeliers, and clothes, and robbed merchants at the open markets in broad daylight. The offi-cers behaved no better, forcing themselves into local business deals, con-fiscating property, and legalizing their theft by paying with worthless Chinese currency. The Chinese occupation lasted six months.

The responsibility for disarming the Japanese in the South belonged to the British, who, like the French, also had vested interests in colonial-ism. After news of Ho Chi Minh's declaration of independence reached Saigon, British General Gracey quickly released and armed French troops who had been, until then, confined to their barracks by the Japanese for six months. A day later, French soldiers seized control of Saigon City Hall. French soldiers and French civilians went on a ram-page, breaking into shops and homes, indiscriminately beating Viet-namese men, women, and children. The last week in September of 1945, Saigon was wrought with hysteria and mayhem between the French and the Vietnamese. Hundreds were killed. In mid-October, French reinforce-ments arrived, and General LeClerc reasserted colonial rule by force. Saigon was reestablished as a French city, but the vast Mekong Delta became a battlefield.

While the U.S. was hesitant to get involved in Indochina and did not favor colonialism, the Americans yielded to pressure from the British and the French and stepped back to allow their Allies to maneuver in Vietnam. The Americans did not protest when the British gave the French their American equipment and transported French troops back to Vietnam. This action pushed the founders of the Democratic Republic of Vietnam further toward the Soviet Bloc. Many Vietnamese saw this American complacency as the seed for the thirty years of war.

From late 1945 to mid-1946, the French, Ho Chi Minh, various Vietnamese Nationalist factions, religious groups, and the Chinese occupational forces continued to maneuver against one another through both political and military means. In an attempt to make his provisional power permanent, Ho Chi Minh hastily held general elections on January 6, 1946, against vehement protests from the Nationalists. Although a National Assembly was formed, the infighting continued unabated. While the Vietnamese bickered bitterly among themselves, the Chinese, who until then claimed to be an ally of Vietnam, switched loyalty and struck a profitable bargain with the French. In March 1946, the Chinese traded the control of the North to the French for huge economic and political concessions. Well-armed French troops shipped in from Saigon replaced the Chinese occupation force. In the same month, the British left the South to the French. Once again, Vietnam fell neatly into the hands of the French.

After its defeats in World War II, France was eager to reassert colonial control and regain some of its former prestige. Having briefly tasted freedom, the Vietnamese refused to relinquish their Democratic Republic without a struggle, and yet they were unable to unify under a single banner. The French formed an alliance with the Viet Minh to eradicate the other factions. In June 1946, with French assistance, General Giap began a bloody campaign to crush all opposition groups, one by one. In July, Giap's troops attacked the Nationalists' headquarters in Hanoi while the French blocked the surrounding streets to prevent Nationalists' escape or reinforcement. The Viet Minh killed and arrested more than a hundred Nationalists. In a single stroke, the Viet Minh eliminated nearly every key Nationalist leader and pushed the remnants of the Nationalist forces into the mountain forests.

At the time, many Vietnamese, Nationalists included, did not know this was the work of Ho Chi Minh's organization and continued to support him. Those who did regarded the collaboration of the French and Viet Minh as an unholy alliance. Later, some would portray the event as a hunt with the masters encircling their prey and then unleashing the hounds to do the dirty work. Others would cite it as the most successful example of the French colonial divide-and-conquer tactic. For the Nationalist sympathizers, it was an unforgivable betrayal between brothers.

With the other opposition groups decimated, the alliance of convenience ended. For months, the two forces controlled the country in an uneasy coexistence. Tension escalated through the fall of 1946. A misunderstanding in Hai Phong resulted in the Viet Minh militiamen slaughtering twenty-three French soldiers. North of Hanoi, six French troops were killed days later. On November 23, 1946, French commanders decided to teach the natives a lesson and butchered more than six thousand Vietnamese men, women, and children in a single day. The French bathed the streets of Hai Phong in Vietnamese blood.

On the night of December 19, the Viet Minh militia retaliated by destroying the power station in Hanoi and attacking French installations. Fighting quickly spread throughout the country. The war began, and all the Vietnamese factions set aside their political differences to join the Resistance headed by Ho Chi Minh's government.

20. THE TRAP

By 9:30 P.M., Viet, Nhan, and I had finished touring the hamlet's defenses. We returned to the community center, excited by the preparation for battle. I was feeling rather positive. My show of confidence for the men lifted my own spirit as well, but as I stepped inside the common house, moans of the injured sobered me instantly.

Nurse Nhi reported that the two seriously wounded men had taken turns for the worse. Nurse Nhung and Thoi had cooked and sent food to the whole team guarding the perimeter. Our meal was set in the classroom.

Viet, Nhan, and I stood around the teacher's desk with the three women. They had cooked a meal of brown rice, green onion omelets, and watery tomato soup flavored with dried shrimp. It was all that was available in the hamlet. None of us had eaten since lunch, and we dug into the food without decorum. I was so hungry I thought it was the best dinner I'd ever had in all the times I spent with my RD teams. I doubted what people said about fear spoiling one's appetite. I had a great meal, even though I was definitely afraid.

After dinner, Viet, Nhan, and I went out to sit on the porch steps with our tea. I wondered aloud why the VC hadn't attacked yet.

"Maybe they left already," Nhan ventured as he rolled a cigarette.

Viet grinned and shook his head. "They're out there. This is their Regional Force; they don't hit and run like the local guerrillas."

"Yes, but their Regionals are professionals. Why would they give us time to get dug in and rested?" Nhan said.

Viet deadpanned, "I guess they have to eat too."

Nhan and I chuckled at the image of our attackers having dinner around a campfire. Somehow it struck me as tragic.

A chilly breeze made the stars seem icy. The moonlight gave shadow to everything but revealed nothing. It was strange not to hear a single dog bark all evening. The silence was unnerving, infectious.

I thought of my wife at home alone with our child. Whatever surprises she'd prepared were long cold now. I marveled at this young woman who hadn't asked me for a single thing in the years we'd been together. She saved everything, spent only for our bare necessities, and wanted nothing for herself. She never complained or showed her displeasure with our poverty in any of the many ways a woman could. I wished I could have worked harder for her somehow. I felt sorry I did not earn more money to make her life easier.

Lieutenant Lan came over the radio and reported the good news that we would have artillery support. Viet and Nhan dashed off to update the men while I worked out the details with Lan. Since our outdated radio didn't have the army's frequency, all requests and instructions had to be relayed through Lan at headquarters, who would radio the coordinates to the artillery batteries out near the runway.

I put the radio down and realized Nurse Nhung had been standing patiently beside me with a teapot. She filled my cup, sat down on the step, and hugged her knees. The litheness of her movements was strikingly childlike. She was quite attractive, twenty-three, and already a widow with a four-year-old daughter. Her husband had been drafted and killed in battle two years before.

"Lieutenant," she said in a tiny voice. "Do you think we will be able to get out of this?"

"Yes, if we don't panic."

She bit her lips and then sighed. "I am not afraid of dying, but I'm very scared of getting seriously hurt. I don't want to suffer like the guys in there. What will we do if they overrun us?"

Our last resort was the river. "Do you know how to swim?"

"Swim? No."

"Can you hide with someone in the hamlet?"

"I know several families, nice people. I helped them many times."

"You should go and hide with them. Take Nhi and Thoi, too, if they want to go with you."

"Thank you, Lieutenant. I will." She fell silent for a moment. "Does Aunt-at-Home know about this attack?" Nhung asked, using the polite term to refer to a superior's wife.

"I asked Lieutenant Lan to tell her I am spending the night in the countryside with my team."

"That's good. It's not necessary to make her worry."

"Are your parents worried about you working in the country-side like this?"

"They understand this is the only way someone without an education like me can support a whole family. What can you do with one pair of hands and four mouths to feed?" Nhung shrugged.

"What about Nhi and Thoi?"

"Similar circumstances have a way of bringing people to similar ends, don't they?" She smiled. She still had the small-town girl smile.

Carbine shots startled us. They came from the east side of the hamlet.

Viet and Nhan returned and reported that the men shot at some movement near the creek. There was no return fire and nothing was spotted after that.

"If they don't attack us during the first hour after midnight, they may not attack at all," Nhan said.

"We will be home free, eh?" Viet sneered. "Let's go inside and get some rest. It's going to be a long night."

Not wanting to be the only man in uniform, I changed into Nhan's extra set of black pajamas. Utterly exhausted, I lay down on the cold dirt floor in back of the classroom. It felt wonderful to be stretched out on my back with my rucksack for a pillow. I immediately dozed off and would have slept well the whole night.

It couldn't have been more than an hour when the ear-piercing rattle of an AK-47 jerked me awake. Viet and Nhan were already bolting out the door. Disoriented, I jumped up, grabbed my rifle, and followed them without thinking. Viet ran off toward the creek-side where he had twelve men posted. Nhan veered toward the paddy-side to join his four cadres. I had four men at the front gate and four at the back side guarding the river. Artillery! A dozen yards down the road, I wheeled around back to the common house for the radio.

"Tiger-one, Tiger-one. This is Tiger-six, over!"

"Tiger-six, this is Tiger-one, over," Lan replied.

"Tiger-one, we are under attack on the creek-side, over."

"How far from the fence?"

"First, shell at thirty yards, then move out up to fifty, over." I headed out, taking the radio with me.

"Roger."

"Do it now! Over and out."

I ran down the main road. There was no fighting at the main gate. I cut diagonally to the creek-side, weaving between the houses, not daring to run along the perimeter. I found Viet and his men holding the enemy at the far bank across the slow-moving creek. The shooting was heavy. The enemies' AK-47s popped in ferocious bursts, mangling the fence of woven branches.

I shouted into Viet's ear that artillery was coming. Grinning, he gave me a thumbs up. Then the fence completely splintered around our heads. I patted him on the shoulder and crawled out. I slipped between the houses, going clockwise around the hamlet, shouting our password as I ran. The river was quiet, as we had expected. Without stopping to talk to the men there, I pushed on toward the sounds of fighting at Nhan's side.

The west side of the hamlet was flanked by open paddies. I joined Nhan in his trench. They had repelled the first probing charge. The VC were gathering behind a shallow dike sixty yards from the fence. What looked like a breeze moving through the rice field was actually dozens of troops crawling in the paddy mud. They had camouflaged themselves with rice stalks. Even with the half-moon, it was nearly impossible to see them unless they moved or fired at us.

Suddenly Nhan started firing. "Here they come again!"

I radioed Lan. "Tiger-one. This is Tiger-six. Come in, over!"

"Tiger-six, artillery support is coming soon. What's your situation?"

"Shell the east side immediately. We're under attack here too. What is taking them so long?"

"Artillery is coming soon for the west side."

"Listen, they've got two guns. Have one shell the creek-side, and the other shell the paddy-side. We're going to be overrun in a couple of minutes! Get on it! Over and out."

It was crazy that it took them so long to fire the damn cannons when they had the coordinates and hours to prepare. I turned to Nhan and shouted, "Hold them! I'll bring more men to reinforce your position."

Leaving my rifle with Nhan, I drew my pistol and held the radio in my other hand. I sprinted so fast the dirt road looked like a velvety moonlit blur, as smooth as leather, elongating hypnotically. It felt as though I was flying, but I couldn't seem to go fast enough. In the back of my mind, I was half expecting one of the villagers, a VC infiltrator, to step out of the shadow and put a bullet through me.

I took two men from the riverbank and another pair from the front gate. When we got to Nhan's side, they were nearly overwhelmed. I deployed the four men along the wall.

Phht. Phht. Phht. Bullets punched through the bamboo walls and zinged past me. In several spots, the VC came within ten yards of the wall. My men hit them with nearly every shot. I dove back into Nhan's trench.

Nhan smiled his weird smile and said, "We're in real trouble now."

I peered through the fence and shuddered. Sixty yards away, the dike swarmed with shadows. They moved toward us like a dark ripple.

"Kill! Kill! Kill! *Aaaaaa!*" they screamed. Their voices merged and climbed to a crescendo, the crazy words overlapping into one continuous chilling note.

The urge to flee was overwhelming. I had never shot or killed anyone. I sighted an attacker coming directly at me, but I couldn't squeeze the trigger. He trudged awkwardly in the thick paddy. It was like watching someone moving across quicksand. He fired his AK-47. The instant the fence in front of me exploded, my finger closed down on the trigger. *Bang!* The figure slumped into the paddy like a melting shadow.

"Kill! . . . Kill! . . . Kill! . . . Kill!" They surged forward without respite.

Nhan turned to me and asked casually, "How many men do you think they have?"

"I don't know. Maybe a hundred and fifty—at least a full company. Probably more in reserve."

One of our men cried and slid down in a heap at the bottom of the trench. Bullets drummed the length of the wall. I fired without debate or remorse. The heavy AK-47 fire kept us low against the mound. I found myself ducking and inching along the fence for cover. Attackers swarmed forward, screaming, "Kill! Kill!" Their covering fire was so fierce, we couldn't aim with any accuracy. Their charge was severely hampered by the mud, but we still couldn't drop them quickly enough. Their machine guns ripped holes in the fence almost large enough for a man to crawl through.

Just as I was about to order the retreat, I heard the gut-clenching sound of incoming artillery: *eeeeeeEEEEUU—BOOM! eeeeeeEEEE-UU—BOOM!*

The bombardment was falling on the other side of the hamlet. I ran over to Viet's perimeter. The shells were striking too far away. I radioed Lan and adjusted the coordinates. Within minutes, shells fell right on top of the enemy. I ran back to the other side just as the first shell came down precisely between our lines and theirs.

The men cheered. Between the explosions and the gunfire, the wounded wailed.

Although I knew the shells would fall outside the fence, I couldn't help but cringe at the whine of every incoming shell. It was like a judgment bugle from above, utterly demoralizing. The detonation was a comforting conclusion: If you heard the boom, you were still alive.

The attackers wavered. Some crouched down into the water; others moved warily as though they could sneak past the bombardment. Feet shackled by mud, they stumbled forward bravely, firing their AK-47s, the muzzle-flashes like fireworks. We picked them off steadily. It was the hour of attrition, our ammunition ticking away with the seconds. I had no idea how long they would last.

The battle raged on, shells screeching down like falling stars, bloodied men sinking into the paddy to nourish the rice grains that would feed children and peasants—both Communists and Nationalists.

We heard Viet's whistle: The enemy had breached our defense. Within seconds we found ourselves being shot at from the flank. I signaled Nhan to retreat. The order quickly traveled along the defense. We scurried from the shadow of one house to the next, exchanging fire with the attackers. Fighting broke out all over the hamlet. It was impossible to know who was shooting at whom. We pulled back to the seven huts surrounding the common house. In the confusion, two more cadres were injured and one was killed.

Viet, Nhan, and I met in the common house to assess our situation. We had twenty-four men left, including ourselves and the three wounded who were still capable of fighting, and were down to roughly twenty rounds apiece. I radioed Lan to cancel the artillery bombardment and report that we had pulled back to our secondary defense position and were in desperate need of reinforcement. Lan relayed that Trieu said he would send troops at dawn. Viet, Nhan, and I looked at each other. Dawn was a death sentence.

I wanted to thank them for using their experience and courage to get us this far, but I couldn't say a word. We shook hands and wished each other good luck before heading back to our separate huts.

My housing was a single-room hut with a thin bamboo partition separating the living from the sleeping area. It had one door, three windows, and a thatched roof. I had four men. I ordered two to stay on guard and the other two to make a hole in the mud wall at the back of the hut. If the enemy set the hut on fire, we needed an escape. Then we waited. Sitting in the dark waiting for the final shoot-out, I realized that the VC had never spent this many men to kill a bunch of lowly RD cadres. It seemed very odd.

There was intermittent gunfire nearby. One of my men shot at four guerrillas approaching our hut. They fled into a hut across the street. The enemy was taking its time narrowing down our location. They didn't mount an attack, seemingly intent only on securing their position. They must have known they could wipe us out with a single charge. A few grenades through the windows would have finished us.

After two hours of inactivity, I sent one of the vets out to check on the other huts. The instant he dashed out the door, the enemy fired so intensely with several AK-47s that I was sure he was dead. He scurried right back in.

I called Lan and reported our situation, but I dared not tell him we were almost out of ammunition, afraid the enemy could catch our conversation.

Lan said, "Trieu wants you to find out how strong the guerrillas are."

"How strong the guerrillas? Strong enough to overrun us!"

Lan tried to placate me, saying that he'd tell Trieu that we tried but could not move at all. I told Lan to ask Trieu when we could expect reinforcement. Lan called back later and said any time in the morning. He said he could not be more specific due to security reasons.

One of my men, an ARVN vet, said, "Oh, don't worry, they will come. Otherwise, it will look very bad if a whole RD team gets eliminated without some sort of rescue effort from the army. But you can bet they will take their time mobilizing, dragging it out as long as possible, because if we're wiped out by the time they get here, they won't have to risk getting involved in the fight."

His words struck me. I didn't have a reply, and all the men knew it. I lay down in a corner to gather myself. I knew my time could come at any moment, yet, at twenty-eight, I was not ready to die. Until now, I always thought I was very lucky. It was a pleasure to stay in the provincial capital most of the time and work with civilians primarily as an administrator. I reported only to the province chief, a lieutenant colonel who, thankfully, was a reasonable man. I got to stay at home with my family. Generally, it didn't feel like being in the army.

I could accept being attacked, but seeing my men being treated like bastards by our very own Regional Forces who were supposed to protect us was difficult. Ours was a half-baked paramilitary force, and I did not blame them for looking out for themselves. It was common knowledge that most platoon leaders from the Regional Force avoided battle at all cost. They practiced the combat philosophy of "live and let live," hoping the Communists would see that they were not the real enemies. With my experience, I strongly doubted this line of thinking. The Communists always attacked when they saw an opening.

With so many depending on me, I felt more helpless than ever. I was ashamed that I did not have any combat experience. It seemed rather senseless to struggle. Even if I survived this, there would be other battles and ambushes. I was stuck in the army for years. I often wondered if it was in my destiny to be killed like my Uncle Thuan, with a sniper's bullet in the chest.

THE hours dragged on. In spite of impending danger, it was a struggle to stay awake in the dark. The house was small and crowded. Every few minutes, I stood up, stretched my legs, and peeked outside. One of the men found some sweet potatoes and a pouch of tea in the hut. He boiled the potatoes, then used the hot water to make tea. At 5:00 A.M., we had our farmer's breakfast. The tea was thick and bracing, with grits from the potatoes.

Outside, an indigo stain spread across the eastern sky. A dense ground fog rose from the paddy and poured into the hamlet and obscured the surrounding huts. We were all very restless, but no one wanted to go out again. The sky began to glow. The fog became a milky soup that obscured the bushes and flooded right to the treetops.

I told my group to hold the position while I went to meet with Viet and Nhan at the common house. I secured the radio strap across my back, checked my pistol, and then crawled through the hole in the back wall. The thick fog and the vegetable garden provided good cover, so I crawled twenty yards to the next house. When I reached the bushes separating the home lots, it seemed safe enough, so I got to my feet. AK-47s cackled ferociously, chopping up the bushes around me. I threw myself down to the ground and scrambled to the common house. Nhung opened the door and I jumped to my feet and charged across the last few yards, tailed by sprays of bullets.

The three women were crying. They had been taking care of the wounded when we sounded the retreat and didn't have time to hide with the villagers. The two injured from yesterday had died. They were laid out on the floor with shirts covering their faces. Our situation looked very grim, so I had to assure them that the rescue force would be with us soon enough, although I had not heard anything new from Lan since the time I called to let him know of our withdrawal.

I waited for Viet and Nhan in the classroom. Sporadic gunfire rang and echoed between the huts. It was gut-wrenching knowing my men were out there.

Viet and Nhan ducked through the door a few minutes later, looking disheveled and worried.

"What's your situation?" I asked.

"My men have about a dozen rounds left each." Nhan smiled apologetically.

"Same here," Viet said.

"With this fog, our chances of sneaking out of the hamlet are better than last night," I said.

"It's very hard to carry wounded people without making noise. We don't have stretchers," Nhan said

"We can create diversions," I said.

"If we don't make it to the hills by dawn, we'd be exposed in the middle of the road," Viet said.

"Staying here without ammo is suicidal," I insisted.

"We know, Lieutenant, but going out there is suicidal too," Nhan said, looking at his feet.

"Yes, it's bad either way, but I prefer to go." I was willing to go alone, but I couldn't. They would think their commander was abandoning them.

Neither Viet nor Nhan replied. We stood there in silence, measuring each other. These brave vets would go into battle on my word. I knew then at that moment that it was a matter of conscience. It simply was not my prerogative to order them into battle. They had signed up to do social work as public servants, not to fight as soldiers—and they were not compensated as such.

"You are the majority," I said. It was a sinking sensation. I was being pulled deeper into this nightmare. "We will stay."

AFTER sunrise, Lieutenant Lan called with a report. Captain Trieu had ordered a two-pronged rescue of two platoons from the district seat and two platoons from the hills several miles away—the same group that had been sharing their campsite with my team. Carelessly relying on daylight to expose the enemy, the regional commanders of both groups brought their troops to An Binh from opposite directions on the primary interprovince road, confident that the VC had vanished before daybreak. The L-19 scout plane, a two-seater prop, didn't spot the enemy camouflaged in bushes and submerged in the paddy water. The truck convoy from the district was decimated crossing a bridge, no doubt by the same machine guns that ambushed us yesterday.

The platoons from the hills came on foot. Suspicious of another ambush, they marched in a single, staggered column and so suffered fewer casualties when the enemy sprung the trap. Even with the air support of two World War II Thunderbolts, they could neither retreat nor overwhelm their attackers. It was a stalemate. Lan relayed new orders from Trieu. We were to evacuate the hamlet and reinforce this platoon.

Everything made horrible sense.

"Bait," I said, feeling ill. "They kept us alive all this time as bait."

"We should have known." Nhan grimaced.

"As soon as they wipe out the Regional platoons, they'll come back here and finish us," Viet said.

Nhan nodded. "We won't have a single bullet left by then."

"They must have relocated their troops and machine guns once they breached the fence. There's probably only a dozen men in the hamlet, just enough to pin us down," I said.

"We stay, we die tonight." Viet said, "This is my fault. I'm the veteran here; I should have known better. You were right, Lieutenant; we should have left before dawn when we had the fog."

"Let's evacuate then. We're not done yet," Nhan said.

Viet proposed that he and his best veterans would create a distraction and cover our retreat. We would time our evacuation for ten minutes. Everyone must get clear of the front gate within that window. Artillery bombardment would cover our escape and block any pursuit. It was a suicide mission, but we couldn't think of better alternative.

Nhan shook Viet's hand and held it awhile in silence. I shook hands and wished him good luck. Viet grinned gamely; he knew his chances.

FIFTEEN minutes later, Nhan took the first group of seven men and moved along the hedges. With a fair idea of where some of the guerrillas were hiding, Nhan picked a path among the bushes between the houses to the front gate. His group promptly encountered heavy fire. They dove for cover and began shooting. Viet, Sanh, Hiep, and Toa sneaked out of the huts, going around the enemies to attack them from the rear.

I led the main group of fifteen. Four men carried the two wounded on hammocks. Three more helped the less critically injured. All three women had decided to come. Bullets zipping all around us, we simply ducked and ran as fast as we could. The noise from half a dozen AK-47s was terrifying. It made you want to huddle behind a wall. The fear was like a poison; once it got into your legs, you couldn't move. I never knew how we did it.

"Run! Run!" I crouched down and fired at a hut across the road. "Don't take cover! Keep running! Run!"

Once we passed their position, Nhan's group followed, firing as they retreated. Somewhere behind us, Viet and his men were engaged in the battle of their lives.

The sounds of gunshots softened and became sporadic after we crossed through the gate. Inside the hamlet, the fighting continued with Viet's group. I ordered the team to keep running until we got beyond range of the enemies' AK-47s.

I kept glancing back, expecting Viet's group to come out of the gates immediately after us. Every second behind that wall increased their chances of dying. Their only hope was that the artillery would fall precisely on time as promised. I had my group hunkered down inside gun range so we could provide covering fire for Viet's group.

I got Lan on the radio, but didn't know what to do next. It took too long to change orders for artillery fire. Then we saw Viet, Sanh, Hiep, and Toa running out the gates.

"Now! Artillery! Get them to fire now!" I yelled into the radio, then picked up my rifle and fired at the gun slots by the gate. The guerrillas chased Viet's group to the perimeter, then hunkered down in the foxholes behind the wall, the very position we had held last night.

Our covering fire distracted them, but it was impossible to hit defenders behind the fortification. Toa fell, as if struck by a sledgehammer. Bullets caught Viet and spun him sideways. Dropping their guns, the other two men wheeled around to pick up their comrades. Sanh carried Toa on his back, Toa's feet dragging in the dirt. Hiep had Viet. They hobbled on three legs. Bullets swept around the men like hail. They should have been mowed down, but somehow they had become untouchable in this act of heroism.

At last, when it was too late for Toa and Viet, the shells howled down directly on the gate. Sanh and Hiep hobbled toward us against a backdrop of explosions and dust. We lowered our rifles. From a distance, you could admire the awesome beauty of falling shells, their wanton, godlike power.

Sanh laid Toa at our feet. He was vacant-eyed; he was dead. Viet grunted, doubled over on the ground, soaked in blood. Nhung cried as she tore up a shirt for bandage. It was no good. Viet had several bullets in him. We had nothing for him except our hands to apply pressure to his wounds.

Lan called and repeated orders for us to reinforce the Regional troops directly. My throat tightened. I couldn't answer him. I knew we should get moving. The VC could still mount a pursuit through the hamlet's side gate. Nothing seemed to matter at that moment.

□   □   □

followed no soldierly code of conduct and wore no uniform. Like a beast, he went bare-chested, regardless of sun, wind, or rain. No one in our village had seen him wear anything other than leather sandals and a pair of khaki shorts cinched with a belt. A gnarled and knotted brute, he had biceps thicker than a man's thigh, a broad chest covered by a thick mat of wiry hair, a cannonball gut, and rippling slabs of meat for a back. His shoulders were piles of muscles. A pistol hung on his hip. A long, curved sword was slung across his back.

It was late in the spring of 1947 when Mohammed and his band of twenty Arab and African legionnaires first established a post along the interprovincial road two miles from our village. Like most troops sent into the delta that year, they had little success in quelling the Resistance. Mobile and intimate with the countryside, their foes struck and vanished into the population at will.

As the weeks wore into futile months, the legionnaires became more severe in their reprisals. Sabotage of roads and bridges brought swift executions of any men caught in the vicinity. Attacks on their encampment were answered with mortar shelling on nearby hamlets. Against a ghost-like enemy, the legionnaires eventually turned their fury on the only available targets—the peasants.

The day Mohammed found Mr. Nhi, my cousins Lang and Tan and I were walking home from school when a man sprinted into the hamlet.

"Patrol! Patrol! Mohammed is with them!"

His cry fell like a blanketing shadow. Words leaped through every house in the settlement. The alarm swept down one street after another, leaving a chilling silence in its wake. The fear was instantaneous, as palpable as an evil presence. I felt it in my stomach.

In the yards, the rice thrashing halted. Folks scrambled to hide their valuables. Women smeared soot on their faces and donned an extra layer of clothes to make themselves unattractive. In the fields, the harvest was abandoned. Older women and children rushed back into the hamlet. The men ran in the opposite direction, taking with them all teenage girls and young women at risk of being raped by the legionnaires. White-faced and empty-handed, they sprinted down the road, not sparing even a second to fetch provisions or weapons. They must get clear of the village before the patrol came within view. Not a single tree or a hill could hide their flights across the open fields. By twos and threes, they dove into the network of tunnels dug into the creek's bank and beneath the rice fields. In moments, the naked land absorbed the peasants.

It was a common practice in every village. Men dared not linger and risk capture, arrest, or execution on mere suspicion of being a Resistance fighter. Women, particularly the young ones, were at risk of being arrested on false charges and taken away, never to be heard from again. Although the legionnaires preferred men for hard labor, any healthy person, woman or adolescent, could be forced into service as a coolie.

My cousins and I were thirteen, small enough to be worthless, young enough to be harmless, but old enough to understand. Lang ran home to warn our mothers in case word hadn't gotten there already. The patrol always stopped at our estate, where they feasted at our table and re-stocked themselves from our supplies. As the wealthiest family in the domain, we were required to provide the French and their legionnaires with whatever they wanted, from rice to money to laborers, without compensation.

"I see them!" Tan pointed at the village gate.

"I wonder if the Resistance sabotaged something again," I said and went to stand under a tree away from the road.

"If they did, we would have heard it by now. The Resistance always spreads news of their work," Tan said.

In our young, provincial eyes, the patrol was a fearsome sight—alien, demonic, powerful, and mysterious. Mohammed strode down the middle of the road at the head of the pack, towering over his men: a dozen Arabs and Africans. Unlike the ragged and hungry Chinese horde that I had seen in Hanoi two years ago, Mohammed's band was composed of well-fed, strong brigands. Some of them wore turbans and had exotic-looking swords and curved daggers stuck into their waistbands. Their rifles were slung across backs or carried over shoulders like shovels, barrels pointing at the sky or the ground at haphazard angles. One held the leash of a large black hound. At the rear, nearly hidden behind the patrol, Thien, the interpreter, and four Vietnamese coolies followed with empty baskets.

In the village, the legionnaires randomly searched houses as the inhabitants, mostly women and children, waited in their yards with their heads bowed. The soldiers grabbed blankets from the drying lines and helped themselves to fruits and vegetables. They shackled two old men on charges of being informants. There was nothing their wives and children could do except wail and kneel on the ground in an attempt to block the legionnaires' way. People averted their eyes, too terrified to move.

As they neared the end of the main road, the commander's dog stopped abruptly, picking up a scent. It lunged forward and barked ferociously at a haystack. Mid-harvest season, every home was flanked by several bales, each as large as a hut. Without warning, the legionnaires fired several rounds into the haystack. A muffled voice came from within.

A legionnaire shouted, *"We've got a rebel here!"*

They dragged a man out from underneath and began to kick and beat him. It was Mr. Nhi, one of our classmates' father. He was a middle-class farmer who owned his land.

We climbed a tree in the neighbor's yard and had a clear view over the heads of the legionnaires who stood just a few yards away. They ignored us, having gotten used to being tailed everywhere by children.

"You little pig," Mohammed said in French. *"Are you a rebel or a spy? Are there others in this village?"*

The interpreter translated the question to Mr. Nhi, but omitted "little pig," which was what the French commonly called Vietnamese farmers. It was a term I had heard French soldiers used both in the countryside and in Hanoi.

Mr. Nhi knelt on the ground with his head bent. "Please, honorable sir. I'm not a spy."

Mohammed turned to the interpreter. *"Tell him, anyone who hides from us must be a rebel or a spy."*

When the Arabs moved to shackle him to the other two captives, Mohammed barked a command and they backed away. He grabbed a machete from one of his men and tossed it on the ground. The interpreter's translation was drowned out by the legionnaires' guffaws. They dropped their packs and formed a circle around Mr. Nhi.

"What did he say?" Tan whispered.

"I think he's challenging Mr. Nhi to a fight." My French was rusty since the Resistance ordered all schools to stop teaching the colonialists' tongue two years ago.

"Not fair!" Tan hissed. "Mr. Nhi is just a farmer. He doesn't know how to fight."

A soldier kicked the machete closer to Mr. Nhi, who looked at it, perplexed. The men shouted. Mr. Nhi flinched and turned to the interpreter standing under the eaves of the house.

Thien was a small, thin-faced Vietnamese from Hanoi, a Catholic who had voluntarily enlisted under the French cause. Certainly, he had envisioned himself posted as an attaché to some noble French lieutenant. No one wanted to serve the lowly mercenaries. The legionnaires treated him like a servant and never allowed him to eat at their table. My mother paid him handsomely to keep us safe from Mohammed. When these men ate at our estate, Mother always made a point to secretly set him a special table with fare superior to what she served the legionnaires. I knew he was all that stood between us and the marauders, but I couldn't help disliking him. Watching the legionnaires foul our home with their drunken vulgarity, I often wished I could just poison the lot of them.

Thien said, "He wants you to stand up and fight. If you kill him, you can live."

Mr. Nhi's face clenched with horror. He shook his head violently, scooted back on all fours, and then pressed his forehead into the dirt. Mohammed came forward, and Mr. Nhi inched away until he had backed into the legs of the Arab behind him. Too frightened to speak, he put his hands together and started bowing to the Algerian, over and over as if he were praying at an altar. One Arab shoved him with a foot. Mr. Nhi tumbled and curled up on the ground, arms raised to ward off blows.

The men laughed. *"What a coward!"*

In front of the home, the family huddled, crying. The grandfather had his two grandchildren in his arms to keep them from running to their father. The grandmother and Mr. Nhi's wife clutched the arms of the interpreter, begging him to ask the commander for leniency. Thien brushed them off and stomped away to stand near the road.

The Algerian dragged Mr. Nhi to his feet by the front of his shirt, then slapped him hard across the face. Mr. Nhi reeled backward. The man finally found his voice and begged for mercy. His mouth was bleeding. The interpreter did not bother to translate. The soldiers guffawed as the Algerian drew his sword and began stalking around the circle. Mr. Nhi crawled around on his hands and knees and got kicked when he came close to the soldiers. Mohammed lunged and made a shallow cut on the man's thigh.

Mr. Nhi shrieked, curling up into a ball. The Algerian shoved him with a foot and then kicked him when Mr. Nhi didn't get up. The soldiers jeered.

Mohammed raised his sword, looming over the small farmer like an executioner. *"Fight or die!"*

Mr. Nhi's father rushed into the circle and knelt between the commander and his son. The old man touched his forehead to the ground at the Algerian's feet. "Please, honorable sir, be merciful! My son is innocent!"

"He shouldn't have hidden," the interpreter said from outside the circle.

"My son is a silly man. He was afraid of the troops. He hasn't done anything. Please spare his life. He has a family to provide for. Take me instead. Do what you want with me."

As if permission had been granted, the Algerian slashed the old man. The blade swept across his arm and chest. The women shrieked. The old man crumpled, his blood splattering dark blotches in the dirt. In seconds, his white hair, beard, and white peasant shirt were soaked bright red. Mr. Nhi wailed and threw himself over his father, shielding the old man. The soldiers stepped aside and let the two women drag the old man into the house. He would die of the wound within hours.

I shuddered thinking what would happen if Mohammed knew my mother was also paying the Resistance just as handsomely as she paid the legionnaires. Would we be hacked to pieces like this family? Would the servants' daughters be dragged away to be raped in the legionnaires' camp? I didn't want to watch anymore, but I couldn't look away.

The interpreter said, "Pick up the machete and fight. I have never seen him let anyone go. Your best chance is to kill him while you still have the strength to try. If you won't fight, he'll cut you in a hundred places until you bleed to death."

Mr. Nhi's shoulders sagged, his chin resting on his chest. At last, he reached for the machete and rose to his feet. The legionnaires cheered. Next to Mohammed, Mr. Nhi looked ridiculously small and childlike, his head level with the Algerian's chest. The eighteen-inch machete dangled at his side, pointed at the ground.

Grinning, the legionnaires fetched whisky bottles from their packs and began to drink. The commander swigged from a bottle and lit a cigar. He made a joke in French and let out a long cackle. The men laughed and wagered on the fight.

The cigar clenched between his teeth, Mohammed circled his prey, the long saber at ready. Mr. Nhi turned, but did not raise his puny weapon. Despite his size, Mohammed was very fast. He stepped forward and, with a snappy tap, knocked the machete out of Mr. Nhi's hand. Before Mr. Nhi realized what happened, Mohammed's fist caught him flush on the mouth and sent him spinning into the dirt. The men threw back their heads and hooted. An Arab tossed Mr. Nhi the machete.

Old men and women who remained in the village gathered in the street and the neighboring houses. I kept looking around, half expecting the Resistance forces to storm the village and rescue Mr. Nhi. The Resistance killed those they suspected of collaborating with French, and the French killed those they suspected of collaborating with the Resistance. And both sides demanded information, resources, and men from the villages. There was nothing a nonpartisan peasant could do.

When Mr. Nhi picked up the weapon again, something had come over him. He rose into a fighting stance and brought the machete to bear on the Algerian. Like many men of his generation, he had some training in martial arts in his youth and was not entirely inept. The Arabs cheered, pleased that there would be a fight after all. Mohammed harrumphed and flourished the saber above his head. He was evidently an experienced swordsman.

Mohammed delivered the first blows slowly so his inexperienced opponent could fend them. Metal rang against metal in a rhythm dictated by the Algerian. It was as if they were playing a game, or the Algerian was teaching Mr. Nhi to fight. Several times, the Algerian playfully slapped Mr. Nhi with the flat of his weapon. Mohammed pulled back and laughed, seemingly pleased. Over and over, he swooped in from a distance, each time gentling nicking his opponent's arm or leg, enough to hurt but not maim. After each cut, he stood back and regarded his swordsmanship. His men hollered encouragement. Mr. Nhi staggered, gasping and covered in blood. In a sudden burst of energy, he lunged, nearly catching the Algerian on his blade. The soldiers parted and tripped Mr. Nhi with a foot. They encircled him again.

The men jeered, *"He nearly got you!"*

"Gut the pig already. We're getting hungry!"

Growling, Mohammed raised his saber high above his head. The blows fell: one, two, three, four. Somehow Mr. Nhi parried them all and mounted his own attack. The Algerian swatted away the machete almost casually. It was a crude and heavy tool for clearing bushes.

It was simply too short to penetrate the saber's reach. Mr. Nhi pressed his attack, but he was hampered by his injured leg. It was futile. With each thwarted offense, he cursed and grew bolder and more desperate.

Mohammed toyed with the man until the game bored him. He feigned a retreat, then lunged, the saber flashing across the gap. The machete fell to the ground. Mr. Nhi's right arm hung limp and useless at his side. The cut on his forearm had gone through to the bone. He wobbled on his feet, breaths ragged. He did not beg; his eyes brimmed with scorn.

A cheer for the dying man rose in my throat. It was a precious moment of awe. He was an insignificant peasant, made from the very stuff that formed all of us. Though nothing remained of him, neither his strength nor his limbs, he stood defiant.

Blind to the valor before them, the Arabs cheered for their commander to finish the kill. The Algerian grinned and circled his victim. He stepped closer, his blade poised high. A steel arc glinted in the sunlight. It swept past Mr. Nhi's face without appearing to make contact, though a red gash started to widen in Mr. Nhi's throat. He clutched it, trying to stem the leak. His legs buckled and he slipped to the ground. Blood gurgled out of his throat. He lay on his side, legs churning as though trying to run. His wife and mother fainted. An audible shudder went through the crowd. We watched him shake and jerk and twitch until his last breath quieted. There was so much blood.

Mohammed puffed on his cigar and watched his victim's death throes. The Arabs passed him the whisky bottle. It had been a good show. The Algerian rolled Mr. Nhi onto his back, then cut open his belly, from groin to ribcage. Coils of intestines spilled out onto the ground. Mr. Nhi died with his eyes open, his bowels a bloody heap in the dirt.

"Look and remember. You can hide nothing from me!" the Algerian shouted, sweeping his saber over the villagers. *"You are to leave this pig here for the birds and the dogs. He is not to be touched until I return."*

"*Roast the pigs!*" Mohammed shouted.

His men torched the hay bales and the house.

"Get out!" the neighbors shouted to the women inside the house.

Screams came from within. As quick as dry kindling, the thatch roof caught fire. Glowing embers and black smoke curled up to the sky. Mrs. Nhi and her mother-in-law dragged the grandfather out the back door. The children followed behind, coughing. Mohammed and his men chortled. Once the house had become a bonfire, the legionnaires gathered their loot and sauntered to our estate, where they would gorge themselves with drinks and foods.

Gusts of heat rolled from the fire. I sweated, sitting in the tree. Villagers hurried to draw water and douse the adjacent houses. During the dry season, a fire like this could wipe out the entire village. We sat in the branches a long time, watching flames consume the house. I looked at Tan. We were not ashamed of our tears. Our world had been irrevocably changed. I surely did not cry out of fear. The giant Algerian had lost his mystery. He was still every bit a monster, but I saw his heart. It was the heart of a coward.

Somehow he had reduced himself with his own brutality. A small, frail farmer had stood up to this giant. We too were capable of fighting.

THAT night, people buried Mr. Nhi with his father. Monks blessed their graves under a pale crescent moon. In the wee hours, more than twenty young men, single women, and boys our age left the village. Tan and I ached to slip into the darkness with them and join the Resistance.

It was as much a desperate act of salvage as redemption. It was a matter of honor.

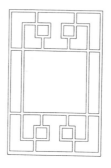

THE NORTH
1948

22. THE RESISTANCE FIGHTER

One night right after the New Year celebration, Vi, the orphan, came back wearing brown pajamas and sandals. We barely recognized him. Gardener Cam's adopted son—our famine project—had grown into a tall, lean young man. His boyish round face had squared into an almost chiseled look. He had shaved off his unruly tangles, leaving only monk's fuzz on his head. Vi used to be as dark as a buffalo boy. Now he was as pale as an office clerk. His voice had broken into a man's baritone. His eyes, however, were the same—small, narrow, and serious. The huge mole in the middle of his forehead was as ominous as ever.

His visit came as a big surprise. We had assumed Vi had died in battle because we hadn't heard from him since he disappeared almost three years ago. Everyone in the estate gathered in the dining hall to welcome him. The women complimented him on how mature he looked and swamped him with questions. Everyone was very nice to him. It was the most attention he'd ever received. Vi was gregarious, joking and tousling the heads of the little ones. He sipped his tea and answered questions patiently like a real adult. He exuded power and authority.

One of my little cousins chirped, "Vi! Vi! You remember when we used to call you Dumpling-Face-Boy?"

The women gasped, mortified, but Vi just chuckled and patted the boy's head. Aunt Thao told the kid to be quiet.

Old Cam asked the one question that had bothered him since Vi left. "Why didn't you write? We were so worried."

"Oh, Uncle, it's against the rules. And besides, we were so busy moving from one assignment to the next, we never had time to write."

"Brother Vi, why don't you have a gun?" asked Chau, the perennial buffalo boy.

Vi laughed easily. "I had several guns before, but I don't need them for my new work now."

Tan said, "Is it communication or intelligence?"

Vi just smiled and wouldn't say anything. The kids clamored for him to tell, but he replied, "I wouldn't be a good Resistance fighter if I disobeyed my orders and revealed my assignment to you, would I?"

Aunt Thuan hushed the kids and turned to Vi. "Well, son, now that you're back home again, we'll prepare a private room for you—in the old guards' wing, because you're a fighting man now."

Vi said he would like that. He was still active in his unit, so he would only come and spend the night when it was safe. He said his group was stationed nearby and that he would be back regularly to gather information on the French. Vi asked my mother when my father would be coming home. She said he wouldn't be back until the situation in the countryside stabilized. I noticed she avoided saying that Father was afraid the Resistance might assassinate him as they did his brother.

Vi didn't stay long that night. He left laden with sacks of food and money donated to his unit by Aunt Thuan and Mother.

□   □   □

□   □   □

GARDENER Cam couldn't stop talking about Vi for days. He was very happy and proud of his adopted son. Most people were glad to see Vi because it meant that the estate had more favor with the Resistance. But some disagreed, saying that we were in greater danger of being punished by the French legionnaires if they found out someone from our estate was in the Resistance. Both the French and the Resistance had their own informants. Khi, our old guard, said the Viet Minh sent members of well-to-do families back home to collect money and supplies, and that Vi's information gathering was just an excuse. The Resistance certainly knew much more than we did. Aunt Thuan and my mother didn't say anything, but I knew they were aware of the precarious balance they had to maintain to appease both the French and the Resistance. Troops from both sides regularly stopped at our estate to eat, rest, and gather supplies.

Over the next five months, Vi visited us once or twice a week, often staying overnight if the French had already stopped at our village that day. The legionnaires never patrolled or entered villages at night. Vi knew their movements and was always very relaxed at the estate. For the adults, he took on the roles of underground liaison and protector. For the young children, Vi was their own hero. For Tan and me, Vi was a guide into the world of the Resistance. He told us everything we had ever wanted to know about fighting the French, the camaraderie of the Resistance, and our patriotic duties.

Slowly but inevitably, the stories of his years away seeped from Vi like unbearable secrets. We listened to him carefully, as though our future depended on his stories—and in a way, it did. We were fourteen and torn between two loyalties: our family's generational allegiance to the Nationalists and our own patriotic need to join the Resistance to strike back at the French. I didn't know it then, but we were searching for the proper rationale to join the Resistance, struggling to conjure a good reason why the Resistance—whose core was the Viet Minh—wasn't responsible for the murders of Tan's father and our cousin Quyen.

Night after night, Vi sat up late with Tan and me by the lake and told us about his adventures. Perhaps he knew it the whole time: Our lives hung in the balance. Our decisions would be based on what he had to say.

THE night Vi decided to join the Resistance, he simply stuffed his worldly belongings into a sack and followed the fighters who had stopped at our estate for provisions. He told no one his plans and did not say good-bye.

Vi was lucky to have attached himself to a crackerjack group— one of the most daring platoons in the local Resistance forces. They were forced to march through the nights, crossing the flatland back and forth at a crushing pace to attack multiple French camps. Their endurance was renowned, their exploits legendary. Villagers fed and sheltered them, celebrating them like heroes. It was an addictive introduction to life as a Resistance fighter.

They sent Vi through an underground network into the mountains, where he spent the next five months at a training camp hidden deep in the forest. There were more than a hundred children as young as ten barracked in makeshift shacks. Vi felt at home among the many orphans. The twenty-six-year-old commander was the oldest person present. The training was difficult and dangerous. The instructors were demanding, but they were also supportive like older brothers and sisters. They taught him the value of independence and freedom, and told stories of Vietnamese heroes and the victorious battles of the people. And there was also time for songs and dances and nights around the campfire celebrating life. In the camp, he found the sense of family and camaraderie. It was the happiest time of his life.

Vi spent the first year in a light-foot brigade based in the northwest region of the rice plain. A beautiful young scout took him under her wing in a sisterly way and taught him the details of guerilla life. She had full red lips and a mole beneath her left eye. The village midwife had said hers would be a life of tears. In her hand, the lifeline faded to nothing at the center of her palm. After her lover was killed in battle, she had vowed not to take another. Vi had fallen for her, and as the seasons passed, the weight of his infatuation became crushing. When she died in an ambush, he knew life held nothing else for him but the Resistance. He was ready to give his life for the cause.

Vi became the enemy's greatest fear, a soldier who could not be bought; a fighter to whom honor, courage, and sacrifice were the measures of a man. He lived the Resistance creed that every leader must have been a proven follower with courage and sacrifices to his credits; that a leader could order no task that he had not performed himself. These were the shining demands Vi willingly fulfilled. With Vi's valor came promotions. A year later, he was a platoon leader with twelve young fighters. Vi was seventeen.

VI's last battle was at Cao Bang. It was part of a major campaign to destroy a French camp that controlled the mountain pass. His platoon was one of the crack demolition units chosen for their expertise in destroying barbed-wire fences.

They marched through the night, passing a number of checkpoints, and arrived at the staging grounds in the early morning hours. While the troops rested, the platoon leaders followed a local guide to survey the enemies' camp.

Just after sunrise, they came to an observation spot hidden in the rocks high on a mountain slope. The rain had stopped. The sky was thick and marshy. The valley mist faded in layers and revealed the French camp in a murky light. It squatted at a fork in the road like a monstrous sentinel, its back against the mountain, drowsy and morose, confident in its invincibility. The enemies were still asleep. A thin strand of white smoke rose from the mess hall chimney. The three barbed-wire fences, each as tall as a man, stretched around the rectangular perimeter of the camp. Between the inner two fences, there was a wide trench filled with stagnant water; it held the reflection of the sky, a dark forbidding ribbon.

He felt predatory. His enemies were not secure; they were bound by their own fences and walls. He knew with delicious certainty that the Resistance would take the enemies. It was a pity, he thought, that the enemies did not know doom was at their gates. He felt a childish urge to shout down into the valley and make his presence known.

Someone handed him a field glass. When he examined the fort, he understood at last the full scope of the campaign, the magnitude of which was several times larger than anything he had experienced. He had memorized the camp's details given at the operation briefing. The minefields surrounding the camp were covered with high weeds. Twenty feet from the innermost fence lay a formidable wall of sandbags that from a distance looked like a raised mud dike. Four machine-gun towers situated at the corners of the camp defended the wall. Within the fortifications several wooden buildings formed a horseshoe facing the camp's main entrance. The buildings were all one story high with sandbags laid like tiles on top of the corrugated metal roofs. The defenders, two hundred legionnaires and fifty Vietnamese traitors, had six mortars and eight more machine-gun nests scattered within and around the buildings. At the far side of the camp were a long storage shed, an underground bunker, and two cannons that the French used to shell the insurgency. On the steep slope rising from the back of the camp, three camouflaged machine-gun bunkers guarded the camp below. These must be taken the moment the attack started. Their entire campaign depended on it.

At nightfall, the Resistance forces began amassing under the eaves of the forest. Two companies had crawled ahead of the main force to the very edge of the minefield. They had been resting in the sodden weeds for hours. This was their honor—the first wave, the suicide squads whose lives would clear a path for their comrades.

The occasional flare popped into the sky, breaking the stillness. The landscape looked mournful in the descending yellow light. From beneath the foliage, the drizzle fluttered in the pale glow like a silk scarf hung from the clouds' bellies. Vi was wet, his straw hat soaked. A chill had wormed its way through the cotton jacket and into his chest. The cold sapped strength as well as courage. He rubbed his arms and chest and stomped his feet to keep warm. He was past exhaustion. His heart thumped like a drum in his chest. He felt the anxious presence of his platoon. It was a desperate mission. They all knew it.

Suddenly mortars exploded in small flashes all over the camp and on the mountainside behind. The enemies launched half a dozen flares at the same time. At the edge of the minefield, the men moved forward, their camouflage looking like a massive ripple in the undergrowth. The mines threw up geysers of earth and bodies—a few at first, then everywhere at once. Searchlights on the towers blazed down on the attackers, and the machine guns followed the beams and began raking the ground. Mortars from within the camp fell on the field, setting off even more mines. The earth heaved under the onslaught. The remainder of the two companies continued to advance, clearing the minefield with their lives. The drizzle thickened into rain.

Snipers in the forest started shooting out the enemies' floodlights. Group commander Tuan signaled the charge, and the second wave moved out onto the open field in nine columns, each headed by its platoon leader and political advisor, who was the second in command. Behind them were four men carrying two dynamite rods on their shoulders in pairs. The others followed closely, ready to pick up the rods when their comrades fell.

It was a difficult charge. A heavy curtain of rain blurred the field. They slipped on the muddy weeds, their rubber-tire sandals finding little purchase on the blast-cratered ground. Men stumbled blindly over their dead comrades. The injured were left where they lay. Enemy artillery screamed down from the French mountain bunkers.

In the crossing, Vi lost two men. His men reinforced the remnants of another platoon hunkered down at the outer lip of the trench. The first group had blown through two fences and laid ladders across the trench, but they were out of dynamite. An enemy plane circled above, dropping dozens of flares and turning night into day. Enemy machine-gun fire pinned them down.

Vi signaled his first demolition crew forward. Two men scampered across the ladder with a pair of dynamite rods on their shoulders. Gunfire killed them immediately. A backup crew dashed across and pushed the dynamite rods halfway through the fence before they too were killed. A third pair slid the dynamite rods through and lit the fuses. They died crossing back over the trench. The explosion breached the fence.

Vi led them into the gap—the one duty he regretted most. Two machine guns converged on that opening, and Vi lost half his platoon within seconds. They would have all been slaughtered then, but the Resistance had breached the camp on another front. Inside, the fighting was intense. Attacks from within crippled the wall defense. The towers collapsed from dynamite, the gunner nests falling one by one.

He led the remnants of his team over the wall. Inside the camp, shots rang out from every direction. Bullets rained down from several machine guns inside the buildings. The fighting was chaotic until the French withdrew into the buildings. When Vi looked around, only Thanh was behind him. He turned to his second in command and nodded at a machine-gun post at the corner of the main building. Thanh reloaded his submachine gun.

They sprinted across the body-strewn ground, Thanh in the lead. Vi had a grenade in each hand, the pins pulled. The gunner sprayed his shots in sweeping arcs. Thanh charged, his gun ablaze, his battle cry drowned. Vi threw the first grenade. It fell outside the sandbagged nest, but the explosion bought them another few seconds. As Vi threw the second grenade, Thanh was hit. He stumbled backward into Vi, knocking him over. The grenade blew out the gunner's nest. Vi rolled Thanh onto his back. Half of Thanh's face had been shattered. The remaining eye was open, perfectly intact.

Vi grabbed Thanh's submachine gun and ran along the wall toward the main door. A shell fell directly on the building. The blast knocked him unconscious. The side of the building collapsed on top of him in a cloud of debris.

Vi woke with a terrible thirst. His head was wracked with pain, his limbs immovable. The clouds had cleared. A searing sun straddled the sky directly overhead. A wood beam lay across his chest, pinning him. He looked at the burnt building—a gaping hole in the wall, the yard deserted. There was no one. The silence was eerily complete. He couldn't hear the birds. The stink of smoke hung in the stillness. A sickening certainty closed upon him: His comrades were already miles away. They had rescued the injured and carried away the enemies' stores of arms. They had missed him. Flies were feasting on his face. He would die there alone, forgotten. He tried moving his arms and lost consciousness.

It was dusk when a noise startled him. He opened his eyes. A small boy was plucking buttons and insignias off the corpse of a Frenchman. Vi called out, but could only manage a guttural sound. Startled, the boy ran away. Vi sobbed. Night came, and he faded into dreams.

He found himself on a straw cot in the care of a village medicine man. A bullet had gone through his right shoulder. His right forearm was fractured. His left leg was broken below the knee. The medicine man nursed him while word was sent to headquarters. Two days later, comrades arrived and carried him away on a hammock stretcher.

The combat hospital was a long, thatched bungalow deep in the forest, housing several dozen patients. The nurses put Vi next to his company commander, who had lost a leg. Out of their 152-man company, seven survived and three members were entirely unscathed. Tuan, the group commander, was shot and killed. Vi's commanding officer told him that the four companies in the first wave were wiped out even before the two buildings were taken. Three companies in the following waves took the camp a few hours after midnight.

For three months he lay convalescing in the bungalow, haunted by the battle that claimed his entire platoon. His mind was beyond repair. Vi would neither lead nor serve in another combat unit again. What was left of him was only suited for darker purposes. He was eighteen.

23. THE TET OFFENSIVE

The afternoon bus from Phan Thiet delivered me to
the Saigon depot at dusk, along with several thousand
travelers and merchants rushing home for Tet—the
Lunar New Year celebration, our most important holi-
day. Everyone wanted to be home with his family and
to be blessed by his elders during Tet. I hadn't been
home for Tet in five years. Anh and the children were
spending the holidays with her mother in Phan Thiet.
Although my family had accepted my marriage, Father
still blamed it for my years in the army.

But I was ecstatic to be a civilian after six years of
service. I had been decommissioned just four months
prior. It couldn't have come at a better time because my
responsibilities had grown more dangerous as the war
escalated. In addition to my Rural Development duties,
I also served at the front as a liaison officer at a Vietnamese Special Forces camp established and assisted by U.S.
Special Forces. During the second half of my service,
my safe and comfortable office in Phan Thiet was taken

over by a corrupt major, and I found myself being sent farther out into the countryside to coordinate the ever-growing RD Task Force. It felt wonderful being decommissioned and knowing that I would never have to sleep through another midnight mortar attack or drive through VC-infested countryside to visit my teams. It seemed incredible to me that I made it through unscathed. I knew I was very lucky and I was ready to start my life all over again as a civilian.

I hopped onto the back of a Honda Cub at the motorcycle taxi queue outside the station. Darkness was settling over the treetops. The streets came alive with neon signs and headlights of cars and motorbikes. It was the drinking hour, and the sweet-fatty aroma of barbecued meats was in the air. Kids were already lighting firecrackers. Heavy traffic gave the city a feeling of prosperity. I hardly recognized the streets. New buildings, dwellings, and shops had sprung up all over the city. Since the Geneva Accord, Saigon's population had quadrupled, from five hundred thousand to two million. Now one fifth of the population of the South was concentrated in Saigon, Cho Lon, and the adjoining suburbs.

My driver squeezed through the bottlenecked intersections, snaking effortlessly through the snarls. After hours of broiling in the bus, the cool evening breeze made me giddy. I was grinning. Freedom was still a wonderful novelty.

Downtown was completely lit up for the holidays. Strings of lights crisscrossed the broad avenues; red globe lanterns dangled from the eaves of buildings. Shop windows glittered with shiny displays. Cars, cyclos, motorbikes, and bicycles clogged the streets. Nguyen Hue and Le Loi Boulevards in the heart of the city were closed off and turned into an open-air market. Merchants dumped their entire inventories of rice cakes, fabrics, fruits, altar implements, liquors, American beers, French biscuits, flowers, white blossom branches, candied fruits, and whatnots right on the ground. During Tet, the populace plunged into a consuming frenzy. Most families easily spent several months' wages in a week on travel, food, new clothes, entertainment, temple offerings, and gifts.

I got off at the plaza and strolled down Le Loi, looking for last-minute gifts. Kiosks, cart vendors, and bistro tables vied for space on the sidewalks. Music blared from a dozen bars lining the street. The stretch of Le Loi from the plaza to Ben Thanh Market was packed with restaurants, cafés, ice cream parlors, and shops. Business was very good and many places stayed open past midnight. The place exuded such optimism and possibilities that it was almost inconceivable that we were at war. Venture a hundred miles in any direction from here and one could promptly stumble into a pocket of insurgency. Six years in the field, I learned one thing: The countryside was swarming with VC.

OUR neighborhood had prospered, much like the rest of Saigon. The crude wooden dwellings were largely gone, replaced by rows of two- and three-story buildings that were built shoulder to shoulder. With the money my brothers Hung and Hong and I sent home, and our stepmother's savings from her lottery ticket sales, Father had torn down the old house two years prior and built a modest but comfortable three-story brick home, forty feet long and fifteen feet wide. The living room, bathroom, and kitchen were on the first floor. The second- and third-floor bedrooms had small balconies facing the alley. The flat roof was used for drying laundry and vegetables. Father spent most of his days and nights in his personal opium chamber, a small room built off the stairwell between the first and second floors.

I came home just in time for altar prayers. With Hung, Hong, and my sister Huong visiting later in the week, it was one of our smallest family gatherings: Father, Stepmother, my brothers Hoang, Hien, and Hau, and my sisters Hang and Hanh and myself. Hoang, Stepmother's first son, was fourteen. Her first daughter, Hang, was nine; her second daughter, Hanh, seven. Twelve-year-old Hien was Father's soft spot. The boy got into all sorts of trouble around the neighborhood and was a real hellion at school, but somehow he always managed to sweet-talk his way out of a well-deserved caning.

Hanh was eight, as cute and precocious as any little girl I'd ever seen. Baby Hau was barely a year old, Father's avowed last child.

Stepmother added my biscuits, cakes, beers, and flowers to the feast laid on the altar. Father dressed and came down to the living room. He lit the first batch of incense and started the prayers. Father was fifty-three, but looked seventy. Streaks of silver had crept into his hair. Age had mottled his skin. The opium had drained his flesh of vitality. Twenty-five years on the pipe had wasted his body, but strangely left his mind sharp.

After prayers, the kids went outside to play while the incense burned down. Father sat me down in the living room. Without telephones or time to write letters, we rarely had a chance to talk. Besides, we were never close. Father wanted to know about my plans for the future.

"After Tet, I'm going to look for teaching jobs here in Saigon. We'll buy a house on a main street and hopefully open a business of some kind for Anh," I said.

"It would be good to have you nearby." He nodded. "Fighting at the demarcation zone has worsened recently. There's bound to be more trouble in the outer provinces. I've heard rumors that there are big anti-war protests in the U.S. If it leads to a decrease in American involvement, it will be disastrous."

"But they'll never pull out completely. The Americans will never desert us," I said, citing the general sentiment of everyone I knew, including my former commanding officers.

"There are many ways of abandoning a cause," Father added.

He was the consummate living room politician, spending all his lucid hours debating war and politics with his opium cronies. I knew he was right. The situation was serious, but I was too happy with my newfound freedom to let it worry me. I had performed and survived my share of duty. The conflict belonged to others now. It was time I started building a normal family life.

"It's bad luck to bring in the New Year with war talk," Stepmother said as she began serving the food.

The incense had burned out. Hang and Hanh transferred the offerings from the altar to the table. We settled around the long makeshift table. The kids bowed and invited the folks to begin the meal. I bowed to Father and Stepmother. They nodded, acknowledging our respect, and gave us permission to begin the meal. Still very much a rigid traditionalist, Father insisted on form and manners. The children ate in silence. Table conversation was an adult privilege.

Father asked, "Are you planning to continue your studies?"

"Yes, absolutely," I replied, a little too quickly. It remained a delicate subject between us. He was disappointed that I had not fulfilled my potential. Even now, he expected much of his first son and little from his other children.

My siblings were doing well. Hung was a high school teacher in Binh Tuy. Hong was working in the Forest Service in the Central Highlands and at the army headquarters in Da Nang. My sister Huong was married to a Catholic man and living in a small town near Saigon.

After the dishes were cleared, Stepmother brought out platters of fresh fruit, biscuits, candied fruits, special Tet sweets, and teas. Sporadic bursts of firecrackers rang throughout the neighborhood for hours. We were sipping our first cups of tea when an explosion rattled the house. Stepmother jumped. It sounded as if a bomb had detonated right outside. There were gunshots. I heard the unmistakable brassy rattles of AK-47s. Mortar or artillery explosions followed in quick succession.

Father shouted for everyone to move to the back of the building. He wanted to put as many walls as possible between us and whatever was happening outside. Stepmother, Hang, and Hanh were terrified. None of them had ever seen fighting. I went to lock the metal grill across the front of the house. In the alley, people were running to their homes. I could hear bullets zipping in the air. Hoang and Hien were right behind me. I pushed them back inside, bolted the door, and turned out the light in the living room.

"Brother Thong, is it a coup?" Hoang said.

I shook my head. It seemed like a VC attack, but the thought of something so bold right in the middle of Saigon on New Year's Eve was unimaginable.

Hien looked at me. The boy knew what I was thinking and ran upstairs, Hoang on his heels. I went after them. The rest of the family huddled in the storeroom next to the kitchen. Stepmother fiddled with the radio, trying to find a station. The baby was crying. Father yelled after me to bring the boys back, but they were already up to the third floor. I caught them on the roof, staring out at the Military Assistance Command, Vietnam (MACV) compound on the other side of Tran Quoc Toan Boulevard, half a city block from our alley.

Explosions flashed around the MACV buildings. Red tracer bullets streaked back and forth across the darkness. Flares lit up the sky like fireworks in half a dozen places across the city. The main MACV buildings were set far back from the heavily fortified fence fronting the boulevard. The Americans weren't firing in our direction. On the boulevard, all of the traffic had vanished. A few figures dashed for the cover of the buildings. Fighting had broken out in other areas of the city. The VC had launched a massive attack.

We stayed awake on the first floor all night. Father had Stepmother gather a few things to prepare to run if the fighting came too close. They were profoundly shaken, their fear infecting the kids as well. I felt very badly for the children. They had waited the whole year for Tet. These were the days for going to the movies, the fair, the stage shows, and the temples. For every child, it was a time for games, toys, new clothes, sweets, and wads of *li xi*—money—earned by bowing to their elders and wishing them good health and good fortune.

I lay on the living room divan, my guts knotted with worry about Anh and the children in Phan Thiet. My wife was a good woman, and I felt terrible for not being home with her. I thought of the five chicks she had bought months ago to raise in our backyard in anticipation of having chicken for the feast at Tet; the new coat of paint she put on the house; the full week she spent cleaning our home to herald the New Year properly. What had become of our country? I closed my eyes, blocked my ears to the explosions outside, and thought of the way we had celebrated Tet during my father's time in Tong Xuyen: two weeks of feasts, games, carnival shows, and dances.

DAWN brought a sense of reality. The battle in our immediate vicinity had abated. The MACV compound was quiet, but explosions and gunfire raged elsewhere. From our rooftop, we saw squadrons of helicopters swarming the horizon and firing rockets into different corners of Saigon. Columns of smoke curled upward from several districts. Police cars and army vehicles raced down the streets.

Life in the city ground to a halt. No one ventured outside. There were no newspapers or food deliveries. The television went dead. The government's radio broadcast was sporadic and filled with propaganda to keep the populace from panicking. A pervading sense of doom settled over the city. It was a very bad omen to herald the New Year with bloodshed.

For the first time in memory, Saigon was stunned and humbled. Disaster hung in the air like smoke. American strength suddenly appeared to be in doubt. The city's sense of prosperity and safety was shattered. During the eight years of war with the French and the fourteen years following the Geneva Conference, Saigon was never in peril. City dwellers expected battles to be limited to the countryside. Saigon had always been the unassailable bastion.

FOUR days later, the government ordered all civil servants to report to work, but issued a dusk curfew. City folks ventured out on short shopping errands. Traffic slowly returned to the streets. All day the planes circled overhead. Helicopters skimmed low over the rooftops. Sounds of rockets and gunfire could be heard from many parts of the city. Fighting continued in Cho Lon's labyrinth of alleys. In Saigon, the attacks centered at Tan Son Nhat Airport, Phu Nhuan, and Gia Dinh, a town on the edge of Saigon.

News trickled in from the provinces. Hung, Hong, and Huong were safe. Anh and the kids were fine. The VC attacks were focused on the opposite side of town from our house. Phan Thiet's downtown market had been burned to the ground. Thousands of Americans, ARVN troops, and civilians had died, but it wasn't finished. The fighting would continue for two more months. The official death toll would be staggering: 3,895 Americans; 4,954 ARVN troops; and 14,300 South Vietnamese civilians. And the VC would lose 58,373 men and women.

On the fifth day, the order came over the radio: All decommissioned officers and veterans were recalled for duty. My four-month-old life as a civilian was over.

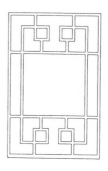

24. THE EXECUTIONER

The last time I saw Vi, he knew he would not be coming back to visit us for a long time. He said the fighting was heavy where he was going. There was a high probability that he would be killed, but that did not factor into his perspective. He had become more fearless than ever.

We were sitting—Tan, Vi, and I—side by side on the grass at the edge of the carp pond. Fireflies skimmed low over the dark water. A tiny breeze rolled through the sweetening longan orchard; the sky was awash with stars. It was late. Everyone had already gone to bed. Vi was in a solemn mood. Something big was afoot; our mothers had the servants load a cart full of rice, salted pork, dried fish, and various supplies. On all his previous visits, Vi had never taken more than money and two rucksacks of food as contribution to his troops.

"Why do you have to leave?" my cousin Tan asked.

"Our work is considered done here. We have a new assignment in another province."

"Is it the same work as what you've been doing?"

I asked. In all his previous visits, no matter how often we pestered him to tell us about his work, Vi always put us off by saying, "Someday when the time is right."

"The same. I've been in this task force ever since my last battle."

"You like your job?"

"It's an exciting way to contribute to our just cause."

His reply sounded like a line from one of the rousing Viet Minh speeches we'd heard in the village. "Just cause" was the Resistance's current catchphrase. People were asked to sacrifice, to join or send their children to the armed forces, to offer their belongings, all for the just cause of fighting the French and defending our independence.

"But what's so exciting about it?" Tan asked.

I said, "You promised to tell us, but tomorrow you'll be gone for a long time."

He thought about it for a few moments and then said, "I'll tell you two, but you must swear not to tell anyone else."

"We swear!" Tan and I replied in unison.

Vi reached inside his shirt and pulled out a knife from the sheath that was tied to his body. He handed it to Tan.

"This is a rice-leaf knife, the weapon of our trade. Every member of our task force was given one when he was accepted into the group."

It was a six-inch, double-edged blade as slender as a rice leaf, polished to a gleam. The wooden handle was stained dark. It looked sinister. I didn't want to hold it.

Tan slashed the air with it. He was very intrigued. "What do you do with it?"

Vi put the knife away, then stretched out on the grass, arms folded behind his head. "I belong to a special squad. We eliminate traitors."

"You kill them?" Tan blurted.

"Everyone in my task force does."

"How can you tell someone is a traitor?"

"Our intelligence people report on collaborators and spies who work for the French. Our commander gives us orders to catch and investigate suspects."

Tan said, "What if the traitor is your friend?"

"Then he is no longer my friend."

I glanced at Tan. I knew he was thinking the same thing: What if someone had reported our mothers and aunts?

"How many guys have you caught so far?" I asked.

"Ten."

"How many guys did you release?" Tan asked.

"None."

I gasped, "Why?"

Vi glanced sideways at me and grinned. "They were all guilty."

"All of them?" I couldn't believe it.

Vi smiled, his teeth glowing in the moonlight. He said, "Let me give you an example."

"Yes!" Tan said.

"Do you remember the teacher they found in the river last March?"

"Teacher Uc," Tan said.

"He was my father's second cousin," I added. Something seemed uneven. Then it came to me. "You came back after he disappeared."

"You killed him . . ." Tan muttered.

I had goose bumps rising all over me.

"I could not avoid it," he said nonchalantly. "We took turns doing the jobs, and it was my turn."

"Poor Uncle Uc. He was a good man. I can't believe he was a traitor."

Uncle Uc had been our only teacher from the time we first started school, right until he disappeared a few months ago. He had always been a good teacher, patient and fair to both of us. Everyone in the village liked Uncle Uc and was very anxious when he disappeared. When a fisherman found his body, people thought it was an accidental drowning. The whole village attended his funeral.

"Do you want to know what happened?" Vi asked us, but he looked at me.

Despite myself, I nodded.

"Last year our intelligence people suspected your teacher could be an informant for the French. Many of our party members in this area were captured and killed by the French patrols. Two of them were in your teacher's village."

"Mr. Nhi was killed by Mohammed. Was he a party member?"

"He wasn't. Whenever something like that happens, we get a big wave of new recruits." Vi sounded pleased. "Last December, my task force leader received an order to investigate your teacher. The preliminary report was over twenty pages. It listed all the names of your teacher's family and friends. It listed many people he talked with—people we knew were not totally supportive of the just cause, people who had connections with the French. Your teacher also talked with the French patrols whenever they came to your school."

"They asked him questions. He had to answer. We were there," I said.

"He could have passed them information on a piece of paper. You can never tell," Vi replied dismissively. "We watched him for two weeks. We were worried that he might become suspicious and flee into the French-controlled areas. I suggested to my team that we capture him on a Friday afternoon on his way home," Vi said with a half-grin, "because I remembered he always came here for tea with Auntie every Friday."

His words slipped into me like cold poison. I felt nauseous. We had brought a snake into our home. I lay down in the grass to hide my revulsion. Vi lay not two feet from me, this boy-man who was once a living skeleton we found in the barn. A nameless orphan without a past with a dark mole in the middle of his forehead.

That moonlit night by the carp pond, for the first time since he came into our lives, Vi revealed himself to us, his two closest adoptive brothers. Vi told the story that haunted my entire adolescence.

□   □   □

YOUR teacher seemed happy riding his bicycle home that Friday. He was whistling. Three of us had been waiting for him behind a bush. We wore farmers' pajamas like the locals. It was near sunset when we spotted him. My team leader stepped out onto the road and waved for him to stop while I and another comrade stayed hidden. Your teacher wore khaki pants and a white shirt, very clean and neat. He didn't suspect anything.

He got off his bicycle. Do you need something?

My other comrade and I stepped out and approached him from behind.

He looked around and realized he was surrounded. What do you want?

Shut up and stand still! My team leader ordered.

Startled, he stepped back, still holding his bike. What do you want? I don't have any money.

My team leader raised the pistol. Stand still!

His face changed then. He was terrified. Who are you? What do you want from me?

Shut up and put your hands behind you, I said.

You've made a mistake. I am a good citizen. He realized we were not ordinary robbers.

My comrade and I seized his arms. Our leader jerked the bike away from him and shoved it off the side of the road. We tied his wrists behind his back.

I am a good citizen. I swear to God I didn't do anything wrong.

We don't believe in God, I said.

There is no God, my comrade joined in.

He took a second look at my face. Oy, Vi! It's me, Uncle Uc! What's going on? I just visited your aunt at the estate.

I was both surprised and annoyed that your teacher recognized me. He had never talked to me when I lived here.

Vi, tell them, I am just a teacher. I don't know anything.

Please be quiet, Uncle. Just follow us and we'll sort all this out.

Our leader tried to calm him, Don't worry, we just want to ask you few questions.

Where are you taking me?

A place near here.

What about my bicycle?

Leave it here. Your family will come for it tomorrow. The team leader picked up Teacher Uc's book bag. There might be proof that he was a traitor.

Can I take my hat? His faded khaki colonial hat hung on the handle bar.

You don't need it.

He hesitated, but he knew he had no choice but to go with us. He followed my leader, but kept looking back at his bike lying on the side of the road. Since it was almost dark, we were not concerned about people seeing us. Farmers had already left the fields. After a few minutes, he asked us if we were with the army.

My comrade said, Are you in a position to ask questions?

That shut him up, and from then on he walked in silence, hunched over, staring down at the dirt road. I sensed that he was very scared and that made me feel very powerful. Catching him was my duty to the party.

When we got close to our hideout, we blindfolded your teacher. He started dragging his feet and whimpering, begging us not to shoot him. My leader said it was only a precaution. We had to make sure he couldn't tell anyone our position when he went home. Captives cooperated better when we gave them a little hope. He calmed down, but didn't stop whining about his family.

Our place was a small cottage just outside a village not far from here. It belonged to a young man who joined the army after two French legionnaires raped and killed his wife. He had left the cottage in the care of a party member in the village.

The four of us had spent two weeks digging an underground chamber inside the cottage. We dug during the day and spread the dirt in the fields at night. We were careful not to raise suspicions among the villagers. The chamber was a square, six by six feet, just big enough to hold one person. We vented the cell into the cottage with four bamboo pipes. The only access to the cell was through a secure trapdoor inside the cottage.

In all, we held seven traitors in that hut. Your teacher was the fourth.

After three hours of walking, we came to our place. We gave your teacher some food, but he didn't eat it. We locked him in the chamber with a bundle of straw for bedding and a clay pot for a toilet. We didn't interrogate him that night or the day after, to keep him confused and scared.

The next day we did not give him food or water. He called out several times in the afternoon, but we ignored him. He tried prying the trapdoor from below. He asked for water and begged to come up. He said he was ready to answer any question. After calling for several hours without result, he broke down and sobbed about his innocence.

I knew it was very difficult to be locked in that cell. I had tried staying in there for a day, but I lasted only a few hours. The cell was hot and completely dark. You couldn't see your own hands. You could lie down, but you couldn't stand up straight to stretch your back. You never felt like you got enough air. It was like breathing dirt, like being buried alive.

Your teacher was like every prisoner we had; he spent the first day pleading, complaining, and whining. It was bothersome to hear, so most of us stayed outside. I usually napped on a hammock under the mango trees. We interrogated prisoners at night. It was safer. The villagers went to bed very early, and there was no risk of a passing French patrol.

That night, we brought him up to our cottage right after dark. Your teacher was so happy to be allowed out, he couldn't stop thanking us. He said he couldn't breathe down in the hole. We gave him a bowl of water and a bowl of plain rice with nothing on it. We untied his hands so he could eat. We made him sit on the ground while three of us sat on chairs in front of him. Our fourth comrade stood guard outside. My task force leader started by telling your teacher that we knew all about him and his family, and the only way he could go home was to tell the truth. Your teacher swore he would tell the truth, and that he did not have anything to hide. We took turns talking very fast to him to keep him off balance.

My leader said, We want you to write down everything you did in the last two years. Anything you said or did with anyone outside of your immediate family, especially your interactions with the French, their VN soldiers, the legionnaires, and people in the Nationalist party.

I will try, but I am afraid I may have forgotten things.

Forgetting is just an excuse to hide something.

Remember that we have been watching you for a long time. We'll know if you tell the whole truth or not.

Write down all the activities you engaged in. Who you met and when and how many times. What you discussed.

We know you're a schoolteacher. We know you talked with the French patrols when they stopped at your school. It's best if you try hard to remember.

They asked questions, but I didn't know anything. I'm just a teacher. I teach children! Vi, tell them. You've known me a long time.

My leader shouted, Shut up! Write your confession. The sooner you finish the report the sooner you can go home.

He stopped eating and put down the bowl unfinished. I will try to remember and write everything down. I'm innocent of any wrongdoings.

We sat your teacher down at a table in the corner of the room and gave him a booklet of paper and a pencil. After a few hours, he handed us his completed report, and we put him back down in the cell.

The routine was the same for all our prisoners. We fed them twice a day, once in the early morning and once at night when we brought them up for interrogation. These were also the only two times we raised the trapdoor to air out the cell. They might have suffocated had we not done so. The prisoners never got to go outside of the hut and never saw daylight the whole time we kept them. When people were afraid, they sweat differently and became very smelly in a short time. We gave each a set of pajamas. We washed the pajamas for them every few days; otherwise, it would be very unpleasant for us to interrogate them.

All the next day, your teacher kept asking if we had read his report. We ignored him. That third night, we brought him up and told him his account was inadequate and inaccurate. We told him to rewrite his report. We did that three more times, each time giving him some events he participated in but did not mention in his report. He apologized for forgetting, but he wouldn't admit that he was a member of the Nationalist party.

Finally, it was time to torture him. No matter what he confessed, we were going to torture him anyway. It was part of the program. Every night we brought him up, gagged him, and bound him to a chair. We put fire ants on him. We burned his eyelids and fingertips with cigarettes. Besides hitting and whipping, there were many, many ways to torture a prisoner, and we had plenty of time to try various techniques on him. You never knew which one would crack a prisoner. They all reacted differently. Your teacher was really terrified when we made him go on our submarine. We tied his hands, hung him upside down, and put his head into a barrel of water.

I didn't have any problem with torture. I knew we must do it to get information. And to have a thorough investigation, we must hurt the prisoner. Torture was necessary to achieve our goal. What I learned was that everyone begged and cried when enough pain was applied.

Your teacher was one of the toughest prisoners I'd seen. After two weeks of torture, the only thing we got out of him was that he was a sympathizer of the Viet Nam Quoc Dan Dang (VNQDD) party. We believed that he was a real party member, just too tough to crack. We tortured him another four days. When my task force leader decided that we couldn't get any more information out of him, we sat down to discuss how we should write our investigation report. Only one of my comrades thought that your teacher could be innocent. The rest of us thought your teacher was just too tough.

My comrade said, He did not admit he was a VNQDD sympathizer until we tortured him for a long time, so he was obviously not truthful from the beginning.

The task force leader said, Two of our party members in his village were killed by the French, and we have no suspect other than this teacher.

We came to the conclusion that we should eliminate your teacher, to be safe. We submitted our report and recommendation the next day and received the approval from our commander two days later. It was in the middle of February. We didn't want to execute your teacher in the moonlight, so we waited another week.

As the big day neared, I practiced the execution with my comrades. I wasn't comfortable because it had been nearly three months since my first execution. It was a difficult maneuver. If I did not do it right, it would be very messy. There would be a lot of blood spilled or maybe even a struggle with the dying man. If I stabbed too high, he would spring upward. The movement wouldn't be violent, and he might still remain sitting. If I stabbed too low, near the stomach, he would bend forward. In both cases, he would be conscious enough to cry out.

But if I stabbed him in the heart, he would jerk up, and fall straight backward, dead without a sound.

The night of the execution we gave your teacher a good meal of rice with a fried fish, two boiled eggs, and steamed vegetables. He was surprised and became very concerned. Our leader said, We believe your confessions, and we have orders to take you home tonight.

He was very frightened and couldn't finish his dinner. He must have sensed that it was a lie, but he didn't say anything. He looked more hopeful when we gave him back his khaki pants and white shirt. Near midnight, we led him outside for the first time in over a month since we captured him. We didn't blindfold him, and it helped him settle down a bit.

In the training course, my instructor said bodies of water had a calming effect on the condemned; a creek or a lake would do, but a river was best. They normally become more relaxed sitting by the river. And it was a good place to dispose of bodies. My leader said it was a kind way to kill someone. The prisoner didn't know that he was going to die, so he didn't suffer.

Although the moon was empty, the starlight was bright enough for us to see by. It was a balmy night. You could hear the toads and crickets for many acres. At the river, my task force leader called for a rest stop, and we sat down on the grassy bank. The water was very dark and didn't reflect the stars. I sat on your teacher's right side, and one of my comrades sat on his left. Another holding a pistol stood two steps behind him. My leader watched us from farther away. This was only my second execution, but he allowed me to do it without blindfolding the prisoner.

I gave your teacher a cigarette and lit one for myself. I asked him, If we let you go home tonight, are you going to tell anyone about us?

No. Never. I'll never tell your Aunties about this. You . . .

Never mind that.

Your teacher was tensing up, so my comrade started asking questions about his wife and kids. That took his mind off the situation. We chatted and finished our smoke.

I pointed to a star in the sky in front of him. You see that star — the bright one that looks like it's shifting colors a little bit around the edges?

Yes, the bright one.

Concentrate on it and make a wish.

Yes . . .

I stabbed his chest only once. He sprang backward without a cry. Even before I looked, I knew I did it right. I felt the blade go clean through. I pulled my knife out and wiped it on his shirt. His eyes were open, looking up at the sky. Blood gurgled out of his mouth. His body jerked. It took some time for him to die, but he didn't make a sound the whole time. It was a good strike. I was happy that I performed my second execution even better than my first. I could have stabbed him again and ended it quickly, but that would have made another hole in his body. It would be messy. We watched him until he went still. My comrade checked his pulse and told us he was dead. We tossed his body into the river and went back to our cottage.

I slept well that night, as I did after my first execution. I never had any problem sleeping. They were all guilty and they deserved to die.

There was no God. We must be ready to judge.

25. Old Friends

In the aftermath of the Tet Offensive, Saigon was silent, convalescing beneath a blanket of unseasonably cool air. It had been a harrowing escape. Downtown, the gunfire had quieted, though the occasional pitched whine of Cobra helicopters swooping low over rooftops could be heard. On the outskirts, there was still fighting, but at the city center, the streets looked almost tranquil. The normal hustle and bustle of morning traffic was absent. Very little trade traveled on the interprovincial roads. Merchants and farmers hadn't started bringing their produce into the city yet. Shops stayed shuttered, the sidewalks were devoid of the omnipresent vendors. The shock of bloodshed was still fresh.

I spent the morning mingling with a hundred other recalled officers in a cavernous waiting room at the army headquarters. We paced and milled about in various states of dejection and nervous dishevelment. One by one, our freshly pressed uniforms wilted with streaks of perspiration, despite the cool weather outside. The creaky ceiling fan mixed the odor of our fear-soured bodies with cigarette smoke and made one dispiriting cocktail.

For the past two weeks, since the first night of the Tet Offensive, I had reported to headquarters and waited for my name to be posted on one of the bulletin boards. Some officers received their assignments earlier than others, but most, like myself, had the pleasure of sulking here for several weeks. The first few days saw a couple of comics trade jokes, but as dangerous posts began appearing on the board, we stopped laughing. A sense of doom straddled the backs of our necks. We chain-smoked, read newspapers, struck up gloomy conversations about the war, and jumped like startled rabbits at every announcement. It was a magnificent and utterly demoralizing waste of time. In the face of such sheer inept organization and bureaucracy, we had little hope our side would win.

If I had had the money to buy an exemption from the first draft, I would have. If I could have avoided this second tour, I certainly would have. Six years of service had shown me too many foolish decisions made by corrupt politicians and inept brass. Good men followed orders and died. Inept men made lousy choices and got promoted. The honest suffered; the corrupt got rich. Putting your life in the hands of brave and intelligent commanders was one thing, but standing up to be cannon fodder for greedy fools was plain stupid. I had no faith in President Thieu, his generals, or even the seemingly well-intentioned Americans—the only people in this whole bloody mess who seemed to believe the South could actually win this war.

After forcing down a plate of fried fish and rice for lunch at the cafeteria, I went outside to wait for an old schoolmate to pick me up. Thu was one of many friends and acquaintances I had contacted in hopes of finding the right connection to keep me from being sent to the front line.

Thu pulled up to the main gate in a brand-new white Toyota Corona. Leaning over, he pushed the passenger door open, grinning as if we had a big night on the town in store. And he was dressed for it, too: a beige silk shirt, black pleated slacks, European leather shoes, a beautiful gold Omega watch, and a heavy gold necklace to match.

"Where do you want to go?" I asked, worried that I couldn't afford the places he frequented.

"Not many places have reopened yet. You want to go to my house?"

"Let's go for ice cream on Le Loi. My treat." It was difficult enough asking for help; I had no desire to beg in front of his wife.

Thu sped down the road, bubbling with cheerful chitchat. We fell into the rhythm of old chums. I had always liked Thu. Jovial and accommodating, he was one of my closest school friends. We studied together during high school and the first two years of college. Unlike most of our old friends, he was posted in Saigon the whole time and knew all the gossip: who got married, who had the lucrative posts, and who was killed in battle.

He stepped hard on the gas pedal, showing off the car's acceleration. We zigzagged easily through the maze of avenues. Thu honked his horn and blew through the intersections without slowing down. The deserted boulevards were such a joy to drive on, we forgot what unsettling sights they were.

Nguyen Hue and Le Loi Boulevards were built for commerce, laid out in the manner of famed French boulevards with dividing islands of grass and trees lining their entire length. When I first came to Saigon, the boulevards had a park-like atmosphere, their strips of greenery and flowery roundabouts as well tended as gardens. These days, the helter-skelter of unregulated development had taken over much of the city. The former jewel city of the French colonial empire was now a jumbled mess. It made me smile to think that in the French civil engineers' wildest imaginations, they never conceived that their precious garden islands would be paved over and used as parking areas for motorbikes and bicycles. Drive down any major Saigon street and it was the same story, as if the moment the masters had left, the newly freed denizens seized the opportunity to assert their own imprints on the greater design.

One aspect of Le Loi Boulevard remained the same: It was still the heart of Saigon, the favorite street for strolling. The stretch between Ben Thanh Market and the plaza was busy all day. Shady trees kept the extra-wide sidewalks pleasantly cool even in the summer. Restaurants, bars, and cafés spilled tables and chairs onto the sidewalk. The stores sold luxury items, and the kiosks lined against the curbs carried cheap knockoffs and trinkets. Among the dealers, vendors, and agents, shoppers could find household appliances, furniture, motorbikes, European fashions, Vietnamese silk, army surplus items, exotic herbal potions, electronics, and just about everything else.

High school and college students swarmed the shops and eateries. Couples window-shopped. American GIs paraded their young Vietnamese girlfriends decked out in outrageously sexy outfits. It was a peculiar sight. The French never did that in Hanoi or Saigon. They kept their association with Vietnamese girls behind closed doors—even with proper girls from good families. Few Frenchmen wanted to be seen in public holding hands with those from the servant class. It was refreshing and rather sweet to see the GIs and their girlfriends enjoying the city like everyone else.

Normally, it was near impossible to find parking on Le Loi. Today, we could have parked a bus anywhere. Without a single fruit vendor on the sidewalks, it felt like a ghost town. Three or four cafés gamely opened their doors in a futile attempt to lure patrons from their homes. In the absence of its usual exuberance, the boulevard had an air of remorse. I picked the ice cream parlor at the corner of Le Loi and Pasteur because the Hanoian owner had a good collection of music. The sidewalk tables looked vulnerable on the deserted street, so we sat just inside the open shop front.

"How are things going at the Customs Office?"

Thu waved a negligent hand. "Same as always—as if nothing happened. My boss, the minister, believes life will be back to normal soon, since the attack clearly failed."

"Did he say anything about the war in general?"

"He doesn't know if we'll win the war, but he said we will never lose unless the Americans let us lose."

"It could go on like this forever."

"Well, the Americans will put more responsibilities on our shoulders. They'll still finance the war. They can't stop until it's over, and he thinks that will be a very, very long time from now. But they will try to cut down the number of body bags they send home."

"That's my problem! I don't want to be in the army for another six years. My luck won't last. If I get sent to the front, they'll be sending me home in a body bag within a few months."

"I understand. I'll try to help you, old friend."

"I know there is no way I could get back into the Rural Development Program. Is there any chance you could get me a place in personnel or logistics?"

"I don't know anyone in army personnel, but several of the big brass owe me favors. You can afford to pay, right?"

"My wife has a laundry business in Phan Thiet. If it's not an outrageous amount, we'll find a way to manage."

"It's hard to find a good post right now. There are so many recalled guys trying to avoid combat units, you may have to take a mediocre post for now, and then change later."

It was true, but I could not help feeling disappointed. "I understand. Thanks. Just do the best you can."

"Sure, I'll try. I haven't forgotten what you've done for me. I couldn't have gotten through the first year at NIA if it hadn't been for you."

I almost blurted out that I wished I had continued my studies at the National Institute of Administration with him. Thu had pleaded with me to stay. After two years of attending two universities concurrently, I left the school in 1958 to complete the more challenging degree in pedagogy. Pure pride. It was the worst decision in my life. Thu stayed on and graduated to become a department head at the Saigon Customs Office. With plenty of opportunities for dealings and

kickbacks—common practices for civil servants in South Vietnam—
he became very wealthy.

The waitress brought Thu his three scoops of vanilla ice cream, his
favorite since high school. I had a crème fraîche, which was whipped
milk served with a preserved strawberry in a wide-mouth goblet.
Creamy and mildly sweet, it never fails to bring back Hanoi memories, the cool afternoons I spent rowing alone on West Lake. Good old
Johnny Mathis was crooning "A Certain Smile" over the speakers.
Those adolescent days before the end of the French colonial era were,
perhaps, some of my most peaceful moments. I remembered that I
knew it then, even though I didn't know what the future would bring.

Thu noticed a man wearing sunglasses sitting at the rear corner
of the shop. "Hey, that's Dung."

"He's too fat to be Dung," I said.

"It's what happens when life's good to you." Thu chuckled and
waved the man over to join us.

Dung came, carrying his soda float. He was pale and paunchy
like someone averse to physical exertions. He wore a sky blue
pullover and dark navy slacks in the current hip style of Saigon,
looking every bit the part of a savvy urban professional. Forty extra
pounds lent him a sense of respectability. The double chin dimin-
ished his pronounced underbite. Faint, striated scars radiated from
beneath the dark glasses.

"Dung, remember Thong?" Thu asked, pulling out a chair for
Dung.

He sat down before extending his hand to me, as one might to a
subordinate. He said, "Thong, you haven't changed much."

"You changed a lot, Dung. I didn't recognize you. You look like a
very successful man."

"He's a manager at the Department of Information and Propaganda," Thu chimed in a tone that implied that they were equals.

"That's great. You've really made it big," I said, trying to catch
his eye behind the glasses.

"Hmm." He grinned. "You don't look too bad yourself, Thong. You look very handsome in your uniform." Dung chuckled loudly. The waitress and other patrons turned. Thu grimaced, but didn't comment.

I was taken aback. I hadn't said anything to insult him. The back-handed joke caught me off guard. We all knew it was appalling luck for a college graduate to be drafted into the army. He must have known that I was fully aware of my underdog status, sitting in my crumpled army khakis next to two guys sporting fancy garb. More than ever, I loathed the way the uniform felt on me. It branded me as a member of the unprivileged class. I was one who could not avoid the army draft.

Dung smirked. "All that studying didn't pay off as well as you expected, did it?"

I held my tongue, blood rising to my face.

We were good friends once. I wondered how a person could change so much. What I saw before me clashed with my heroic image of him. For years, whenever I thought of him, I remembered a daring Dung wrapped in the red and gold of the South Viet Nam flag leading a charge into a fray of demonstrators, just moments before the bomb exploded and robbed him of his right eye.

THE Nguyen Van Dung I knew was a colorful, char-ismatic figure, the most popular student in high school, central to the student body as well as the faculty. This was a monumental achievement considering the fact that he was short, bony, and dark skinned—an unflattering combination of attributes that would have relegated anyone else to the bottom rung of the social ladder. He had a thin face and a pugnacious underbite, the sort of tractor jaw that you wouldn't want to crack your knuckles against.

Dung was a single child in a devout Catholic family from the North. Before their migration south, they had a comfortable lower-middle-class life in Hai Phong, the primary seaport city for Hanoi.

His father had been a warehouse clerk, his mother a produce seller at an open-sky farmers' market. In Saigon, their livelihood was reduced to a tiny food stall at the neighborhood market. His father, like many northern or southern Vietnamese, could not find employment in Saigon's trading, shipping, or warehousing industries, which were largely closed to non–ethnic Chinese Vietnamese.

During the summer of 1955, Diem's faction was preparing a referendum to overthrow Bao Dai and establish Diem, a Catholic, as head of state, in a campaign openly endorsed by the church. Dung's father worked as a paid grassroots organizer in Diem's political machine and later recruited his son into the group. Dung quickly became a Diem fanatic and star promoter who brought politics into our high school even though most students weren't old enough to vote.

During the first two months of our senior year, Dung rarely attended a full day of class. He was shuttled in and out of school like an important courier, picked up and dropped off by adult drivers in shiny cars. The teachers frowned, but dared not reprimand him. The rest of us sat miserable in our stifling classroom and thought how sweet it would be to thumb our noses at the teachers the way Dung did. There wasn't a single one of us who wouldn't trade places with him.

He was a natural leader with a talent for winning key figures over to his side. It wasn't difficult since Chu Van An was the most prestigious of the high schools set up for refugee boys. If some of the students and teachers weren't pro-Diem, most of them, being northerners, were certainly anti-Communists. Dung had plenty of money, food, drinks, and even girls—party members from the girls' schools. He made political activism hip, and we scrambled to volunteer in the campaign, march at rallies, and scuffle with Communist sympathizers at every opportunity.

In Saigon, Election Day for an interim government came like a festival. Diem swept up 98 percent of the votes amidst charges of widespread fraud and intimidation. At our school, Dung threw a lavish party at the teachers' lounge one evening and invited the faculty, girls from our sister school, and fifty of us who had contributed the most to the campaign. In spite of the school's strict ban on alcohol, Dung made sure there was plenty of 33 beer. The schoolmaster had no choice but to turn a blind eye. Many teachers drank and mingled with the students at the swell back-patting event with Dung as the star.

During the celebration, Dung took me aside. We went out and stood in the courtyard to sip our beers, thumbs hooked on our belts like adults. It was a splendid feeling to be on the winning side for once.

"Thong, I wanted to thank you for helping us with the speeches. They were fantastic."

"Oh, it's nothing. Just doing my bit."

"You were a real player at that last rally. Thanks for standing with the team. We gave those Communist sympathizers a good beating, didn't we?" He laughed and patted me on the back.

"You threw the first punch."

"No, I didn't." He grinned. "I smacked that fool over the head with my picket sign."

We chuckled, and he leaned forward conspiratorially. "We can really use a man like you. You're one of the top students in our class. They look up to you. I want you to be one of our core team members."

Schools at the time still practiced the French method of ranking all the students in the same year, from the top scorer to the lowest. The system created competition through segregation and effectively fostered an air of prestige and mystique around the best students. Student body council membership, club presidencies, and sports team captaincies were posts that went naturally, like prizes, to the top academics.

"Thanks, Dung. That's fantastic. You know I'm always there for the rallies. I truly want to join, but I don't think I can take any more time away from my family's noodle shop."

"A core team member must dedicate himself to the work." He nodded solemnly. "You know, there are enough perks to offset your not helping out with your family's restaurant. Think it over."

Dung was referring to each core team member's stipend and share of all the freebies and goodies the government organizers doled out to grassroots groups. Smiling, he winked and shook my hand like a real politician.

WE all had high expectations for Dung. Even the teachers thought he was on a stellar trajectory to government appointments. Dung had street smarts and was very adept at motivating people. As the political leader at one of the most prestigious schools in Saigon, he was also a de facto leader for all the groups from other schools. He had successfully mobilized and led Diem's young but very visible and vociferous support group.

After the referendum to remove emperor Bao Dai from power, Dung quickly fell back into anonymity. The political organizers stopped picking him up from school. Dung's political funds dwindled to nothing. His core team disintegrated. The months passed, and we busied ourselves with exams. Dung was still popular, but without a clear purpose, he grew irrelevant.

Once installed, Diem initiated a swift campaign to eliminate the remnants of the Communist party in the South. Within a few months, tens of thousands of South Vietnamese farmers suspected of being Communist sympathizers were rounded up and interrogated. Many were jailed or sent to re-education camps. Although the U.S. had already signaled to the world that it would renege on the Geneva Accord and cancel the scheduled election to reunite the country, the South Vietnamese still hoped for a miracle, believing the Americans and Diem would yield to international pressure. Public protests cropped up in Saigon and other major cities where Diem couldn't exercise drastic measures due to the presence of international bodies. As the July 20, 1956, deadline for the general election drew near, the political atmosphere in Saigon was intensely charged. Every week there was at least one major demonstration. With the foreign press on hand at every event, Diem couldn't use police force, so groups such as Dung's were summoned to stage counter-protests.

Suddenly Dung was back in the local limelight. This time he

received even stronger support from the student body because we suspected that most South Vietnamese were likely to elect Ho Chi Minh simply because they disliked Diem and his cronies. As refugees and survivors of Communist atrocities, we felt it was our duty to educate the public about the real faces of the Communists. Despite looming graduation exams, we plunged into the campaign. Every time anti-government groups staged a protest, Dung and his organizers sounded the battle cry and we would pile into the waiting convoy of trucks to be transported to the demonstration site. The trucks were always loaded with snacks and drinks, as well as an ample supply of rocks, bottles, and sticks. We were ready to brawl at a moment's notice.

Swollen with pride and purpose, we became messengers of true knowledge. We stormed the town in government cars, loudspeakers blasting slogans, tossing leaflets out the windows, howling with a glee that had nothing to do with politics. We plastered Diem's chubby face on windows and walls. Without realizing it, we became Diem's little henchmen.

Like rival gangs, we clashed with any group that opposed us, fighting in the usual places, Ben Thanh Market or the municipal theater, at either end of Le Loi Boulevard. The casualties were numerous, but that thinned neither our ranks nor theirs. The demonstrations and the ensuing fights intensified as the Geneva Accord deadline neared. Our opponents were desperately appealing to the international media and foreign diplomats. Our mission was to silence them.

We beat each other silly, vying for the world's attention.

I was too young to realize that it would make no difference.

It was early June when Dung received emergency summons to organize a counter-protest. His political handlers sent a convoy to pick us up from school. We piled onto the flatbed trucks, jammed shoulder to shoulder like cattle, excited at the prospect of a good fight. Thu distributed armbands, strips of fabric torn from a yellow cloth, so we wouldn't mistakenly attack our own members in the heat of battle. Cam, Dung's second lieutenant, chanted slogans over the loudspeakers. Swaying from side to side, we clung to each other, howling and hooting as the trucks caromed across Saigon to the city center. Above us, a blistering sun.

The trucks dumped us in front of the municipal theater, where several of our associate groups had already gathered. A thousand demonstrators and counter-demonstrators packed the plaza, with twice as many spectators gathering nearby. The cacophony of chants between the two factions sent thrilling shivers down my spine. Dung howled and lobbed a bottle high over the heads of the crowd into the center of the protesters. We poured from the trucks and merged with our faction. Our side began to encircle the protesters. As usual, the police stood far off, pretending not to notice that fighting had broken out.

Our mission, as rehearsed many times, was to neutralize the protesters. When they started moving toward the Hotel Majestic at the corner of Tu Do Street and Ben Bach Dang, Dung led the core teams in an attempt to block their path. With the South Viet Nam flag draped over his shoulders like a cape, he charged the marchers, brandishing a long stick. For a small guy, he had a lot of guts and never failed to lead the paid members into the thick of a fight.

I saw Thu moving away with another group to attack the protesters from the flank. He shouted at me, but his words were drowned out by the cacophony. I waved him onward and joined up with another group. The fight was gaining momentum.

It felt like heat, but a sense of madness had descended over us. Bottles, rocks, shoes, sticks, boxes—anything small enough to be thrown—were hurled in all directions. Nearby spectators were pounded with barrages of debris. Suddenly the gap between our side and theirs closed, and I found myself throwing punches. There were no single opponents; we struck at whoever was in front of us.

A man grabbed the collar of my shirt and I hammered my fist into his face. I had stopped thinking. My fists were fighting all the fights the child-me had been unable to fight. I was defending this last stand of freedom. An animal of fury rose inside of me. It howled in my ears, sent jolts of energy through my arms, made rocks of my fists.

Something cracked against my back. I turned. A middle-aged man had struck me with his picket sign. A roar rolled from my throat. I smashed my elbow into his face. I pounded him until he fell, then turned to another enemy.

Power surged through me in rapid, violent pulses; I reveled in a chaos that was swathed in yellow and red ribbons.

A rock struck a glancing blow off my head.

I heard a dull hum—a sound that reminded me of the sea. Then I was leaning against a wall, my head throbbing. The fight swept onward; the street was strewn with broken placards and trampled signs. It seemed unfortunate to me that our faction was mostly northerners and theirs was mostly southerners. I liked southerners. They were easygoing and hospitable. They had warmly received us northern refugees with open arms, making us feel welcome in their neighborhoods. I doubted we would have given them the same treatment in the North had the situation been reversed.

A girl slumped down on the curb near me. There was blood on her face. It stained her white *ao dai*. Too bad the dress was ruined, I thought. She had the round dark face of a southern girl. She was sobbing like a child, inconsolable.

I slipped off my armband and let it fall to the ground. I wanted to say something to her, but I didn't know what to say. And I was ashamed, though I did not know why.

A deafening explosion—a bomb. I felt the thump in my chest. Up the street, a clearing appeared in the crowd. Gray smoke permeated the air with the bitter tang of gunpowder. Screams rose and swelled into a long keening crescendo as the crowd turned and fled. They fled empty-handed, dispersing in all directions. Some bolted into stores nearby. A wave of people rolled back toward the theater square. They pushed and shoved, tripping over each other, with terror on their faces. Discarded on the streets were banners, placards, and weapons. Opponents ran shoulder to shoulder, the fight forgotten.

Panicking, I struggled against the instinct to flee along with the crowd. Where were my friends? Torn, I stood still, my back against the concrete wall amid the pandemonium. A young man stumbled past, supported on both sides by friends. His shirt was soaked red.

The street cleared within moments. Blood and bodies marked the blast area. The injured wailed and moaned. Someone raised a bloodied arm beckoning for help. A few managed to get to their feet and limped away. Bystanders lingered at a distance, not daring to approach as if fearing another explosion.

The police finally emerged and walked through the carnage. They didn't offer assistance to the wounded but instead began cordoning off the area.

I recognized Cam staggering out of the blast area and grabbed him by the shoulders. He was covering a wound on his arm with his good hand, blood dribbling down his right side.

"Where's Dung?" I asked.

Cam looked dazedly at me. I repeated the question, and he nodded in the direction of the blast. "Over there."

"Is he alive?"

Cam shook his head. "I don't know. I don't know. The bomb was right on top of him."

"What about Thu and the others?"

"I . . . I have to go." Cam sobbed, his face blanching as he hurried away.

Ambulances arrived, followed by a fire crew. I waited to see if I could recognize Dung when the paramedics carried him to the ambulance. More police came in patrol cars and began grabbing people for questioning. That was when all the bystanders started running.

No one claimed responsibility for the first-ever bomb to be unleashed on demonstrators. The homemade device had injured more than fifty people.

Dung had shrapnel in his chest, abdomen, arms, and face. He lost one eye and was lucky to be alive. Dung never recovered from his injuries. The Geneva Accord deadline passed while he languished in the hospital. Dung failed his graduation exam and faded from view.

"You want to see my eye?" Dung said.

Before I could decline, he removed his sunglasses. His chubby face swelled over the empty socket like rising dough, narrowing the hole. The lazy eyelid fell down and reduced the opening to an eerie black slit. It was his winking eye.

I must have winced because he laughed.

"Took me a long time to get used to it myself. I was lucky the doctor was able to save my other eye." He ran his tongue over his front teeth, then said, "I only need one eye to see everything I need to see."

I noticed that he had sat down slightly sideways so he had both of us in his good eye.

"That looks painful," Thu said, leaning closer.

"No pain. I don't even miss it anymore."

"Why don't you use a glass eye?" Thu said.

The corner of Dung's mouth curled up marginally. "This is more useful in my line of work."

I forced a smile, shuddering to think what a high school dropout must have done to rise into the upper echelons in the Secret Police, whose notoriety surpassed even the Viet Cong's.

Outside, an ambulance siren was approaching. We paused. Everyone in the café turned to the boulevard. Two army Jeeps and a truck full of VN soldiers thundered past, a white ambulance trailing behind. We waited for the sound to recede into another part of the city. You never knew where the Viet Cong could spring up next. They had cells everywhere. Fighting had erupted throughout Saigon.

The war had entered another phase. It was far from over.

I quelled an impulse to reach out and pat Dung on the shoulder. The front line wasn't the worst place I could end up. Yet I found myself still envying Dung—not for what he had become, but for those glorious days when he stood at the center of our world. This cursed war, in its own measure and manner, would eventually claim us all, but at least Dung had his time. I envied his one precious year.

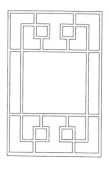

26. THE CHAMPAGNE BOTTLE

When I was fourteen, my mother gave me a bottle of champagne three months before my graduation exam, just before her death. At the time, she had already grown cumbersome and round in the third trimester of her pregnancy. That afternoon, she called me to the koi pond in her private garden. We sat together on the wooden bench, her favorite reading spot. The swell of her belly made her lean back against the support pillow. Mother unwrapped a cloth bundle and showed me a dark green bottle with gold foil wrapping at the top. I knew immediately it was the special bubbly beverage of celebration that called for the delicate glasses Mother kept in the cabinet.

"Is Father coming home?"

Several months ago, we received news that Father, while on his way home from Hanoi to celebrate the New Year with the family, had been captured and conscripted into service as a porter and translator for the

French. Mother had sent two investigators to locate Father and purchase his release, but he had vanished without a trace.

Mother's face fell briefly. She gathered herself, mustered a smile, and tousled my hair. "Do you know what this bottle is?"

"Champagne!" I guffawed. I felt bad for reminding her of Father. We were all pretending that he was well somewhere and would be home any day. I held the bottle up to the light and read from the label. "France, nineteen-forty-six. Father and Uncle Thuan always have a good time when they drink it."

Mother chuckled. "Well, this is for you, for a very special occasion, my dear."

"Father never lets me drink alcohol."

"I think he will if you pass your exam."

"I haven't even started studying for it yet!"

"Yes, I know. And I know you will pass. I'm already proud of you," she said and squinted in that peculiar way of hers. It made her look as if she was smiling at me.

The middle-school exam was a major obstacle. The colonial school system required a majority attrition rate to restrict students from acquiring higher educations, which was seen as a danger to the colonial government. Although the new government under Ho Chi Minh had changed the curriculum, they kept the multiple exam levels. Passing the exam was still enough of an achievement for most families to throw a celebration dinner, but I couldn't imagine how it warranted a whole bottle of champagne, worth several months' wages for a laborer. None of my friends had ever tasted champagne. It was a momentous feeling.

I hugged her. "Thank you, Mother. I won't just pass it, I'll score high marks for you!"

"That's a big promise! You're an extravagant one, aren't you?" She perked up with a small happy laugh that I rarely heard from her. It made me very happy. She gathered me into her arms. "I know you will. You have never disappointed me. We will open this champagne to celebrate your graduation, and we will have a big cake to go with it. You can invite your cousins and all your friends."

"Even Hoi?"

Besides Tan, Hoi was my best friend, and I knew she was very worried that I might fall under his influence and join the Resistance. Hoi was the leader of the local Uncle Ho's Youth Brigade. His group and the Resistance fighters, in general, had become very popular in our village, since our domain came under the Resistance's control. People were swept up in patriotic zeal. After a year of suffering under the Algerian Mohammed and his marauding band, the peasants credited the Resistance for driving away the legionnaires, even though the legionnaires' retreat was part of the general pullback of French forces to the perimeter of the Red River Delta.

"Yes, son, if you wish." Mother sighed. "I cannot protect you forever. Sooner or later, he will want you to join his group. You must decide for yourself."

I avoided her eyes. Hoi had already asked me many times. I didn't like the awkwardness of making excuses to postpone joining the Resistance. It was difficult for me to concentrate on school when all my friends were doing exciting activities in Uncle Ho's Youth Brigade.

"We're safe as long as we provide the Resistance with everything they request," she said, holding my face in her hands. "I can give them land, livestock, rice, and gold, but I cannot give them my son."

Even though I knew the Resistance had murdered Uncle Thuan, my cousin Quyen, and Uncle Uc, I still wanted to be a member of this great movement that was cleansing our country of foreigners. It was a new and wonderful feeling not having to live in constant fear of a patrol coming to plunder and rape our people. I hated the sight of the legionnaires eating and drinking in our halls, despoiling the sanctity of our temple and home.

"Son, don't be quick to kill or be killed for someone else's rhetoric. A day will come when you and Tan will be responsible for our entire clan. Remember that any decision you make, you make for all of us, from your ancestors to your family to the folks faithful to our estate—everyone, including this baby in my belly."

It was a bewildering thought. I stared at the ground. It was unimaginable how anything could be in my control. It would be so much easier if I could simply pick up a gun, fall into rank, and fight the enemy.

"I think we all have the duty to fight for our independence," I insisted.

"Oh, my dear son, he who seeds the wind reaps the storm." She sighed again. "I am afraid the time for you to fight will come. When it does, you can contribute more to the fight if you're educated." Mother wiggled to sit up straight, then clapped her hands. "First, you still need to pass your exam so we can drink this champagne."

"We have to hide this! The legionnaires might want it if they come back."

"Don't worry, I doubt the French will patrol our domain again any time soon. Besides, we're going to bury this bottle."

"We can just hide it somewhere. I have a few secret places."

Mother chuckled. "The champagne will taste better after aging awhile under ground."

"Are you sure?"

"The French keep wines in underground chambers to keep them cool and at a constant temperature so they age properly. I read it in a book." She winked at me. "You know I have a whole library of books that you haven't read."

"Yes, Mother. But if you bury it, the water may seep in through the top."

"We'll seal the top with wax and bury it upside down."

"You won't tell my brothers, right?"

"Of course not. This is just between us. It's a reward for your efforts."

Mother brought out a lamp and a lump of wax. We sealed the bottle. She levered herself slowly from the bench and led me to her prized guava tree. We dug a hole and buried the bottle wrapped in cloth. She picked out a large flat black stone from the edge of the koi pond and had me put it over the spot as a marker.

THE day Mother went into labor it rained heavily. An unseasonable storm came from nowhere. Dawn cast little light on steely clouds that quickly burst into torrential rain. Midmorning, Mother told the maid that it was time. Aunt Thuan, Aunt Lang, and Aunt Thao descended on our house like a gaggle of geese, asking questions and shouting directions at the servants. Mother said the baby was coming earlier than the doctor had predicted, but she wasn't worried, as this was her fourth child. Aunt Thuan put her hand on Mother's forehead. Aunt Lang placed her hands on Mother's belly to feel the contraction. The women knew what needed to be done and quickly mobilized the staff to prepare for the delivery.

"Have you sent for my doctor?" Mother gasped.

"The roads are blocked. There's been heavy fighting for the last three days outside the district. No one can get through the French line," said Aunt Thuan.

Aunt Thao agreed. "It's a long way. The roads might be washed out."

"Try! I want my doctor," Mother insisted. He was the family physician who had delivered all the children on the estate.

Aunt Thao said, "I'll have Noui go with our contact in the Resistance. He will have to go around the blockade."

"Let's send him by horseback," Aunt Thuan said. "In the meantime, we'll fetch Midwife Nga from the village."

A sense of expectancy loomed over the household. With the storm gathering strength outside, there was little work to be done. The men stoked the kitchen fire to boil a cauldron of water, and then sat around mending tools and milling rice flour. The women brought out fresh linens, ground medicinal herbs, put fresh fruits on the ancestral altar, and lit the prayer incense for a safe delivery. The Aunties took turns sitting with Mother.

It was a Sunday, so there was no school. I studied in the living room, but couldn't concentrate with Mother's muffled groans coming through the wall. Outside, the afternoon had gone dim. The downpour was so thick I couldn't see across the courtyard. Thunder rumbled across the underbelly of the sky. The water was ankle-deep and rising. I grabbed an umbrella and waded across the courtyard to the Ancestral Temple. I lit three incense sticks and prayed to Grandfather's spirit.

A runner arrived with a message that Noui had not found a way across the French line, though his connection expected to get him into the district town during the night. It was bad news, and the Aunties were very worried. Late in the afternoon, a young woman carrying a basket arrived. She took off her hat and shed her raincloak of palm leaves. She was in her early twenties, very young for a midwife.

She bowed to the Aunties and Mother, and said, "Mrs. Nga went to help with the Resistance's hospital. I'm Trang, her apprentice."

"You're the herbalist's youngest daughter," Aunt Thuan noted with raised eyebrows. "I didn't know you started training with the midwife."

"I've been her assistant for five months, but I have never delivered a baby on my own."

The older women glanced at each other. It was bad fortune and dangerous to have such an inexperienced midwife. Perhaps the doctor from the district would arrive in time.

"Isn't there anyone who could help you?" Aunt Thao asked.

The girl shook her head, looking at the floor. "There are no healers or midwives left in the village. My father went with Midwife Nga to tend wounded Resistance fighters."

Mother's face was flushed and wet with perspiration. "Sister Trang, listen to me," she moaned. "You will have to deliver this baby. It's coming!"

The women closed around Mother and chased all the men and children away from the house.

□ □ □

IT was dark when Kim, the cook's daughter, fetched me from the Ancestral Temple where I was hiding from the awful sounds of birthing. She said I had a new baby sister. I splashed across the calf-deep water in the courtyard. In her room, Mother was propped up with cushions. Beads of sweat ran down her flushed face.

"Mother, are you in pain?" I sat on the divan next to her and held her hand.

She smiled wanly, too exhausted to talk. She squeezed my hand. Her fingers were soft.

"It's a girl, Mother, so her name is Huong, just like you decided."

Mother seemed to want to say something, but her eyes closed to sleep. Aunt Thao whispered that Mother needed her rest. Trang frowned as she tended Mother. That was when I noticed there was a lot of blood everywhere. They were wiping it up, but it kept coming. In the light of the oil lamp, it looked dark like pitch on the straw mat; on the white rags, it was red. They called for more hot water and fresh linens. Trang gave Mother an herbal concoction, and the Aunties were panicking. The bleeding wouldn't stop. The wind howled around the eaves, struggling to get inside. Within the flickers of the oil flames, fate shifted. Mother closed her eyes as if to rest, but her spirit sped away, slipping over our world, gone from me.

The women wailed. The storm did not relent, the sky pouring through the night.

THE day burned white, the sky as clear as blue glass. The ground steamed. A reddish film of dried mud left by the receding floodwater coated the grass and bushes. Along the creek, brown water filled the breached dikes. Roads disintegrated into miles of slop and puddles. The gravediggers had waited three days for the water to ebb before breaking ground on her resting plot.

As her firstborn, I led the funeral procession out of the Ancestral Gate. It was difficult walking backward in the mud. I kept slipping and falling, holding up the whole column of marchers, monks, relatives, friends, and servants. My white mourner's robe was completely brown. I struggled to perform the funeral rites—the same one Tan had done for his father. I walked backward in front of the casket bearers. I stopped, knelt, pressed my forehead into the mud, and cried: *Please, don't leave us, Mother. We are lost without you. Please, stay and watch over us. We love you. We need you. Please, don't leave us, Mother.*

When the coffin reached me, I rose, took ten steps back, knelt down, and repeated the pleas.

Towed by their nannies, Hung and Hong wailed. Cousin Tan was walking next to his stepmother, head down, sobbing into his chest. He was closer to my mother than to his stepmothers, Aunt Thuan and Aunt Lang. The rest of the household followed behind as we went out of the estate. Villagers lined the road to pay their respects. The peasants adored her—the soft-spoken outsider from another province.

I lost my sandals and cap. I was covered in slime, mud in my mouth and the hot smell of earth in my nostrils. A heavy sun. The villagers, my childhood friends, my relatives, the monks, the servants, the heady incense, the mourning chants, the cymbals and tolling bells. Nothing could fill the hollowness within me.

We came to a crossroad. To the left was the dirt path to our Ancestral Cemetery in the village—a modest park enclosed by a low brick wall, with a few trees and stone benches where Uncle Thuan rested with his forefathers. Places for Father and Mother had already been chosen long ago.

If I walked straight ahead, I would come to the interprovincial road that led back to Mother's ancestral home. Her family had a splendid cemetery there, much nicer than my father's family's. It was a beautiful flower garden with statues, gravel footpaths, trees, and a fishpond, all enclosed by a high wall and tended year-round by a caretaker. Former senators and mandarins and village chiefs of her line had been laid to rest there. She would have been among family.

To the right, in the middle of a rice field, lay the plot Aunt Thuan had picked out for Mother. During Mother's wake, the Aunties had a monk augur the family's fortunes. In the tea leaves and chicken bones, he predicted dangers ahead, so the Aunties summoned a feng shui master who said that the estate was exposed to ill elements from the north, and that if they buried Mother in the northern field, the estate would be protected from evil. I protested, but they would not hear of it. Auntie Thuan said Mother's spirit had the duty of safe-keeping the household. As head of the clan, she had the right to decide my mother's resting place.

My knees buckled. I couldn't make the turn. I couldn't lead them to that grave, the lone mound of red earth in a blue paddy-sea of sky. Crumpling in the mud, I was useless. I opened my mouth, but no words came. Dry sobs seized my throat. The bearers stopped, the shadow of her casket falling on me. Guards Canh and Khi pulled me to my feet and walked me backward down the path the Aunties had chosen.

The monks chanted and the bearers lowered her into the ground. Aunties burned paper chariots, fake money, and gold foil to send Mother's spirit to heaven in comfort. I wondered if water would get into her casket. I could not stop shaking.

I STUDIED as I had never done before. I bent my entire being into the text, poring over the equations and chapters as if Mother were in her garden, waiting for me to pass the exam. Within the pages, I could pretend that nothing had changed, that Father was safe in Hanoi, and that things would return to normal soon. My escape portal was through literature, history, and mathematics. The tighter my focus, the easier the texts became. In grief, I discovered my mental stride. Learning was transformed into an act of pleasure. It was Mother's last gift, her wish for me to love the quest for knowledge.

Week after week, I stayed in our house, ate meals the cook set out for my brothers and me, and avoided the Aunties. Boyhood games lost their hold on me. I stopped going into the village. My friend Hoi came and urged me to join the Resistance and avenge my mother. He did not know that I blamed the war for everything and that I loathed both the Resistance and the French. I told him that I had promised my mother I would finish school.

I TOOK the exam. When the results came back, I had the highest score in the district. I told no one and brought my grade card to Mother's garden. Her rosebush had grown wild with blooms. The birds were absent. Mother would have been thirty-two the next month, this poor woman who had shed more tears than laughter in the brief time I had known her. I sat beneath the guava tree and thought of Mother and her smiling eyes. The stone marker was still there, beneath it our secret promise as fresh as the day we had committed it to the earth.

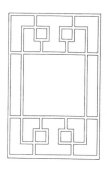

27. THE SLAVE

It happened at the apex of his life; he was thirty-one, in his prime, a country nobleman at large in the city with the riches of generations at his disposal. It happened on a journey home to see his pregnant wife. He had stopped midway to spend the night at the estate of his cousin-in-law. The next morning, a French patrol passed through the village, looking for guerrillas. Warned by scouts, most of the village men, regardless of political affiliation, had fled with their sisters and daughters. French forces were known to plunder and rape villages suspected of harboring rebels.

They herded a handful of elders, cripples, drunkards, and one oversleeper into the courtyard of the community temple. Three captives were shot on suspicion of being Viet Minh sympathizers. When they put a gun to the man in the silk pajamas, he protested in fluent French, claiming to be the brother of the late magistrate of the Pham Domain in Tong Xuyen, candidate apparent to that seat and sworn enemy of the Viet Minh.

It amused the soldiers. For the colonialists, native nobility was merely a convenience. The French commander was delighted. He had lost his interpreter to a sniper's bullet and was in dire need of a replacement. Dismissing the man's identifications and promise of a cash reward, the commander shackled him in his silk pajamas to the line of coolies.

Within months, his wife would die and take with her the secret burial site of the vast ancestral fortune.

The nobleman's new life began as a colonial slave. His lineage, wealth, education — even his family's long-standing obedience to France — didn't save him the indignity of being led from village to village on a chain. He was fed when he worked, whipped when he refused. No more than a useful piece of equipment or a whore, he was handed from one commander to the next, pressed into one tour after another in an endless series of raids and battles staged across the expanse of the Red River Delta. They gave him no respite and paid him no wages. On the march, he was a pack animal for the regiment's supplies. In the villages, he was an interpreter of French demands and threats. He translated the interrogator's questions and penned homesick letters for illiterate legionnaires.

The scorching sky turned rainy, then wintry; the campaign dragged across a full year. Once the old colonial masters had retrenched themselves, the coolies, the cooks, the errand boys, and the strange interpreter — the learned barbarian well-versed in Voltaire — were unshackled and released back to the land. Freedom was their compensation.

My father returned to us, a barefoot beggar with neither a bedroll on his back nor a single piaster in his pocket. As raw-boned and light-shadowed as the famine victims that once roamed the land, he staggered through the Ancestral Gate, sunburned and covered in bleeding scabs. No one dared touch him. Lice lined the collar of his shirt and nested in the stitching of his pants.

Few men had fallen a greater distance.

The house guards bowed, eyes lowered, reluctant to look upon his debasement. He seized his youngest son in a crushing embrace and wept. The boy could not recognize his father and wailed in terror on the steps of the family temple. Servants gathered round and bowed. The head of the clan had returned from the dead.

That evening, I walked him to Mother's grave. We kneeled down in the bed of gardenias and lit incense. We brought Mother her guavas and green mangoes from the garden she loved so much. Father was bent over, his newly shaven head in his hands. He was talking to her, face as wet as rain, hands shaking as I had never seen them shake before.

I left him by her graveside, for the first and last time.

The sunset sky had turned upside down in the autumn paddies, and he was afloat on her island of flowers, engulfed by the burning eaves of heaven.

28. A Lull of Silence

It was the summer of 1971. It seemed unreal to me that Tan and I had not seen each other for ten years. We ran into each other at the fountain square on Duy Tan Street, just a few months before the Americans started pulling out from Vietnam. Anh and I were on our way to the park at the center of Saigon for ice cream. The children were at home with their nanny. Tan had just gotten out from his classes at the law school across the street. He was dressed smartly in a civilian suit, already looking the part of a worldly lawyer. Broad-shouldered and barrel-chested, he had developed into a modern image of his father. Since his decommission, Tan worked for an American company maintaining U.S. fighter planes and was attending evening classes for his law degree.

"Are you all right, Thong?" Tan asked, squeezing my shoulder. "You look very thin and tired."

"Really? I'm in the best shape of my life. I was very lucky with my second tour. It was only a year and a half. They stationed me here in Saigon to train the City Civil Defense Force. If they sent me to the front again, I doubt I'd still be alive. I just got released last year."

"Me too."

At last, South Vietnam appeared to be secure. The failed 1968 Tet Offensive had been a major setback for North Vietnam. The NLF suffered heavy casualties because they were used as the main force to attack the cities. Their underground was also exposed and decimated. In the following year, the U.S. took the offensive, hoping to force Hanoi to the negotiation table. By 1969, the impact of the Tet campaign, which had come close to toppling the government of the South, was largely forgotten. Confident that peace was forthcoming, the U.S. cut aid to South Vietnam. With the apparent stability and a shortfall in the budget, the government reduced its armed forces. Old army reservists like myself were decommissioned once more, and senior regulars like Tan were retired.

It didn't seem unreasonable for us to expect a peaceful future. Tan no longer worried about being sent to some remote airfield where shelling occurred nightly. I no longer dreaded the prospect of being assigned to a combat unit. Tan was planning a career in law. I had a tenured teaching position and owned a house.

"It's really good to see you," he said.

I smiled. "Very good to see you too."

We were standing beside the fountain, grasping each other's forearms. There was no need to say more. I had missed him. Time had swung away from us. We were closer than brothers. Our roots were entwined since birth. As boys, we had shared the same bed, eaten from the same bowl, gone to the same school. Our adolescent fears, shames, and thrills came from the same page. Between us lay all the secrets and pains that were ours alone. It was a profound comfort to know Tan was alive and well.

"We should go somewhere for a drink and celebrate," Anh said.

Tan turned to her and grinned. "My apartment is just around the corner from here. Would you like to see it? I've got a small bar."

It was getting dark. The streetlights came on. People emerged to stroll in the cool evening air. Couples lingered around the little squares, chatting and laughing. Vendors selling snacks, drinks, barbecued meats, and noodles lined the sidewalk.

Tan lived in a new luxurious high-rise. We took the elevator up to the seventh floor, well above the treetops. His modern one-bedroom apartment was as spacious as a top-notch hotel suite. Anh squeaked with delight. One of her wonderful qualities was that she was always genuinely happy to see someone else succeed. She peered out one window after another, telling Tan what gorgeous views he had. She skipped around the apartment, excited as though it were ours. Beaming with pleasure, he recounted every feature of his lavishly furnished home. He showed her his brand-new hi-fi stereo system and television. There was everything a man could want in a bachelor's pad.

It occurred to me then that perhaps his life was rather lonely. Our paths had diverged. Tan had amassed a life of material comfort and pleasures. I had created a family for myself. He had known, possibly, hundreds of women. I'd been with only one. The influences from our formative years, like minor deflections at the beginning of a long trajectory, had borne significant consequences.

Tan opened his refrigerator. The shelves were stacked tightly with Coca-Cola and Budweiser. Anh went outside and brought up some street-foods: stir-fried cubed steak, sweet-smoked fish, peanuts, and ice cream. Tan asked about the family. I was surprised he hadn't visited them more often. Somehow, through all these years, I believe he still considered himself an orphan. Being around the family only made him lonelier.

I told him the family had never been better. Hung and Hong had both graduated from college. Hung was a high school teacher, Hong a department manager of the Forestry Service. Hoang was in the police academy, and Hien was in his last year of high school. The three sisters, Huong, Hang, and Hanh, were in school. They kept things going smoothly at home and took good care of Father. My youngest stepbrother, Hau, was the same age as my first son, An. After selling lottery tickets on the street corner under the full brunt of the sun, Stepmother finally had her own ticket kiosk and was doing well. Hung, Hong, and I had rebuilt the house for them. Father, however, had never made the slightest attempt to free himself from opium.

Inevitably, the conversation strayed to the good old days: the foods we ate in Hanoi, the playground fights, our youthful games and pranks. We ran out the evening on only the pleasant memories. When it was late, Anh took the car key and went home to relieve the nanny. Tan poured us another round of beer. He reached out and squeezed my shoulder, grinning. The view from his sofa was spectacular, Saigon spreading out like a big garden; city lights and neon signs winking through the tree boughs.

From here, it was easy to discount the bad news in the papers, the rising anti-American sentiments in the countryside, the reports about American bombing campaigns indiscriminately wiping out whole villages, and the wanton spraying of dangerous Agent Orange that was poisoning the peasants and their land. Just a few hundred miles north of Saigon, huge tracts of lush land—thousands of acres—had been reduced to parched scrub plains in order to deprive the VC of cover. It was unimaginable to read in the newspapers that Vietnam, the rice basket of Asia, had to import rice from America to feed its people. All that seemed far away from us. Perhaps we didn't want to believe it. I had worked indirectly for USAID, and Tan worked for the Americans. We were too intent on our own survival, eager to at last have a chance to live and plan our lives.

"Do you plan to go back to school?" Tan asked.

"Of course, after we've settled down a bit. I have five kids, the youngest barely a year old."

Tan nodded. "That's good, because I don't think you'll be happy as a high school teacher."

His disappointment was palpable. Tan knew how much I wanted to be a professor. He did not expect me to end up as a second-tier high school teacher.

"You're right. I haven't had much time to think about a career. Eight years in the army with a family to care for, you don't think of much else other than getting out alive."

Sensing my discomfort, he changed the subject. "Do you think there will be peace soon?"

It struck me as comical that this had become our lifelong concern. When will we have peace? I chuckled. "It's never for us to decide, is it?"

Tan leaned back into the sofa and cocked his feet on the coffee table. I noticed that his posture had been Americanized, as had his taste for décor. There was more of a swagger and bigness about him. It suited Tan. I was happy for him. Someday he would become a judge like his father. Uncle Thuan would have been proud of his son.

He said, "The Americans I work with think the peace negotiations might bring some changes to the South Vietnam regime. The Communists are drained after their Tet Offensive. They're willing to negotiate now. There could be peace soon."

"If Minh wins, I think we will have peace. Even my father supports Minh and, you know, my father hasn't said a single good thing about Diem, Thieu, Ky, or their cronies."

Duong Van Minh was a famous figure who had led the junta that overthrew Diem in 1963. He had the support of powerful Buddhist and Catholic leaders. People saw him as an honorable man, a character capable of negotiating a peaceful end to the war. The NLF even mobilized a campaign to get out the vote for Minh and made him very popular in the countryside. However, Henry Kissinger, the American Secretary of Defense, distrusted Minh.

Tan grimaced. "If the Americans allow a fair election, Minh will win. But I don't think that will happen. Thieu used the Americans to eliminate Ky from the race."

With the help of the CIA and the U.S. embassy, Thieu had already rigged the election by bribing the legislature with CIA money to pass a law effectively barring Ky's candidacy.

I sighed. "Minh has to win. It's the only peaceful way."

"I hope you're right."

WE never got the chance to vote for Minh.

After discovering Thieu's plot with the province chiefs to defraud the electoral process, Minh went to the U.S. embassy seeking assurances that the Americans would follow through on their promise of forcing their man, Thieu, to allow a "reasonably" open election. The embassy refused, and Minh withdrew his candidacy.

Faced with the embarrassment of having their candidate running in a "democratic" one-man race, the Americans offered Minh millions to stay in the election, but he declined to lend his name to the charade. The Americans convinced Thieu to reverse the rules and allow Ky to run in the election, but Ky refused.

So Thieu ran alone and took 94.3 percent of the vote.

Although talks were held, Hanoi never made another serious attempt at the peace negotiation. Vietnam had lost its best chance for peace. The war would continue, resulting in the deaths of hundreds of thousands and the sufferings of millions of Vietnamese.

As ordinary citizens, we were oblivious to the details of high-level machinations. But as we had expected with Thieu entrenched in the presidency, there was more fighting. Life did not get any easier. Unemployment and inflation worsened rapidly. Over the next two years, Tan and I kept in touch. We were nervous about the future.

I often came to Tan's apartment to find out what his American colleagues were saying. As usual, we sat in his sofa and drank Budweiser, staring out his panoramic window. We talked about a recent newspaper story about how the salary of an ARVN soldier wasn't enough to support a family of four for half a month.

"What's happening to the economy? I'm getting poorer by the month," I said. My teaching salary, once adequate for supporting my family, now could only cover a small fraction of our budget. Inflation was outstripping workers' wages.

Tan said, "Whatever it is, our own leaders know about it. Don't you see every single one of them trying to steal and rob the country as much as he can, as quickly as he can?"

I shrugged, having grown indifferent to politics and corruption—they had become synonymous to me. "Corruption has been a disease since Diem's regime. I don't see much change."

"Are you blind? It has gotten much worse lately. Before they were just milking the cow and stealing the cream. Now, they're butchering it."

"Yes, I know, but that doesn't mean something big is going to happen. This is the most peace Saigon has had in years."

Tan shook his head morosely, staring out the window. "It makes me nervous seeing the top leaders blatantly ransacking the country. They don't seem worried about their political careers. They must know something we don't."

It had been a long time, but I still recognized that anxious, piercing look on his face. It was disconcerting. Tan had the premonitions of a survivor. Orphaned as a child, he had become a keen observer of the world. He could discern patterns where I found none. I had often resented that and accused him of being a pessimist, but looking back, I realized he had been right all along, from the very beginning when we fled from Tong Xuyen.

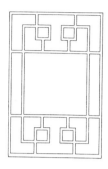

29. CROSSING THE FRENCH LINE

"Our village is no longer a safe place for the family," Father said. "We must cross the front line and go into Hanoi and wait until the war is over."

The French had withdrawn from Tong Xuyen. The Resistance was gaining considerable strength. Fighting in the Red River Delta became more fierce and more frequent. Soon every man, woman, and child would be required to join the Resistance and fight the French. Anyone who refused would be considered a traitor.

We were sitting with Father in his study. It was the first time he explained his intentions to Tan and me. Father had been home less than a week and was still reeling from the shock of Mother's death. He hadn't spoken much about his year of servitude in the French regiments.

"Viet Minh have left us alone because your aunts and Mother helped them when the French were stronger in our domain. Now they will demand more material and financial support, but I haven't found where your

Mother hid our family's treasury. It may take me months or years of digging up the entire estate before I find it. By then we may run out of money to contribute to the Viet Minh."

"Father, we don't have any enemies in the village. Do you think they will rise against us?"

"War changes people, son. Even if they like us, they can't refuse an order from the Viet Minh. I'm sure it's only a matter of time before the Communists kill me. I will leave tonight to find a way to cross the French line. When it's safe, I will send for you and your siblings." Father turned to Tan. "Nephew, you can choose to stay with your stepmother, but I think it's best if you come with us."

"I'd like to go, Uncle," Tan replied without hesitation.

THE next morning, Father was already gone, having departed quietly during the night. A week later a messenger arrived from Hung Yen province with news that Father was at Uncle Loc's house, which was half a day's walk from the province seat. Aunt Thuan instructed our old guard Khi, Tan, and me that we were to leave the next day. I had picked out a few items to take along, but Khi said not to take anything expensive. Traveling as peasants, we would have no way to explain owning something of value.

At the first crow of the rooster, we set off without breakfast or good-byes. There were five children in our group: baby Huong, Hong, Hung, Tan, and me. We were accompanied by three adults: Khi, Noui, and Vien. Khi led our little expedition. Noui, a man in his early twenties, was an adopted member of our extended family. He knew the back roads to Hung Yen. Nanny Vien was a young widow whose baby had died prematurely. She had been hired to nurse Huong.

Under the cover of darkness, we left the estate through a secret gap in the bamboo hedge. A mist hovered over the fields and obscured the footpath on top of the dikes separating the paddies. Nuoi led us in single file. Vien followed behind him with baby Huong in a fabric sling across her chest. Hung and Hong trailed behind her. Tan and I came behind the boys to keep an eye on them. Khi brought up the rear. It was difficult to see my own feet, but Noui pressed onward at a fast clip. We needed to get clear of the local fields before the peasants started coming out at dawn to work. There was always the chance of being recognized by the villagers. Eight-year-old Hong tired after half an hour, and Noui carried him on his back. Hung was ten and didn't last much longer than his younger brother. He soon rode on Khi's back.

Stumbling along behind Tan, I kept wondering if I had done the right thing by leaving the champagne bottle behind. What if someone dug it up? Would he sell it or give it back to us? At last, I decided that I would never know if someone took it, so in my mind the bottle would always stay safely buried in Mother's garden. I could hold on to it forever this way.

We turned onto a smaller road and suddenly the hackles rose on the back of my neck. This was the place where Uncle Thuan had fallen. The sky was shifting to a deep shade of lavender. The air took on a heavy swampy odor. The big tree loomed like a monstrous shadow at the bend of the road.

Tan paused, staring at the tree. We had come here together once after his father's assassination. Tan looked at me. He was visibly shaken. His life had been changed irrevocably in this place by a single bullet. I shuddered as we passed the spot where his father had laid. I muttered a prayer to Uncle Thuan and Mother to safeguard us on this journey.

After sunrise, Khi slackened the pace, but didn't let us rest for another hour. We sat behind some bushes and ate rice balls with a sweet powder of sesame seeds, peanuts, and sugar. Later in the morning, a group of Resistance fighters stopped us on the road and asked Khi where we were going. Khi said we were a peasant family going to live with our relatives in a village outside the province seat. At the time, there were many peasants on the roads displaced by intense fighting so they found our answer credible and allowed us to go on our way.

We skirted several villages, taking mostly footpaths through endless, unchanging miles of rice paddies. I had never walked so far. My feet blistered. Khi pushed us steadily onward. We reached Uncle Loc's house by sunset.

Uncle Loc was my mother's youngest brother. As the family's only son, he inherited the majority of his family fortune, which included his countryside manor. He was married and had five daughters and one son. He was one of the last relatives on my mother's side to remain in the countryside, most having moved to Hanoi a year ago.

Khi went back to the estate the next day. The rest of us stayed with Father at Uncle Loc's house. Early in the morning of our third day, a guide arrived at the manor. He took all nine of us by foot on the main road toward the province seat. Hung Yen at the time was a twilight territory much like our village had been a year ago. The French controlled the countryside during the day, the Resistance during the night. We stayed on the well-patrolled highway, avoiding back roads that were watched by the Resistance. The Viet Minh considered people crossing over to the French area as traitors and regularly executed them as such. Our guide knew the French troops at each checkpoint and was able to bribe our crossing all the way through to the province seat, where he again helped us to buy French papers that allowed us to travel.

The passage was surreal. It happened in a blur of exhaustion and confusion. Before I realized it, we were sitting on a bus rolling toward Hanoi. I opened my burlap bag and took out the flute Hoi had given me the day before we left home.

THAT evening, Hoi had come by to see me. He waited for me by the old banyan tree just down the road from the rear gate of our estate—the same place where, since we were boys, he had always turned back after walking me home.

Hoi was still skinny and half a head shorter than me. His teeth had grown in unevenly. Sometimes I found it incredible that my shy, undersized friend, who was always the last boy to be picked for soccer teams, had become the most respected teenager in the village and the leader of the local chapter of Uncle Ho's Youth Brigade. The boy who could never recite his lessons in front of class without tripping up a dozen times could now give rousing lectures about the evils of colonialism.

"I heard your father was released by the French," Hoi said.

Surprised, I said nothing. My family had kept it a secret.

"Those long-nosed thugs! You must avenge . . . " Hoi sighed, looking away. He had asked me to join Uncle Ho's Youth Brigade many times.

Since the French withdrew from our domain, Hoi's family had emerged as the chief Resistance organizers of our village. In this new sphere, his family was more powerful than ours. Only recently did I realize the small considerations that my family had shown his over the years were what kept us safe while elsewhere in other domains, wealthy families were targeted for retaliation by the peasantry. Hoi never mentioned it, but I knew he kept the other boys at school from bullying me when I avoided joining their Youth Brigade.

It was strange to see that we were at opposite sides of a sudden chasm, though it did not feel that way, not between us.

I wanted to give him my school supplies and books, but he had no use for them now that he was an important Youth Leader destined for greater things. I handed him a compass on a lanyard. I could tell he liked it by the way the grin grew across his face.

Hoi gave me a bamboo flute he'd fashioned. When I saw the two words he had seared onto the barrel with a hot iron, I knew that he knew we were leaving. *Friends Forever.*

As we grasped each other's forearms, Hoi smiled. I smiled. It was all here. Hundreds of cricket fights. Innumerable days roaming the muddy paddies, fishing, catching frogs, flying kites, roasting grass-hoppers. I could not count the number of *banh da* I had eaten at his house. How many thousand sunny days were we allowed in one childhood? Were there ever enough?

Fourteen years old, we were more boys than men.

I did not know I would never see Hoi or Tong Xuyen again. As always, we parted in the shadow of the old banyan tree. It was amazing how a bend in the road could obscure a lifetime to come.

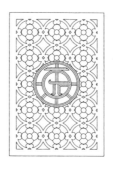

30 . The Fall of Saigon

Sixteen years of fighting had reduced the war to a troublesome liability. We accepted it like an offshore storm that never left. The battles, the bombs, the highway ambushes, the countryside insurgency, the draft cycles, and the ever-mounting casualties had become the ebbs and flows of a long, long war. We never expected victory—our leaders were too corrupt for that— and yet defeat never entered our minds. We convinced ourselves that the ever-present, powerful Americans would never desert us. We had become too dependent, lazy, blind, and selfish to save ourselves.

The end came swiftly. The cities didn't fall; they tumbled, one after another in quick, horrific succession. On March 13, 1975, the first to go was Ban Me Thuot, a key hold in the Central Highlands. Five days later, Pleiku was lost. In three more days, the enemy overran Quang Tri. Hue, the capital of central Vietnam, was abandoned two days after that. President Thieu and his staff of incompetent generals accelerated the downfall with their order to abandon the 1st and 2nd Corps. The stalemate was over. The tide had turned permanently. Within three weeks, eight provinces were forfeited; 40,000 troops were massacred during the retreats. It was devastating, but no one could predict that the Viet Cong would sack Saigon's presidential palace in another twenty-six days.

My brother Hong was working at the Forestry Service of Phu Bon, a province in the Central Highlands. When the VC took the province seat, he escaped to Bao Loc on an L-19, a two-seater propeller plane; it was sheer luck that he had caught his army pilot friend in time. Had he tried to escape by road, he would have been among the tens of thousands of civilians who perished in the forest on their exodus to the coast. From Bao Loc, he caught a bus into Saigon. Hong walked through the door of my father's house empty-handed. He had lost his home and everything he owned. Days later, my brother Hung, a high school principal, fled Ham Tan, a mere sixty-five miles from Saigon. The news Hong and Hung brought home was terrifying.

Madness had descended on the city. People were in a selling and buying frenzy. Refugees sold whatever they had. Others liquidated assets at a fraction of their cost to raise money for passage out of the country. Former northerners like my family, who had lived under Communist rule, were the most anxious to leave. The majority of southerners, however, did not think that a Communist takeover would be disastrous. They snapped up cars, motorbikes, houses, and staples at bargain prices. I sold my car and was in negotiation to sell our four-story house. The prospective buyer backed out of the sale when the Viet Cong approached Phan Thiet.

A day later, as the Viet Cong began encircling Phan Thiet, my wife's mother, brother, and sister fled on their neighbor's fishing boat and arrived in Saigon the next morning. When they came to stay at our house and gave us the news, I immediately rode out to Vung Tau on my Honda motorbike to see if I could find a fishing boat to take us out to sea. The highway was busy in both directions with refugees from the outer provinces heading to safety and Saigonians fleeing to the coast in search of passage out of the country.

Army trucks rumbled into Vung Tau along with hordes of expensive civilian cars. The wealthy and the powerful were flocking to the coast. Vung Tau's population had tripled in the past month. I scoured the docks, but it was hopeless. Every single vessel, including motorized dinghies, was already booked or bought outright. The hotels and vacation houses were filled with people waiting to board their boats; some were already living on them. Vung Tau officials declared the city closed to new refugees.

The cost of buying passports, tourist visas, and plane tickets out of the country had skyrocketed out of our reach by the time we saw that a collapse was inevitable. It had become the choice of the super-rich with weighty government connections. Many folks lost their savings in passport cons. Saigon was full of scam artists and opportunists offering the gamut of escape options, from airplanes to ferries to overland border crossings via trucks. Every day, my brothers Hung, Hong, Hoang, and I crisscrossed Saigon looking for contacts and deals. The pall of desperation had fallen over us.

My best friend Tat, the handsome buddy from my high school days, came to me with a proposal. His brother Han, who worked at the Ministry of Transportation, had a deal with the captain of a small coastal merchant ship belonging to a Chinese company. The captain, a Vietnamese of Chinese origin, agreed to take twenty passengers at the price of ten gold leaves each. Tat didn't have the money for his family and suggested that if I loaned him the gold, I could take seven members of my own immediate family. We had been close friends for more than twenty years, so I agreed to his terms. I wanted to meet the captain. Han said the captain refused to meet anyone until it was time to go and that the full fee would be due upon embarkation.

Bach Dang pier was near downtown Saigon, and there were many boats and ferries bringing refugees in from other parts of the country. Tat and I found our ship not on the pier but moored offshore on the other side of the Saigon River. It was a pathetic sea-going junk. Packed to the gunwales, it might carry thirty passengers. Without any other viable alternatives, I swallowed my misgivings and hoped for the best.

A week before the city's collapse, I went over to Tat's house. Neither of us had a telephone, but we lived only three blocks apart so it was easy stopping by to see each other several times a day to check on the status of the boat. I thought it was very safe and fortunate that Tat lived only two minutes by motorbike from me. It was going to be very close because southerners like our ship captain were complacent and had no idea of the dangers of waiting to the final hours.

Tat said, "The captain announced that he'll go as soon as the Americans start to leave."

"That's very risky. We don't even know for certain if he would take us. We haven't even met him."

"I told Han the same thing. He said the government hasn't allowed ships to take people to sea yet. The chaos must begin before the captain can leave without permission. By then, no one will care."

"Why can't he bribe the officials? Your brother can help him find the right contact in the Ministry."

"I doubt the captain will want to part with any of his gold. Besides, he probably can get more money at the last moment when people will pay anything to leave."

"So we wait for the end."

"Yes, we wait for the Americans."

PRESIDENT Thieu and his cabinet fled well before the Americans. On April 21, 1975, Thieu abandoned his office and country. He flew to Taiwan with his family, taking along fifteen tons of personal luggage, rumored to be the wealth of the country. His disgraceful exit delivered a detrimental blow to the troops' morale, and on the following day, Xuan Loc, a critical defensive point merely thirty-five miles from Saigon, crumbled into the enemy's hand. It would be remembered as an epic battle, a display of heartbreaking courage against overwhelming odds. Our trusted American allies never came, but the embattled and impoverished ARVN had gallantly fought on alone, outnumbered and outgunned.

Refugees poured into the capital, running from the shelling and fighting in the adjacent towns that formed a defense line around the city. The number of refugees swelled dramatically as the Viet Minh pushed the ARVN back toward Saigon. Reality was fast disintegrating into nightmare.

State-controlled television and radio broadcasts lied to keep citizens calm. Even the Voice of America was no longer trustworthy. Only the BBC remained factual, and none of their reports bore good news. Like everyone else, I spent my days dashing back and forth all over the city, gathering information and rumors wherever I could. The latest and most credible news was the firsthand accounts from the tens of thousands of refugees seeking shelter at pagodas throughout the city.

XA LOI Temple near my house had more refugees than it had celebrants during the New Year prayers. Hundreds of people huddled and slept wherever they found space. Plastic tarps were strung up in the courtyard and along the sides of the temple to shelter the newcomers. They were all in very bad shape. Some were injured. Many were missing family members. Women sobbed, their children crying inconsolably. Old men sat like statues, staring off into space. These people had run for their lives.

At one corner of the yard, a middle-aged man sat alone, calmly smoking a hand-rolled cigarette, oblivious to the chaos around him. His shirt was torn; dried blood stained the sleeves; his pants were caked with mud. I asked him if I could sit next to him. He glanced sideways at me and kept smoking. I sat down and waited for him to talk. Usually, people were anxious to talk about their ordeals, but the man just rolled another smoke. I finally asked him where he came from.

"Nha Trang," he replied without turning.

"Is your family here with you?"

"They didn't make it."

"The VC captured them?"

He closed his eyes and sighed. "They killed them."

Not knowing what to say, I blurted, "Do you think we'll be safe here?"

He ground the cigarette beneath his sandal, stood up, and walked away.

BY April 27, 1975, it looked as if the end of the world had arrived. The Communists had surrounded the capital—the final foothold of the South's forces. Artillery shells, rockets, and bombs tore up the outskirts of the city. ARVN jet fighters screamed across the overcast sky and swooped along the edges of the city, trying to turn back the advancing Communist forces. North, south, and west of Saigon, columns of black smoke curled upward, the blazes spreading. Torrents of refugees poured into the city on every road. Terrified, traumatized, and exhausted, they rolled toward the last sanctuary. They came like an undulating human carpet, filling, choking the new Bien Hoa superhighway as far as the eyes could see.

On April 28, Duong Van Minh took over the role of Chief of State. Fully armed South Vietnam troops appeared on Tran Quoc Toan Boulevard, where the Military Assistance Command, Vietnam headquarters was located right around the corner from my father's house. These were the "Red Beret Angels," the South Vietnam elite airborne force. They were our very best men, known for their courage and seen in every parade. They were our heroes, symbolic of South Vietnam's pride and power. Their dedication, ferocity, and sacrifices were legendary. They were the ones who had shown us that we could fight the VC and win. It shook me profoundly to see them sitting on the curb with their heads hung low, their rifles on the sidewalk. Without their confident swagger, they seemed so young, more boys than men. Had it been fifteen years since I was drafted? I walked up and down the street, trying to catch their eyes. I recognized that look of battle fatigue. Their morale was broken. Hopelessness pulled on their limbs. It was plain on their faces; the war was over.

I got on my motorbike and rushed over to Tat's house, determined to convince the captain that we must not wait any longer. I was prepared to pay a premium to make the captain see reason. The moment I saw Tat sitting outside his house, I knew our hopes were dashed.

Tat wouldn't look at me. He mumbled, "They confiscated the boat."

"Who?"

"The police."

"Why?

He shrugged. "They have family and need to escape too."

"When did you find out?"

"Yesterday evening."

I was speechless. We were dead. It was as simple as that. I sat with him fifteen, twenty minutes, dumbstruck. I could feel the seconds ticking away. I was angry that he hadn't told me earlier, even though I knew I couldn't change a thing.

I said, "We must not give up. We must keep looking. Let me know immediately if something comes up."

He promised he would, and I left on my motorbike.

I didn't know where I was going, but I needed to go somewhere, anywhere. My stomach was souring. Where to start looking all over again? I revved the engine, and sliced and weaved through the bustling streets. I joined the throngs of tens of thousands looking for an escape route. All of Saigon, including the hundreds of thousands of refugees, was on the road, coursing manically in a dozen different directions. Cars, trucks, motorbikes, bicycles, and cyclos jammed the avenues. Accidents clogged the intersections. No one cared, no one stopped. We were like animals trapped in a burning cage. But there was nowhere to go. Fighting blocked the highway to Tan Son Nhat

Airport. Streets leading to government and military sites were barricaded. I found one dead end after another.

On Mac Dinh Chi Boulevard, a sprawling mob of Vietnamese and foreigners swarmed the American embassy. They surged at the gate, begging to get into the sanctuary. White foreigners pushed through the crowd and were allowed in first. The Vietnamese clamored and shoved each other to get to the guards, waving documents and shouting their qualifications: employees of American companies, contractors, relatives of Americans, wives and children of American soldiers. I watched from a distance, knowing that a decommissioned officer had no priority, regardless of my service. My office had provided a cover for CIA operatives. If the Viet Cong caught me, I expected to be tortured and executed. My wife and children would be sent to live in the jungle.

I had never felt so much envy toward foreigners as I did at that moment. Since I was a teenager, I could never escape the feeling that they glided on some other plane above us; their dignity, living standards, and privileges thriving in another stratum beyond our reach. I had never bothered looking upward until now. Even other Asians—the Filipinos, the Taiwanese, the Koreans, the Japanese—were passing right over us. My people were at the bottom of the hierarchy, and we were about to sink even lower once the Communists took control.

I WENT home, put my arms around Anh, and told her the bad news. Rather than breaking down as I'd feared, she insisted that we see our physician, who was a good friend. We had known Dr. Nguyen Duy Tam for the fourteen years since he opened his first modest clinic. He had become one of the most successful doctors in Saigon and had powerful connections. His clientele consisted of generals, politicians, and business moguls. He was also a prominent congressman.

When we arrived at his modern clinic in an upscale neighborhood, it was nearly deserted. Three patients were attended by two distracted young nurses who seemed on the verge of bolting out of the office. Dr. Tam took us into his office and confided that he had plans to go to France. He offered to take my family if we had one hundred bars of gold for the fare. The agent would need twenty bars as a deposit. We rushed home and brought back the gold. The flight would leave the next morning. Dr. Tam said he would send a car for us.

In the evening, I went over to my father's house. My brothers were out roaming the city, looking for an escape. Father was sipping tea with his opium cohorts. Father's cousin and confidant, Mr. Tri, droned on about his theory that the Americans would strike a deal with the Viet Cong once the fighting was over. According to Mr. Tri, there was no need to flee the country. Father's two neighbors, both southerners, insisted that at least with the Communists there would be less corruption in the government. They couldn't see why the Communists would want to take revenge on former northerners like us for migrating south twenty-one years ago.

I sat with them as long as I could because I wanted to spend some time with my father. I considered telling him about Dr. Tam's offer, but in the end, I couldn't bring myself to do it. He had become extremely cynical, and he believed solely in Mr. Tri's counsel. My stepmother and sisters could do nothing. Their fates lay squarely with him. Father wanted Hung, Hong, Hoang, and me to escape, because life for us would be very dangerous under the Communist regime. As for himself, Father had decided that he was old enough to die. He had the resigned calm of someone stricken by a terminal illness. He had decided to face the Communists together with his neighbors and Mr. Tri, his most trusted friend.

THAT night of April 28, Anh and I stayed up and watched over our three-year-old son, who was very ill with a high fever. We didn't talk. There was too much to say and nowhere to begin. Our entire life was here in this house, all the years of hard work, the memories, our families to be left behind. What to bring, what to leave? Too many difficult choices, so we packed nothing, save some warm clothes for the children and one envelope filled with photos. Anh brewed a strong pot of tea and we sat together looking out our second-floor window at the dark street.

It was 7:00 A.M., just after dawn, when the first convoy of military vehicles thundered down Ly Thai To Boulevard in front of our house. Private cars sped after them toward the center of the city. Something was afoot. I had a strong urge to jump on my motorbike and follow them, but I was afraid we might miss Dr. Tam's car. It was nerve-racking to see hordes of people heading toward downtown while we sat still. By 8:00 A.M., I couldn't wait any longer and I took Anh to see the doctor.

A smell of rot permeated Saigon. Trash, clothes, baggage, housewares, blankets, baskets of food, and just about everything else littered the streets. A horse-drawn cart full of luggage and trunks was ditched on the side of the road, the horse gone. A beautiful hardwood chair and sofa were left on the sidewalk. Cars parked crookedly, their doors hanging open. Overnight, the ARVN soldiers had vanished into the alleys and byways, their uniforms and weapons discarded in the gutters. Unlike other surrendering cities, there were no robberies or looting by renegade soldiers or gangsters.

In Dr. Tam's clinic, the head nurse sat alone at the front desk reading a novel. She greeted us with a sad smile and said that Dr. Tam had left with his family at around 3:00 A.M. They had gone to Tan Son Nhat Airport by helicopter and flew out of the country on a civilian plane. I felt the earth drop away from my feet. Anh clutched my arm.

"He promised us," Anh insisted. "He promised to take us with him. There was supposed to be a car. This morning, he said."

"I'm so sorry, Sister Anh. The doctor told me to tell you that he tried, but couldn't negotiate to take anyone else besides his own family. He's very sorry he couldn't help you."

Anh turned to me. "He promised us."

I put my arm around her shoulder and led her out. The nurse stopped us at the door and handed us a small box sealed with tape—our gold deposit.

AFTER taking Anh home, I was going over to my father's house when I saw a helicopter lifting off the MACV headquarters. The once-busy compound was empty, the main doors closed. The steel gates were shut, the familiar U.S. MPs gone. Anyone who was going to be saved was already inside the main building. On the rooftop, helicopters were evacuating American personnel and some lucky Vietnamese who worked for them. Watching them rising away effortlessly, I thought I could smell the stink of death seeping into the city. It was truly over. The Americans weren't just leaving, they were running, flying, bolting out as fast as possible.

Father was in the living room drinking tea with a neighbor. He said Hung had gone over to my home to tell me that there were ferries taking evacuees out to sea at Ben Bach Dang. Hong was already there, and Hoang had just left. Hien was still at the police academy in Thu Duc. Father had decided that my stepmother, three sisters, and youngest brother would stay in Vietnam with him. Escape was too dangerous for them. I rushed back home, missing Hung by minutes.

"We have to go to the ferries now!" I said to Anh.

"We don't have a car," she said.

"Get the kids ready. Tell your brother, sister, and mother that if they want to come with us, they must be ready in ten minutes."

"You go first and find us a place on the ferry. I'll get a car and follow you. We'll meet you there."

"I'll wait for you by the pier, at the lamppost next to the banana vendor."

THE eight-mile drive to Ben Bach Dang took twice as long as usual. Traffic was crazy. I saw half a dozen crashes. Throngs of people were fleeing to the pier. The military vehicles and cars that I had seen early this morning were now parked haphazardly by the riverside. The dock was littered with abandoned cars, bicycles, motorbikes, and luggage. No one even bothered to pick them up. I arrived just in time to see the last ferry cast off its moorings. The ship was dangerously overloaded, every inch of its deck packed. People hung onto the railing, calling to friends and relatives who didn't make it aboard. Some jumped into the churning water and swam after the ship. I pushed my way to the edge of the dock. Hoang was on the ferry. I yelled and waved at him, but he didn't see me. I didn't see Hung anywhere. If Hoang was on this last ferry, there was little chance Hung was on it as well. After telling Hoang about the ferries, Hung had wasted more time crossing the city to look for me. My heart pounded violently in my chest. What if Hung had gotten into an accident on the way back here? I screamed out his name, my voice lost in the cacophony. Hung had taken an immense risk trying to help his brothers escape. In this desperate panic when everyone was solely focused on his own survival, my dear brother Hung did not think of himself, but instead jeopardized his last chance of escape to save me. I felt nauseous. My single wish then was to see Hung standing on that ferry. But it was getting farther and farther from me. I kept looking at it until distance fused the passengers into a single mass, between us, a stretch of brackish water as dark and forbidding as an abyss.

I was drowning on the dock. Another chance to escape had slipped through my fingers. If only I hadn't counted on Dr. Tam's help. If only he had sent word to us when he knew he couldn't keep his promise. If only I had trusted my instincts this morning and followed those cars. If, if, if . . .

I CAME to see Tat. His house was locked. No one was home. His neighbor told me that Tat and his brother Han, our Ministry of Transportation insider, had known about the evacuation and left early this morning with his huge family and relatives—more than forty people. They had boarded one of the first ferries. Tat's house was three blocks from mine. We had seen each other several times a day for the past month. My best friend had left without taking a moment to share the information that would have made a world of difference for me. I would have had plenty of time to save not only my own family, but also my brothers and in-laws. This was someone whom I had tutored and guided throughout high school and college. I had seen Tat through the death of his father, performing many of the duties as though I was a member of his family. When he had been summoned to the draft center, I held his full-time teaching position to keep the school from replacing him. After bribing himself another exemption, Tat returned, and I gave him back his job and the entire month's salary that I had earned teaching his classes. He was like a brother.

It broke my heart. I couldn't bring myself to tell my wife the news.

ALL through the darkest night, the most quiet and peaceful night Saigon ever had, I wrestled with fate. Dawn revealed a ghost town. I looked out from my second-story window at the vacant street. I couldn't eat and hadn't slept in two days. I felt detached, drunk with fatigue.

Mid-morning, a convoy of camouflaged trucks roared through the street, heading to the city center. The North Vietnam Army was entering Saigon without resistance or a single gunshot. It was chilling. The air had somehow gone bad.

The victors entered Saigon in the late morning on a medley of vehicles: American Jeeps, army trucks, civilian pickups, and sedans. They were the South Vietnam Communist troops, the PAFL, paramilitary units, and Saigon's own underground Communists. They brandished weapons and wore mismatched uniforms, black pajamas, T-shirts, and even jeans. Pickup trucks with loudspeakers declared the surrender of the South Vietnam government, announcing that we were now "liberated" from tyranny and capitalism. Cheering packs of Saigon youths followed the convoy with their mopeds and bicycles. People stepped outside timidly. They stood drowsily in front their homes as if they were just waking up from a long sleep.

Late in the afternoon, my father came riding his creaky bicycle, dressed in a pair of gray slacks and a white shirt. Bent over the handlebars, he looked ghastly thin—as vulnerable as a pauper. I hadn't seen him pedaling his bike for years. I was afraid he was going to fall over. He came to make sure I didn't do something crazy like commit suicide or hike to the Cambodian border. Father knew that sooner or later, the Communist's ax would fall on my neck and he wanted to be there with me when bad things began. He had always said that our family had been extremely blessed compared to all those around us, the countless others who had suffered heartbreaking losses. He believed it was karma. He came to remind me that we had lived with good intentions. He wanted to give me hope.

We climbed to the fourth-story rooftop together. He said he believed Hung had escaped on the ferries along with my cousin Tan and my brothers Hong and Hoang. Father sighed and admitted that his trusted friend and confidant, Mr. Tri, who had advised everyone to stay, had fled without a word of good-bye or warning. I could tell the betrayal wounded him deeply. I felt very sorry for Father. I wanted to comfort him, but it wasn't our way to show weakness or emotion. I was forty years old. Father was an old man entering the last stage of his life. This was the most serene silence we shared, standing shoulder to shoulder in the fading light.

The sun simmered on the skyline. The day was closing, and with it an era. I could feel the city, my city, kneeling down. The vast orange heaven, pillars of smoke, the ragged cityscape. It was a beautiful sight. It was like standing at the helm of a ship. The whole city was sinking.

Father turned and stared at me. The unforgiving years had carved themselves into his gaunt face, deep scars of a life I had known but never dared study. I saw it then, the immense sorrow brimming in his eyes. It was staggering. I could tell he wanted to say it, but didn't know how. All at once, our barriers fell, and I saw through the blurred seasons of our history, our pains, his disappointments, my childhood fear of this distant man. For the first time in my life, I felt the fullness of my father's love. It was crushing, the lateness of the hour.

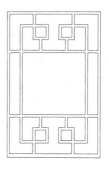

31. THE WIDOWER

I had always thought that some of Father's best years were in the second phase of his adult life when he became a man at the very ripe age of thirty-two. Broke and widowed, he was forced to confront not only the responsibilities of being a parent, but also, for the first time in his life, the hardships of earning a living. His playboy days, for the time being, were over.

Father returned to Hanoi with four children and two servants in tow. The first six months were difficult. He had an extravagant home, but barely enough money for food, certainly none for the luxuries he had once enjoyed and now missed. He had servants, but no means to pay them. Slowly, he sold his antique porcelain, gold wristwatch, gemstone cufflinks, and the various little vanities he had collected during the highlights of his life.

On the verge of bankruptcy, Father at last swallowed his pride and turned to his relatives, most of whom had fled to Hanoi early with their fortunes intact.

He had no reason to think that they wouldn't reciprocate the generosity he had shown them when he was wealthy, so it came as a bitter disappointment when none extended him even a small loan to start a business. It was suggested that he sell his villa and live modestly off the proceeds. Their polite spurns and distant silence wounded him as deeply as betrayals. Once I heard him say to a friend that being born rich was a privilege, and that he had no idea how important money was until he didn't have it.

Looking at Hanoi, he saw that the city had been rejuvenated. People breathed easier—even the villagers who migrated here to escape the fighting. He knew that wartime was also boom-time for those not caught in the cross fire. In fact, Hanoi was in bloom. Its population had doubled. There was no sign of war. There were no gunshots. City life was rather pleasant. In Hanoi one didn't get anxious about French patrols randomly arresting people or mortars suddenly dropping out of the sky. There were no Communist cadres to make everyone attend the dull and repetitive nightly meetings. Furthermore, foods and goods were plentiful in Hanoi. The streets were awash with merchandise; shops stocked wines, spirits, butter, cheeses, sausages, chocolates, and exotic European foods. Throbbing with the bustle of business, Hanoi's population swelled with Vietnamese peasants displaced by the war and foreigners, both civilians and soldiers, including a large number of French administrators, businessmen, and expatriates. Hanoi was also a vacation city and a portal for the hundreds of thousands of French troops, Algerians, Moroccans, and African legionnaires brought into the country to crush the Viet Minh.

Mother's closest cousin, Uncle Toa, who was a former senator, came to Father's aid with a loan to convert our villa into an inn. At that time in Hanoi, there were two types of hotels: the large, expensive establishments catering to rich businessmen and diplomats, and the modest inns serving French expatriates, merchants, and soldiers on leave. Ours fell into the second category. It suited Father for three reasons. First, it was a business where he did not have to work every day. Second, his villa was situated on a major thoroughfare suitable for this industry. Third, Father was fluent in French and had two French-speaking workers handy, namely Tan and me.

We renovated the servants' bungalow at the rear of the property and moved into it, leaving our four posh bedrooms to rent out as deluxe suites. Father put in eight smaller rooms, bringing the total to an even dozen. The living room was remodeled into a lounge equipped with a hardwood bar with polished brass trims in the same French style as the house. The patio had iron bistro tables and chairs to take advantage of the rose garden and the shade trees. Father upgraded the kitchen and hired a cook to serve simple French fare. Two maids and a handyman were added to the staff, and Hao Inn was opened nine months after our return to Hanoi.

Our place was at the junction of two major avenues. The area was once a fashionable French neighborhood, now quickly becoming a commercial area catering to foreigners replete with shops, bars, restaurants, and opium lounges. Big trees lined the wide sidewalks on both sides of the street. A vendor sold beverages and fresh and pickled fruits from a kiosk erected on the pavement outside our villa. Within a week of our opening, the pimps and their girls congregated at the kiosk every evening to attract French soldiers staying at our inn. They made such a commotion that Father had to hire a burly guard and posted him at the gate to keep them from coming inside uninvited.

At the middle and the end of each month when the French soldiers and legionnaires got their pay, our street corner deteriorated into a wild all-hours party. They drank, laughed, screamed, sang, danced right in the street, and collapsed intoxicated on the sidewalk, doing their best to squander months of wages in a few days and with only two things on their mind: sex and alcohol. Fights broke out regularly between soldiers for the same girl, between drunkards from different units, between French regulars and legionnaires, and between two girls over one generous drunk. Sometimes, the chaos lasted through the night.

It was a rougher business than Father had imagined. Once the inn was established, he left the entire operation to Tan and me, and branched out, through his contacts, into government contracts, which, though sporadic, were very lucrative and required little work on his part. Within a year of coming back to Hanoi, Father constructed a comfortable new life. He bought a French bicycle and a motorcycle, neither of which he rode more than twice. He also owned a sleek Peugeot sedan. The handyman washed and polished it twice a week and parked it in the driveway in front of the cottage where Father could admire it from his room.

He took Hong, Hung, Tan, and me to soccer games, boxing matches, French cinemas, and restaurants. Father introduced us to life at the higher stratum, where he was most comfortable. He was as much a man of the city as his brother had been a man of the country. Where people had feared his brother, they were drawn to Father's amiability. Father's earlier reputation as a generous host was revived as his fortune rose. New as well as old friends, including those who had spurned him only a year earlier, started coming round for dinner parties that lasted into the wee hours of the morning.

Father soon succumbed to the grip of opium, the intoxicant of choice among the Vietnamese elites. Though outlawed in France, it was a vice legalized and encouraged by the colonial French, some said to calm the natives. At first he smoked with small groups of acquaintances at the opium lounges, then at home. As he grew more inactive, Father began inviting friends, many of them scholars and high-ranking officials, who could bring him news of the war and the outside world. Gradually, most of his days and evenings were spent lying beside his opium tray with closest friends. Between their lucid dreams, they talked about life, women, the war, politics, French colonialism, and the past World Wars. They discussed and debated everything, but they did nothing. The irony of opium was that it robbed an addict of his energy, wasted his body, hollowed out his heart, sapped his will until nothing remained, and yet it left his intellect intact.

□   □   □

□ □ □

Ms. NGUYET was one of Father's old girlfriends from his rowdier days. She was a retired *co dau*—a sort of courtesan—a night blossom whose beauty and charm were renowned in the best clubs and opium lounges of Hanoi. Although she was in her early thirties, well past the sixteen- to twenty-five-year-old prime of a hostess, Ms. Nguyet had kept her stunning good looks and elegance. She had a thrilling laugh. She knew how to intrigue a man, how to read his mood, and how to talk to and treat him accordingly. She could have snared any wealthy merchant for marriage if it weren't for her opium addiction, a common occupational hazard of her trade. So, she set her sights on my father, an eligible widower with children in need of a mother.

From the first day she came to one of Father's parties wearing a burgundy *ao dai* that accented her slim curves, Tan and I liked her instantly. She was nearly as tall as Father and had an oval Chinese face with porcelain skin. She complimented Tan on his developing musculature, since he was beginning to lift weights at the gym. She talked to me about school and my education plans. It was a part of her charm. I knew that Father could easily be seduced by Ms. Nguyet, a compatriot in his addiction from his bachelor days, who could satisfy both his sexual and companionship needs.

NANNY Vien knew immediately that Ms. Nguyet threatened her own ambition of being Father's next wife. Since Vien came to live with us in Hanoi, Father treated her as a member of the family. He instructed us boys to call her Auntie Vien and afford her proper respect. Unlike other staff members, she ate with us both at home and at nice restaurants. Father paid her a generous wage because a milk-nurse was a rare find. He also allowed her to make most of the household decisions simply because he was too lazy and consumed with work, then later with opium. His passiveness led to Vien's natural assumption of a supervisory position over the other servants. Little by little, she assumed all the responsibilities and prerogatives of a wife except for sharing Father's bed—but it wasn't for lack of trying on her part.

Although she was capable of surges of gaiety, Vien had a down-turned mouth averse to smiling. You instinctively wanted to cheer her up. She had a round, attractive face and the healthy, tanned complexion of an active woman in her mid-twenties. Endowed with ample bosoms, she usually wore her blouse with the top buttons open. When she did household chores, she liked to wear the peasant *yem* top, which exposed her entire back and left her breasts to move sensually beneath the thin fabric. Sometimes she would find ways to feed Huong near wherever Father was sitting, and then leave her breast exposed. Throughout the day, she brought Father refreshments and devised little errands into his room, making herself available at every opportunity.

As the frequency of Ms. Nguyet's visits increased, Vien's frustration grew into anger, then outright hostility. "Oh, here comes that freeloading harlot again. She had better not expect me to wait on her hand and foot," Vien would say to anyone nearby, loud enough for Ms. Nguyet to hear, but not my father.

Vien was from a poor peasant family and did not know how to suppress or express her fury. She was fiercely territorial and lacked the subtleties that were expected of a woman at the time. The more aggressively she pursued Father, the more he sought refuge in Ms. Nguyet's soothing companionship. Vexed, Vien screamed, cussed, and vented her anger by being rough with the baby. Eventually, things reached a climax after Ms. Nguyet spent five consecutive nights at the house.

The moment Ms. Nguyet left, Vien confronted Father as she served his breakfast. She poured his tea and announced, "Mr. Hao, I cannot work in these conditions anymore."

"What conditions would those be?" said Father. I could tell by his tone that Father was irked that Vien was not educated enough to know that mealtime was never the appropriate time for a row.

"Ms. Nguyet is a bad influence on the children," said Vien.

Hung and Hong ate their chicken rice porridge, oblivious to the adults' undercurrents. Tan and I glanced at each other, but didn't dare say a word. Vien's claim wasn't true on two counts: First, the inn was full of prostitutes. Second, Ms. Nguyet always sequestered herself in Father's room with the opium as soon as she arrived at the house, especially after Vien began baring her claws.

"The children are fine. You shouldn't worry about them," he said, reaching for his tea.

"Well, I refuse to work like this. Either Ms. Nguyet stops coming here, or I quit. I can easily find better employment elsewhere!"

Sighing, Father put down his teacup and canted his head in contemplation. There was much tension in the house, and yet he would have preferred to do nothing. It was his character. He never acted unless forced—as Vien was doing then.

The longer he took to reply, the smugger Vien looked. She thought she had trumped him. If Ms. Nguyet were banished from the house, it was only a matter of time before Vien would become his wife—a disastrous scenario. My mother had been a quiet woman. I had never heard her yell or speak harshly to anyone—servant or stranger. I shuddered at the thought of a loud, brassy stepmother like Vien controlling my life.

Father nodded and said, "Ms. Vien, you have been a wonderful nursemaid for my daughter. I appreciate everything you've done, and obviously, you've made up your mind so it wouldn't be fair for me to keep you any longer. You have every right to seek better employment elsewhere. Naturally, I will include a good bonus with your severance pay."

□   □   □

□   □   □

WITH Vien's departure, the household came under a peaceful spell. Father found another nanny for the baby. Our business was doing well. Tan and I proved ourselves capable managers. Carefree, Father eased deeply beneath the opiate currents with Ms. Nguyet at his side. It was perhaps the happiest period of his addiction. They slept, made love, smoked opium, dreamed, ate, and chatted in uneven, looping hours. Their curtains were drawn against both the sun and the moon. Time was not their concern. Servants brought them all they required. For months, ages really, they led a serene, almost connubial life, enwrapped and enraptured by each other. Day and night, they curled around the warmth of the yellow flame, the opium between them as precious as a child.

UNCLE Tao, who often smoked opium at our house, saw that—short of a miracle or his own intervention—Ms. Nguyet would become Father's next wife. Knowing Father's passive nature and Ms. Nguyet's background, he feared that the woman would seize our family business and mistreat his nephews and niece. It was clear to him that our chances of being in financial ruin were real and significant.

At one of their opium sessions, Uncle said, "Nguyet wants to marry you. She's after your money."

They were coming out of the reverie from the first round of opium. It was the usual period when they liked to talk. Father was lying on his side. He smiled. "Do you know any woman who doesn't want money?"

"But this one is a devious professional. Sooner or later she will give your money to a younger lover."

"Any wife can cheat on you if you cannot satisfy her needs."

"But the chance of adultery is higher with *co dau* than with a virgin wife."

"I know, that's why I paid her for every visit, even though she refused the money."

"That's not the point. If you keep letting her come frequently like this, one day you'll wake up and decide that you want her around permanently. You won't be able to stand the thought of her serving other men."

"I know you're right, but I need a companion."

"A woman like her won't raise your children well. You must find a woman to marry quickly or you'll fall into her trap. Isn't there anyone you fancy?"

"The butcher across the street has a very nice daughter."

"Oh, heaven! That beauty queen is far out of your reach! Besides, even though he's only a butcher, he won't ever let her marry an addict like you no matter how big a dowry you offer."

"Ah! You see my problem? No one wants an addict with four children, and I don't have the energy to look for another woman."

Uncle Tao chuckled. "You're a hungry man who can't be bothered to cook."

"And I'm a finicky eater too!"

They laughed. Uncle Tao promised to help him find a suitable wife.

AN old and wily politician, Uncle Tao had numerous friends and acquaintances in Hanoi. Like most successful public figures, he had a knack with people and understood them. Being a heavy opium user himself, he knew Father needed a young obedient wife raised with traditional values, who would not have the temerity to question Father's ever-deepening addiction. She must be prepared to work diligently as a wife. In other words, she must be a traditional Vietnamese mother who was willing to sacrifice herself for her children and family.

A few weeks later, Uncle Tao introduced Father to Mr. Cuong, who had a daughter of marriageable age. Mr. Cuong was a former

magistrate of a small domain in Hung Yen and enjoyed a good reputation as an honest and fair man. Traditional in every way like the
mandarins of his generation, he had married three wives, one after
the other, when they failed to give him a son. His third wife finally
produced a male heir and thus kept him from taking a fourth.

Father, who was thirty-five years old, decided on Mr. Cuong's
eldest daughter, a sweet, petite girl of twenty-one. At the time, the
age difference was not unusual for second marriages, so Uncle Tao
made the proposal to the girl's father. Mr. Cuong agreed, seeing that
the suitor, though not young, was a man of means and could provide
for his daughter. The girl, whose name was Sanh, met with my father and, with her parents' encouragement, found him acceptable.
Arrangements were made quickly and they were married within two
months of setting eyes on each other.

Father now had a young wife to look after the household, and I
had a stepmother, a wonderful and kindhearted woman only three
years older than me. She asked us children to call her "Auntie" and
adamantly refused to let us address her as "Mother," saying that she
was too young for that title. The following year, she gave birth to a
baby boy, Father's fourth son. Selfless, industrious, and cheerful, she
became the pillar of our family.

32. THE CAPTURE

After a frantic night of preparations, we drove out of Saigon at daybreak on May 2, in my in-laws' Volkswagen Beetle. It was a very tight fit with four adults and seven children. Uncle Khanh was driving. I was in the passenger seat with my two sons, An and Huy, on my lap. Our wives shared the cramped backseat with Tien and Hien, and Khanh's two young daughters. With our reluctant blessings, our daughter Chi had opted to stay behind with her grandmother.

On the surface, life in Saigon had returned to near normal within two days of "The Liberation." The residential streets were peaceful and quiet. Army uniforms, file cabinets, and debris left by refugees had been pushed into piles on the curbs. On the major avenues, most shops reopened for business as usual. The restaurants, however, had a booming trade. Fear did wonders for the appetite. People packed the noodle shops and dumpling diners, wolfing down meals as though they had just emerged from a fast. Rumors circulated that there were no block-ades on the roads.

The conquerors were busy. They made no new laws or declarations regarding travel restrictions. High-ranking officers were availing themselves of the empty mansions and the clubs of the deposed elites. The victorious army that had paraded into Saigon two days before had settled into makeshift camps in the city parks and at the government buildings. They kept a surprisingly low profile. Their green uniforms had a camouflaging effect, blending them with the trees and bushes in the parks. If I hadn't been looking, I wouldn't have noticed them lounging in hammocks and cooking over camp-fires in the middle of the city.

They kept themselves largely out of sight, leaving the local paramilitary units to control the streets. I was very impressed with the Communists' discipline. There was no pillaging, commotion, or any type of public disturbance. The soldiers didn't wander the city, celebrating their victory. I would have been awestruck if I had known that they had endured unimaginable hardships during the war. Later, I would learn that many of them didn't even know how to use a flush toilet, and that some high-ranking cadres had never seen a color television.

Saigon felt almost serene. Some refugees began leaving the city to go home. Traffic was very light. Like us, many were looking for an escape route. Some headed to the nearest coastal cities of Vung Tau and Phan Thiet. Our destination was at the very southern end of the country, a coastal town called Rach Gia near the Cambodian border. Uncle Khanh claimed he had a contact there.

Uncle Khanh was actually twelve years younger than me, but since he married Aunt Han, my stepmother's younger sister, I was stuck calling him "Uncle," which at first made both of us a bit un-comfortable. Although Uncle Khanh was an army colonel, he wasn't rich. His assignments in the Special Forces kept him on the front line for the length of his service, so he was the poorest colonel I knew. He had this Volkswagen Beetle and a modest house. His parents were southerners and lived in the same alley as my father. They worked out of their home as bamboo-screen weavers. Most nights, they could be found sipping beer, playing guitar, and singing *vong co* in front of their house. In every respect, they were the same as their working-class neighbors who were enthusiastically cheering the Viet Cong as victors in an unwanted war. But Uncle Khanh had served in the South's army, and now he was on the run like me while his family in Saigon waited fearfully for the Viet Cong's retribution that would surely come.

We'd barely cleared the outskirts of Saigon when the left rear tire went flat. The women and children sat on the side of the road while Uncle Khanh and I changed the tire with the spare. Sensing the adults' mood, the children became very quiet. Anh and Aunt Han were talking fiercely.

Aunt Han finally said what was on everyone's mind: "This is a bad omen. We're not even an hour from the city."

"Do you want to turn back?" I asked her. She looked at Uncle Khanh.

He shook his head. "If we turn back, we'll be caught at home sooner or later. If we push on, there's at least a chance we can get out of the country before they tighten their border control."

I said, "Uncle Khanh, are you sure your friend can find a boat with a good skipper?"

"I've known him five years. He was one of my best commandos."

Without Anh and me, Uncle Khanh and his wife couldn't afford to buy the boat. It was risky, but it was all we had. Looking at the dozens of middle-class cars going our way, I figured we weren't the only ones with this plan.

I took Anh's hands and looked into her eyes to let her know I would do whatever she wanted. Anh wouldn't be here if I hadn't been in the army. She closed her eyes a moment and took a breath to gather the courage to go against an omen. She nodded.

□ □ □

□ □ □

RACH Gia at dusk looked like a beached fishing trawler, barnacled underbelly exposed, rigging askew, and spilling bilge muck. It was an unsettling sight that hurried us into the nearest hotel by the city square. We took two rooms, but were afraid to leave our money in the hotel. We stuffed our gold, cash, and jewelry into home-made bandoliers and wore them underneath our clothing. The streets were dark and a smell of smoke was in the air. We walked to a restaurant half a block down the street. During dinner, there was some commotion in the street. Down at the fisherman's wharf, a gunfight broke out between the local VC regiment and some South Vietnam officers in civilian clothes trying to board a ship. A South Vietnam major was killed, his men captured. We retreated to our rooms. Uncle Khanh's contact would have to wait for morning.

At 2:00 A.M., Anh woke me and said, "I had a dream. The Viet Cong came to our room and arrested us."

Drowsy, I didn't understand what she was trying to say. "They came to our house?"

"Not the house. Here in this room!" she exclaimed. "They jailed us."

I shot out of bed. Anh often had uncanny premonitions. There was nothing we could do except hide our gold and cash. Leaving the hotel at this hour would surely get us shot. We woke Uncle Khanh and his wife and told them to hide their money.

A Viet Cong patrol came to the hotel within the hour and began searching. We stood with the children in the corridor while they ransacked the rooms. They missed the gold and money hidden among the children's clothing. They were looking for weapons and ammunition and said that out-of-towners had been seen in a restaurant nearby wearing bandoliers of ammunition hidden under their clothing. It was possible that someone had mistaken our gold belts for ammo.

Around five in the morning, a car with loudspeakers circled the town, announcing that the government had declared martial law and ordered all non-residents of Rach Gia to leave the city and go home. Hopes dashed, we left for Saigon at dawn, not suspecting any deception.

The previous day, the checkpoint right before Rach Gia only had a couple of guards who waved us through without a word. Today, it was staffed with many soldiers in PAFL uniform and civilians with red armbands. They signaled for us to stop. Two other cars had stopped in front of us, the occupants sitting on the side of the road with their luggage. Civilians with red armbands were searching the luggage. A man told us to step out of the car. He collected our identity cards, saying that they were looking for soldiers of Thieu's regime with concealed weapons because those "traitors" still did not see the revolutionary light and refused to surrender.

Uncle Khanh kept saying that we should be fine because we didn't have any weapons. I didn't reply, but I thought we were certainly in trouble. Aunt Han and Anh were busy looking after the children. My son An was old enough to sense something wrong, but the other young ones started chasing each other around the car and going over to look at the two cars stopped in front of us.

The guerillas frisked us and then searched our belongings. I was impressed with their discipline. They found wristwatches, cash, and jewelry in our luggage, but they did not take anything. After about half an hour of searching without finding weapons, they told us they must take us back to the city to wait for orders from their superiors. Some very young men with AK-47s rode motorcycles to escort us back to Rach Gia along with the two other civilian cars.

It was clear then that we were under arrest. Whoever engineered the capture was very devious. Arresting all the out-of-towners last night would have caused considerable commotion. Some might have escaped. But today, by ordering non-residents to leave Rach Gia, they netted everyone since there was only one road out of the city. Catching people at the checkpoint was clean and efficient.

"Why did you leave dollars in the open?" Aunt Han asked Anh right after we got in the car. "They must have arrested us because of the money! They probably don't know that people could buy U.S. dollars on the black market in Saigon. They could charge us for being spies!"

"I'm sorry. They must have fallen out from one of the pants," Anh replied, feeling guilty. She had sewn several small clips of U.S. $100 bills into the children's clothes. Somehow one clip fell out in the search. We didn't know at the time that all non-residents of Rach Gia who tried to leave the city that day were arrested.

"What should we tell them?" Uncle Khanh asked.

"Tell them we were returning to Saigon because we heard there was no more fighting," I said.

"But they will say there was no fighting when we left Saigon."

"They don't know when we left."

"They could ask us to prove when we arrived here and where we stayed."

"In this chaos, they won't have the time to check what we say. I think if we take the chance and if they believe us they may let us go."

"If they believe us." Uncle Khanh was skeptical.

His face was taking on a sick pallor. Beads of sweat trickled down from his forehead. He was terrified for good reasons. As a former high-ranking army officer in the Special Forces, he could certainly expect serious punishment if caught. Seeing him in distress made me think about my own situation, which, in fact, was worse. I had worked for USAID, a well-known front for the CIA. It would not matter to the Communists that I was drafted.

"Maybe we should not tell them that we are related," Aunt Han said. I knew she was afraid the Communists might suspect that she and her husband were American collaborators like us. We had U.S. currency. Normal people working for the Americans were not paid with U.S. dollars.

"Yes, that's a good idea. Maybe we should say we gave you a ride," Uncle Khanh said. I was disappointed to hear him say that.

Even if he claimed he gave us a ride to make some cash, the Communists would not believe him.

"That's fine with me." I said quietly, trying to hide my annoyance. Anh was not argumentative. She rarely expressed her thoughts, but I knew she was disappointed too. A heavy silence fell on all of us. The fear and tension in our car was so palpable the children became very quiet, no longer laughing and playing like this morning when they thought we were going home.

As we re-entered Rach Gia, the lead escort turned down a side street.

"They are not taking us to the town hall!" Uncle Khanh cried.

His wife gasped, "Are they going to torture us?"

Our convoy turned toward the gate of a huge compound enclosed by walls and barbed wire. There was a sign at the gate: RACH GIA CITY PRISON. My heart jumped in my chest. Uncle Khanh slowed the car. I could tell he wanted to flee, but there was no escape.

"This is a prison!" Aunt Han wailed.

The escort had us park next to a dozen other civilian cars and ordered us to leave everything in the car. Anh and Aunt Han begged them to let us take some belongings, pointing out that our little children needed clothes and food. The escorts relented and they were able to pack a small bag for each of the adults. Khanh locked his precious Beetle, still thinking that we would be released soon. I did not realize that we would never see the car again and that our fifteen years of hard work and savings were forever lost to the VC. Almost our entire fortune, stacks of gold leaves, lay hidden in the door frame of the Volkswagen.

IT was a typical small-town prison, a compound of four long, single-story buildings forming a square and enclosing a large courtyard. The main entrance had a thick iron door. In the courtyard, a crowd of about two hundred sat, guarded by fifteen guerrillas and civilians with red armbands. We were told to sit and wait. The escort gave our identity cards to a clerk.

At first, the crowd reminded me of the refugees that flooded Saigon the past month. They had small bags and luggage by their sides, babies crying in their arms. Their children ran around playfully, oblivious to the situation. But instead of fatigue and sadness, I saw fear. An ominous air hung over them. They gathered in family units and whispered among themselves. Some glanced at us when we sat down next to them, but they didn't say a word or even give a signal of acknowledgment. Everyone was waiting his turn to be called into the gazebo at the center of the courtyard to fill out some sort of declaration form.

Since we got inside, Uncle Khanh and Aunt Han really seemed to want to distance themselves. They did not converse with us or even look our way. The four of us sat in silence. I glanced at Anh and knew she felt very uncomfortable, but she didn't complain. I was miserable because I had brought her into this predicament. Why wasn't I wise enough to see the risks in Uncle Khanh's idea of finding a boat through his contact? Anh wanted to go because she was worried for my safety under the Communist regime. She knew that her Uncle Ha, a high-level Communist official, would keep her and our children out of harm's way. Although my grandmother-in-law had not seen her son for more than twenty years, she could make Uncle Ha protect Anh and our children at any cost. I was angry with myself. My bad decision had pulled Anh into this ordeal. Even if Anh got out of here, we had just lost a major part of our savings. How could she survive and raise our children in the difficult years ahead?

Our turn did not come until sunset. There was barely enough light to fill out our declaration forms. We were not allowed to talk. Although the Communists had been telling us all day over the loudspeaker that the more truthful and complete we were in our declarations the sooner we would be released, I did not trust them. Judging from the number of detainees that day in the courtyard, I figured they had at least five hundred forms to review. And they would likely have many more in the coming days. I became very depressed. This could be the end for me.

Once we finished with the forms, they immediately took us to our cells. They put Anh and Aunt Han in the two wards reserved for women and children. Uncle Khanh and I went to two different wards reserved for men. He was in one on the right-hand side. I was in the one at the back facing the front of the compound.

My cell was a single large room, roughly 30 feet wide and 140 feet long. At one end of the room was an open washing area equipped with only one squat toilet and a cement tank filled by a single faucet. The person using the toilet had to hold up a sheet of newspaper for a modesty screen. A bank of small windows with iron bars lined the inner wall above head height. To look outside, one had to jump up and grab hold of the bars. During the day, they opened the outer sheet-metal door to air out the cell. Twice a day, guards passed food through the inner door's iron bars: mildewed rice and a foul broth that gave everyone diarrhea.

As one of the first inmates, I was able to pick a spot on a raised cement platform far away from the toilet. Our captors had arrested so many people that they didn't even have time to search our bodies. All they did was take our names, then incarcerate us. With only the clothes on my back and a money belt lined with thin gold leaves hidden beneath my trousers, I took off my shirt and laid it down on the floor to mark my place.

My neighbors were a young man in his late twenties and another man my age, both of them northerners. I could tell they were of the middle class by their mannerisms and speech, which was a relief since it was unlikely that they were spies planted among the inmates to gather information. Tong was a twenty-six-year-old ARVN sergeant who had fled Saigon with his wife, whose family was from Rach Gia. Bang was a forty-year-old police officer. His wife had a gold shop in Phu Nhuan, a lower-middle-class district in Saigon, midway between downtown and Tan Son Nhat Airport. Like me, they were banking on finding a boat to escape.

The jailhouse quickly filled with detainees. The Communists were sweeping the entire province for anyone they deemed loyal to the former regime. They didn't assign us numbers for identification and didn't call us "prisoners" or "inmates." They called us traitors. "Traitors come to the cell door." "Traitors eat." "Traitors shut up."

WITHIN days, the huge room became crowded with traitors. At night when we lay down to sleep, it was impossible to walk across the room to the toilet without stepping on bodies. There was not even space to hang-dry our clothes, so despite the mosquitoes, we wore only undershorts. We slept next to each other, cramped, a jumble of elbows and knees. We exercised by standing up and sitting down.

As I had feared, an announcement finally came over the loudspeakers: "Attention all traitors: You now have a chance to confess your crimes against the country. You will be judged on your honesty. You are to write down every detail of your life, jobs, family, and background. Any inaccuracies will be considered an attempt to deceive the liberation government and you will be severely punished. If you lie, you will be executed."

They brought us outside a few at a time, sat us down at the rows of tables, and handed out pencils and booklets of paper. I pretended to scribble for the benefit of the moles among us, but I couldn't write a word. I couldn't bring myself to reveal my service record, but I was equally afraid of being caught in a lie. What came to my mind most clearly was Vi, the orphan who became my adopted brother. He had said that there was no forgiveness in the Communists' canon.

If they knew my background, they would have executed me already. Ironically, if I had been caught in Phan Thiet, the neighborhood informants would have promptly exposed me. In Rach Gia,

I had the singular advantage of anonymity although I did not know how long that would have lasted.

I suspected three things: First, the VC had no qualms about executing anyone they deemed guilty. Second, they gave no honor to their enemies, so in their minds, promises made to prisoners were meaningless. Third, I had never heard of Viet Cong showing mercy to those they could not brainwash.

I wrote that I was merely a high school teacher who was exempted from the draft.

THE following day, we were given another chance to write down our crimes against the country. They repeated this tactic several times, trying to find discrepancies in our confessions. During the first week, they held public trials and executions in the town's market square.

I'm a teacher. I'm a teacher, I insisted unvaryingly in my tablet.

I was a high-stakes gambler at a roulette table, the little white ball going round and round. In a room so crowded, you couldn't move two feet in any direction without touching someone, yet I felt utterly alone. My secret settled in my stomach, as indigestible as a rock.

AFTER a few weeks, they started releasing the women and children. When Anh got out, I felt my chances of survival increased significantly. She walked out of the prison gate and went directly to the market. With the money she had sewn into the lining of her pants, she bought food, medicine, a straw mat, and toiletries, and then came right back to the prison. She brought me the first of many supply packages that kept me from succumbing to illness. The next day she took the kids back to Saigon and began the long, arduous bid to secure my release.

In the coming months, Anh would spend most of her energy riding buses back to Rach Gia from Saigon—which was now renamed

Ho Chi Minh City—to visit me and bring the necessities that kept me alive. The new regime issued drastic curfews and travel restrictions that even limited movement between neighboring districts. The simple act of going from one province to another now required permits from several offices. A prospective traveler must first bribe himself through a labyrinth of bureaucracy before queuing for hours to buy a ticket on an overcrowded bus.

With my son An, Anh braved the round-trip journey once every two weeks. From Saigon, it took two ferry crossings of the Mekong River and ten hot, dusty hours on a rickety bus packed to the ceiling with people, produce, and livestock.

In Rach Gia, most hotels and guesthouses had either been ordered to close or simply shut their doors due to the lack of business. Anh stayed for days at the home of a sympathetic woman whose husband was also imprisoned for being drafted into the South Vietnam army. The jailers allowed supply packages, but did not permit prisoners to have visitors. Still, she came to see me without fail, bringing me food and medicine. Knowing that there were hard times ahead, she had scoured the city and bought huge quantities of pharmaceuticals: painkillers, aspirin, anti-diarrhea pills, quinine, ointments, and antibiotics. Without her, I would not have survived.

My strength was ebbing. An overpowering lethargy pressed down on me. My face developed a strange puffiness. My legs swelled up and became heavy. I lost the enamel on my teeth. Near the gums, my teeth blackened. I could wiggle the incisors with my tongue. My whole mouth ached when I ate something hot or cold. I didn't know it at the time, but I was in the early stage of a disease brought on by severe vitamin deficiency.

Many other inmates were in worse condition. At the peak of incarceration, the Viet Cong kept more than a thousand men in the prison, packing people into all four buildings until there was no space left to walk. We were kept like diseased beasts waiting for slaughter, unworthy of the least measure of compassion. We lay on bare concrete. The reek of feces and urine from the clogged toilet was unbearable. The mosquitoes feasted on our flesh. It was so crowded in the cell that we couldn't hang mosquito nets even if we had them. Lice were everywhere—in our clothes, hair, armpits, and crotches. The itching bites and rashes were enough to a drive a man mad. I chewed my nails to the nub to keep from clawing my skin to shreds. In here, a simple infection could lead to gangrene or an agonizing death.

Once a week, they let us outside for ten minutes to bathe and wash our clothes at the large cement cistern in the middle of the prison. It was such a relief to cleanse the grime from my skin that I sometimes forgot what a pitiful sight we were—dozens of pale, withered men in their boxer shorts frantically soaping themselves and scooping water with their rice bowls under the scrutiny of armed guards.

PRISON was the cruelest of man's inventions. Within the walls, the days stood still. We played games and made up trivia quizzes. We invented dozens of little devices to ease our suffering— the best of which was a candle stove made from a Guigoz tin, a can of baby food powder.

Mostly, we filled the emptiness with words. We talked, knowing well that there were moles among us. We could not help ourselves. We talked because infinity didn't span centuries, it lay within each second.

I shared my dreams for the future, the fine food I would eat with my family, the vacations we might take, and the bungalow I'd like to build by the sea. In my mind, I had sealed off my past. I never talked about my childhood. I did not give a single hint of military knowledge. So I became the ardent listener, casting myself as a silent character in the lives of other inmates and losing myself in their past dramas.

But reality returned every evening after dinner. The loudspeakers came on and called out the names of those who would face judgment. A stage had been rigged right outside the prison for the public trials and denouncements of traitors—a ghoulish entertainment.

When it was over, someone would strike the first match. The tiny flare of the flame brought us out from the darkness. We stirred as if the light were a confirmation of our existence. Each man fussed over his own Guigoz to boil some water for coffee or tea. It helped to be busy. It helped to have some caffeine and sugar in the blood to brace the spirit.

In the flickering candlelight of hundreds of Guigoz stoves, the names of those who had just vanished from our midst were never spoken.

POOR Uncle Khanh, a leader of men and a man of his word, believed the Viet Cong's promises. He confessed, and they sent him to a reeducation camp in the north. His service in the Special Forces bought him ten years of gathering human waste from the latrines and fields to make fertilizer. They forced him to use his bare hands to scoop up the excrement and refused him soap to remove the stink. He buried his hands in the mud banks, crushed leaves in his palms, and scoured them with pebbles in the creek until they bled. The reek of feces could not be banished. He could not bear to touch himself with those hands, even to bathe. Without utensils, he ate food off his plate like a dog.

IN another building at the prison was Gia, one of my colleagues from Phan Boi Chau High School in Phan Thiet. He was a nice fellow from a good family who had once been madly in love with my sister Huong. He had wooed her for three years without success. Drafted into the army, Gia served several years as a lieutenant in the logistics department in Saigon before his decommission in 1972. With his harmless, non-combatant background, Gia thought they would not consider him an enemy of the country. He confessed his rank and army service. They rewarded him with years of hard labor in the mangrove swamp—a disease-infested cesspit so vile half the prisoners did not survive their term.

□   □   □

ONE by one, my cellmates were called away by the loudspeakers, each leaving behind a few items of clothing, sandals, toothbrush, candles, and a Guigoz stove. These bits and pieces were all that was left of them. Those of us who remained dared not use their belongings for fear of inheriting the same bad luck. Next to the toilet, a pile of goods collected like bones.

I REMEMBERED how, in my impassioned youth, my heart had swelled with pride at the sight of brown pajama–clad fighters, our brave young men and women—*our Resistance*—coming to my family's estate for supplies. How thrilled I had been when they defeated the Algerian Mohammed and drove the French from our land. How I had wanted so desperately to join our Resistance, to fight injustice, to strike back at the oppressors. I would have become a part of this.

Do the ends truly justify the means?

And to what ends had we arrived?

They had won the war, the populace, and the country in its entirety. This was barbaric. This was ridiculously vindictive. It was all so senseless.

MY time came after sixty-five days of confinement. Dawn brought smoky clouds. A drizzle haunted the long afternoon, fading at twilight. The loudspeakers screeched to life and began calling out names. Pham Van Thong. I heard it as clearly as I had heard it in my nightmares.

I put on my slacks and shirt, the same garments I had last worn as a free man. Everything else I left behind: my extra clothes, straw mat, food supplies, toothbrush, toothpaste, even my precious Guigoz stove. And there against the wall, rolled up in my ragged undershirt, a small fortune in gold.

I had thought I would be terrified. I had expected to soil myself or vomit or scream. But when they came for me, I wasn't afraid. Perhaps I was beyond fear. There was only an overwhelming sense of sadness that I would never see my wife and children again.

A numbing emptiness calmed my limbs. I did not think of my father, my siblings, or anything else. I did not think about whether the execution bullet would be painful or whether death, in its ultimate mercy, would come quickly. I did not think about where my soul would go, or if a heaven existed beyond this hell.

The sky was dark, starless, the air scented with deep, heavy earth. I felt a piercing love for my dearest ones. It did not occur to me to say a prayer.

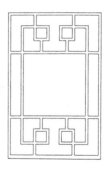

33. THE PEASANT GIRL

There were three rules to managing a French whore-house.

First, never say no to a soldier.

Second, never challenge a soldier.

Third, never fall for a girl who went with soldiers.

Mai first came to sit outside our inn late in the final colonial winter. I saw her on a stormy afternoon, coming home from school. She was huddling alone beneath the awning of the beverage kiosk; her blue dress, drenched from the waist down, clung to her legs. In the pale, bent light, she seemed half melted into the puddle at her feet. It was a striking image and I couldn't help but ask her permission to take a picture. Photography was my new hobby.

She said no, but smiled, pleased.

We stood under the drumming rain. Then I blurted, "Miss, please come inside. You'll catch a cold out here."

"Thank you. I'm fine here." She smiled.

She was soaked and shivering, purple-lipped from

the cold. Her fine black hair lay matted across her forehead like a wet silk scarf, the wind lashing droplets onto her face. It wasn't going to ease. This was the middle of the wet season. I smiled. She looked confused when I made no attempt to go.

"I'm fine, thank you," she insisted through chattering teeth.

I held my umbrella closer to her. I couldn't leave her standing in the miserable January rain. It was the sort of cold that bored into one's chest to dwell. She must be new. Most girls didn't bother waiting for clients in this bad weather.

"Miss, would you like a cup of tea?"

"No, thank you."

"It's very cold out here, if you ask me," I said.

"At home, we worked the paddies in weather worse than this. We just got used to being wet the whole season. At home, this would be just an afternoon shower."

"Around here, people accept a cup of tea when offered."

Old man Nghi lifted the rain flap of his kiosk and cried, "For heaven's sake, go sit in the inn, you silly girl! It's going to rain through the night. I want to close shop and go home. Quickly, quickly, before both of you catch an ill wind."

She stood up and smiled awkwardly.

The afternoon passed with jasmine tea and biscuits in the lounge. The inn was nearly empty. We sat cozily on the sofas as though it was a normal social visit. Wrapped in blankets, she was an ordinary peasant girl. The rain had washed off her makeup. There was no perfume on her. Mai had weathered farm hands and big brown eyes like giant longan seeds. She had perfect doll-like lips. In from the cold, her cheeks turned rosy like freshly steamed dumplings. When she giggled, her eyes went squinty. She was a country girl. Emotions lit up her face like primary colors. Her expressions were untutored, somehow still uncorrupted. It was like talking to a girl from my village.

Mai's sharecropping family had lived in one of the villages recently ravaged by the fighting. Her father and older brother had been killed while working in the paddies. Separated from relatives on the other side of the front, her mother had fled with Mai and her younger sister into Hanoi. They had lost everything. Her story was not so different from the hundreds of girls working these streets, but Mai was unique. She seemed unaware of her beauty, and she loved books.

I was the only reader in my family and had a whole library to loan.

WHEN we first opened the inn three years prior, a group of six girls and two pimps came and sat at the beverage kiosk in front of our place. There was one tall stunning girl from Ninh Binh named Ly with shiny river-stone eyes. She was eighteen and had the sort of striking looks that in peacetime would have made her a star of the stage regardless of talent. Tan and I were sixteen then and smitten. We vied for her attention, not caring that we were making fools of ourselves. We behaved like silly pups, so Cung, our inn gofer, took it upon himself to free us from our romantic notions.

At the time, Cung was a lanky seventeen-year-old. He was an orphan from Hai Phong. Sharp and street-smart, he came and asked for a job a week before we hung up the inn sign. Father hired him out of pity, and Cung soon showed that he had a talent for communicating with the soldiers and placating the drunks. Within weeks, Cung made himself indispensable. He became intimately familiar with the running of the inn. While Tan never talked casually with the soldiers, and I avoided all but the nice ones, Cung was everyone's friend and confidant, from the French regulars to the North African legionnaires, to the sub-Saharan legionnaires, to the girls and their pimps.

One day Cung said he had a surprise for us. He led us upstairs to the linen closet at the rear of the villa, put a finger to his lips, and winked. The hallway was empty. Cung unlocked the door, and we crowded into the five-by-six-foot room. It was pitch-dark and stuffy, reeking of cleaning solvents. Muffled noises from the next room came through the wall. Cung struck a match. Tan was grinning excitedly. Cung reached for a small wooden dowel jammed into the wall and then smiled at us. We bobbed our heads vigorously. He blew out the match and removed the dowel. A thin finger of light passed through a hole in the wall. Cung peered into the opening and sighed with pleasure. Illuminated, his eyeball looked like it was floating in space.

Tan was next. He stayed glued to the peephole until I shoved him aside. Ly was in the next room. I felt a distinct sharp pain in my chest. It was the first time I saw a naked woman. The legionnaire was behind her, rising above the pale sweep of her back like a dark shadow. Pain twisted her features. His grunts passed right through the wall. Suddenly, I could discern—and understood—the vibration I felt through the floor.

Somehow, any virginal idea I had about sex was destroyed at that moment. Here, a few feet away from me, was an act of depraved needs, of desperation—a sort of carnage as horrible as the Algerian raping the women in our village.

Cung's breath was hot in my ear. He whispered, "It's shocking at first, but once you get used to it, it's the best show in the city."

With the strand of light between us, I could see Cung grinning, nodding, enthusiastically proud of the hole he had drilled in the wall. I felt robbed, betrayed, soiled. At that instant, I loathed him profoundly.

Tan and I turned away. We left Cung in his peeping closet. Tan and I never talked about what we saw, but neither of us could look Ly in the eyes again.

Our ways parted from Cung's after that day. For him, it was the beginning of a headlong dive into gambling, whoring, drinking, and smoking opium.

MAI didn't wait outside our inn again. There were dozens, if not hundreds, of other places in the city, and I didn't ask where she worked. But she did visit me every few days to return a book and borrow another. She had her pride and would not accept gifts.

We wandered the city's lakes and picnicked on little pâté baguettes sold from pushcarts. We discovered a common passion for food. She allowed me to take her to my favorite ice cream shop. I introduced her to chocolate ice cream, peach melba, and crème fraîche. We spent many misty, languorous mornings at the waterfront cafés listening to Johnny Mathis. We chose places without foreigners. She never talked about how she spent her days or nights; I never talked about our inn.

Mai dreamed of becoming a teacher. Extremely bright, her mind leapt from topic to topic with ease. Although her family could not afford to give her more than a primary education, Mai had continued to study on her own. She hadn't given up, even in her current situation. Each time we met, she had a list of questions for me. I never had to explain anything twice. We slipped into the roles of tutor and pupil. It was a constructive charade that created a space where there was no pain, no history, and no expectation, as if on some unspoken level we understood or agreed that this was all we were allowed: a stroll around the lake in the pearly drizzle, a poem read on a park bench, a moment of early morning stillness sitting side by side.

AFTER his second marriage, Father slipped deeply into his familiar opium currents, content with his new wife. And he found that she was, indeed, a good woman, competent with her household duties and raising his younger children. He left Tan and me to manage the inn and its staff of five workers. With his inattention, Tan and I had access to as much spending money as we wanted. We went to cinemas, boxing matches, soccer games, shows, and new restaurants. We went sculling on the lake. On holidays, we cruised the countryside on rented motorcycles. Once, on a whim, we caught a bus out to Hai Phong for our first glimpse of the ocean.

We were young, educated, and eligible. Tan was handsome and powerfully built, like his father. He was confident and could talk to girls with ease. I was tall and fair-skinned, like my father. Academically, I was at the top of my class, which in the competitive French system had a certain prestige. We could have courted pretty girls from good families, but we felt unworthy. We were ashamed of our family's business, and couldn't imagine how we would explain it to girls' parents. We ran a modest inn, but the soldiers had turned it into a whorehouse. There was no polite way around it, and no way of denying the ugliness that pervaded everything.

It was very difficult for Tan. Since childhood, Tan was raised to succeed his father as head of our clan and magistrate of the domain. Serving thugs and mercenaries was demeaning work. At the inn, Tan never smiled, joked, or chatted with the guests. He became obsessed with bodybuilding and fashioned himself a fierce image to ward off any friendly overtures from the soldiers. Tan never said it, but I knew he resented Father for getting involved in such a lowly industry, unbefitting of our station.

"I hate this business. We shouldn't be here. We should be out there!" Tan told me late one night as we cleaned up the bar. There had been a brawl between French regulars and African legionnaires, and we had to call the French military police. The place was a wreck. "We should be shooting these bastards instead of serving them!"

I was fed up with the inn as well. It was ridiculous trying to keep full-grown men from smashing each other to bits. I said, "Maybe we should have joined Hoi's group."

"I'll fight the French, but I'd never join those treacherous Viet Minh," Tan growled.

Neither of us could stomach fighting on the side that had murdered his father, Uncle Uc, and my cousin Quyen. But if we were in Tong Xuyen now, we would have been drafted into the Resistance. Aunt Thao sent news from home that there were only children and old people left to work the fields. No boy or girl over fourteen years old remained in the village. Anyone capable of carrying a gun had been drafted. They were all gone—all our schoolmates, boys and girls, even poor Chau, the estate's buffalo boy.

"It's terrible that the Nationalists can't reorganize themselves," I said.

"Forget it!" Tan snapped. "It'll never happen. The Nationalists have turned into a bunch of living-room revolutionaries like your father's friends. They talk themselves silly while Ho Chi Minh outwits them on every front."

I sighed. "True, the Communists assassinated all their best leaders."

The Nationalists had degenerated into a hopeless cause. The Viet Minh, masquerading as the Resistance, was our only option, but Tan and I were infected by our elders' distrust of Ho Chi Minh's brand of Communism, the Viet Minh's deceit, and their political rhetoric. Alternately filled with impotent rage and general apathy, we trusted no one; we couldn't even be proud of our own country. Furthermore, it was impossible to feel very patriotic working in the inn and serving the enemy.

Tan chewed his lower lip. "This war won't last much longer."

Running the inn was like having one's finger on the pulse of the war. For the last several months, French forces had been returning from the front looking ragged and beaten. Their swagger, so prevalent two years ago, was gone. In the bars and clubs catering to foreigners, a sense of agitation had replaced the usual festive air.

As the war crept closer to Hanoi, more troops and refugees moved through the city. Hundreds of wounded soldiers wandered the streets, waiting to be shipped back to France or Africa. Half our guests were convalescing wounded. Even the healthy soldiers on leave were in bad shape. Fear and exhaustion showed plainly in their eyes. They drank and spent money with reckless abandon, making the girls happy and nervous at the same time. The soldiers were more generous, but they also had hotter tempers. Brawls were a daily occurrence at our inn. The French regulars fought with the African legionnaires, one unit against another. Blows were exchanged over the slightest provocation: an attractive girl, a spilled drink, or an insult.

One had to be blind not to see the coming of the end.

THE last time I saw Mai was late in the spring. She hadn't been by to visit in two weeks. I was very busy with school exams and didn't think much of it. That day I was on my way to a friend's house. I almost didn't recognize Mai standing outside a hotel four blocks from ours. I had never seen her with full makeup. She wore a red Chinese dress. She was with three French soldiers. They were laughing, pawing at her. One draped a proprietary arm around Mai, his hand straying down to her buttocks.

I was nineteen and had begun to wish for the ordinary. The cosmopolitan faces of the city, its French villas, bistros, nouvelle gadgets, and fineries, no longer impressed me. I would have given anything for carefree days in the fields, the sun on my face, paddy mud between my toes, a fishing pole in my hand. Perhaps someday I would meet my love somewhere out there on a creekside beneath a full moon. I would serenade her at the Mid-Autumn Festival. I was a man-child, waiting for that first kiss.

It was difficult to breathe. The city had become a vacuum. I pedaled down the wide avenues, gasping. The mist was burning away. Sunlight tumbled between the tree boughs. Strangely, there was a scent of guavas. There were no birds in the branches.

I came to the lake outside the city, dropped my bike on the pier, and climbed into a boat. I put my back into the oars, my legs, arms, my whole body. In mighty strokes, I sculled across the glassy water, gliding to escape velocity. I could not see where I was going, but I saw what I was leaving behind. Marvelous, inexhaustible youth. There was so much of it to burn. Incandescent.

Pull-exhale, glide-inhale; pull-exhale, glide-inhale. Lap after lap after lap. The water could go on forever and it wouldn't be long enough.

Far from every shore, I lay down at the bottom of the boat. Spent, nothing left in my limbs. In the womb of the lake, the world faded away. Above my face, a blue ceiling; lazy, puffy clouds; a caressing breeze. It was like being held. I felt my mother's spirit there at the center of the universe.

34 . REEDUCATION

Tin said, "Surround him. Careful, he's poisonous!"

"The bush!" Tung shouted as the snake slithered toward me.

I slammed my shovel into the ground in front of the snake. It coiled up, hissing.

"Cobra! Cobra!" someone shouted.

Tung and I stepped around to block its retreat into the paddy, our shovels ready. It was more than four feet long and as thick as a man's wrist. Tin had found it under the brambles we were clearing. Within moments, half a dozen other inmates converged to help. There was no way we'd let that much meat escape us.

Tin lured the snake to him with a stick. A machete was poised high over his head. The snake struck at the stick. Tin swung and missed.

I came from behind and pinned the snake with my shovel. It squirmed violently to get loose. Tin brought the machete down and severed its head. The body writhed, flopping and gushing blood.

Tung reached for the snakehead, but Tin batted his hand away. "You don't want to do that. It can still bite and pump you full of poison."

As was the custom, Tin dug a hole, scooped up the snakehead with the shovel, put it in the hole, and filled it with dirt. We all went back to work, grinning. More often than not, we considered ourselves lucky to get mice or frogs. A snake this big meant that there would be a few bites to go around. A year ago, I would never consider tasting the snake meat that was offered as a delicacy in the top Chinese restaurants, but now a cobra looked as tasty as a rope of sausages.

I picked up my shovel and rejoined the crew in the irrigation trench. The sky was blue, the day just beginning to broil. We were outside working in the fresh air, waist-deep in creamy mud. I felt very lucky to be here.

I had thought my life was over when the guards took me from the cell that night in Rach Gia. But instead of putting us on trial as they normally did, they loaded us into a tarp-covered truck bed and drove us out of the city. We had expected to be executed at a mass grave in the woods. The truck bounced over the rutted road for half an hour and delivered us to Minh Luong Reeducation Camp.

Our new home was an old South Vietnam military training site. It was where the Viet Cong kept "low-grade" traitors like South Vietnamese regional soldiers and former low-level officials. Compared to Rach Gia and other prisons where they sent the "high-grade" traitors, Minh Luong was a resort. The doors of our cells were not locked and we were free to move around within the compound. We worked outside daily and had opportunities to scavenge in the fields and streams.

Forgotten diversions of my countryside childhood came back to me. I remembered how to snatch grasshoppers from rice leaves, how to flood crickets from their burrows, how to spear frogs in the ponds. Fellow prisoners taught me how to catch mice, snakes, small fish, and small blue paddy crabs. We picked wild berries, greens, herbs, yams, onions, morning glories, and sour leaves. Some things we pocketed to be cooked later, others we popped in our mouths like candy treats. My favorites were crunchy termites and buttery sparrow eggs.

AT lunch, the guards let us build a little fire. Tin tossed the snake onto the flames. The smell of burnt meat soon drew in the crowd. He gave everyone a small piece. We ate it with our tin of rice.

Tin, Tung, and I sat downwind from a cow grazing the grass on the side of the dirt road. It smelled so sweet and milky that the snake meat tasted just like steak in my mouth. Tung said he could sit here breathing cow-scent all day long. Tin and I laughed at the thought of Tung pining after the cows like a lovesick puppy. Tin and Tung were my two closest friends at Minh Luong. Tung was an army corporal, married with a son. Tin was in his early thirties and single. A recent arrival at Minh Luong, he said he was a government official in Saigon. I suspected he was hiding something because he was very intent on finding a way to escape. He discussed his plans with us, trying to convince us to go with him. Of all his plans only one had any chance of success, but it was such an obvious route that every prisoner already knew about it. I had noticed it my first day inside.

Situated on a rice plain, Minh Luong Camp was enclosed by two layers of barbed-wire fences. The back side of the camp had a creek about three hundred yards from the rear fence. One of our first tasks as inmates was to clear the minefields surrounding the prison, so if a prisoner could get past the fence and stayed unnoticed by the guards, he could reach the creek and float away for miles. It was as clear as an open door. It left me wondering why our jailers hadn't bothered to erect some sort of barrier.

"The ground is very wet and soft. We can dig just enough space to crawl under the fence and then swim down the creek with the current," Tin said quietly. "We would have at least six or seven hours before they mounted a search party."

Tung shook his head. "It's a trap. It's just too easy."

"Do you have someone nearby who can help? You can't go far without money," I said. The new government had issued a new currency.

"I know some people in Rach Gia," Tin said.

Tung was not convinced. "Do you really have to go?"

Tin seemed on the verge of saying something, but thought better of it. I was relieved. I didn't want the responsibility of someone else's secret. We recently heard that the Viet Cong had captured the entire data file of the South Vietnam army, containing hundreds of thousands of personnel service records. Countless men would suffer because the bureaucrats who manned the personnel offices had fled without destroying the files. I had heard two of my team leaders in the RD program had been arrested and executed. I suspected that, like me, Tin had been less than forthright on his confession. It was simply a matter of time before they investigated our service records.

"You know you can't go home. That'll be the first place they look," Tung said.

I nodded. "There's no place to hide. Where can you go?"

The country was practically under martial law. People needed permits to leave their hometowns. Each neighborhood had its own party member representative—and spies who knew every resident.

"Cross the border into Cambodia," said Tung.

I looked at Tin; he had already arrived at this conclusion. He grew up in the countryside and was very resourceful in the wilderness. If anyone had a chance crossing the jungle alive, it was Tin.

He had every reason to flee. If I were Tin, a man without a wife or children, I would have been gone yesterday. He was still healthy and strong, as fresh as I had been six months ago. The longer he waited, the greater the chance he would become one of us sickly inmates.

Life in Minh Luong was harsh. Every day we woke in darkness. They marched us out of the compound to work at the crack of dawn. We cleared minefields, exploded charges, cleared brambles, dug irrigation ditches, and repaired roads. Our first meal of the day came at noon with an hour of rest. We labored until dusk. We had two hours to bathe and eat dinner. Some nights they held trials and sentenced those of us whom they claimed had discrepancies in our confessions. Other nights, they sat us down for three hours of reeducation where a party official lectured us about their battle victories; the struggles of the Vietnamese, first against the French Colonialists and later against the American Imperialists; and the ideals and advances of communism. On special evenings, we watched propaganda movies about VC heroes, battles, Ho Chi Minh, and the success of socialism in Russia and China.

Occasionally, they summoned us from the field, a dozen at a time in the middle of the day, and put us through investigation sessions. We filled out scores of repetitive questionnaires about our family, friends, colleagues, jobs, social views, and political inclinations. We wrote detailed essays on our lives and thoughts. The more we answered, the more precarious our situations became.

"PHAM Van Thong. Come to the door!" the guard shouted.

I jumped, startled. Other prisoners gestured for me to hurry. I came to the door in my boxer shorts. The guard, a young fanatic with an AK-47 slung over his shoulder, stood next to an old man dressed in the ascetic pajama slacks and black cotton jacket of the revolutionaries. I could tell by the deference the guard showed to the stranger that he was a high-ranking party member. The man was in his mid-sixties with hair streaked with white. He was wiry and straight-backed. He had calm eyes.

He introduced himself as my wife's uncle, and I immediately saw the resemblance. Although we had never met, I was well acquainted with my wife's family history. Uncle Ha was my mother-in-law's cousin. During the Great Famine, Anh's entire extended family fled south. When the French came back to Vietnam, Uncle Ha joined the Resistance to fight the French. After the Geneva Accord, he regrouped to the North with the Resistance forces. Uncle Ha returned home after the Liberation to see his family for the first time in twenty years. His mother had always maintained that her son was first and foremost a patriot. Their reunion was a godsend for me.

"You should try to eat more vegetables," he said.

"Vegetables?" I was confused. Prisoners did not get enough food.

"You have beriberi. I've seen many cases. It was a common condition for our Resistance fighters. Unless you get more vitamins, your face and legs will keep swelling, then your vital organs will break down."

I thanked him for the advice. "How is my wife? Is she well? The children?"

"They are all doing well."

"Did Anh come with you?"

"She's at the inn. Spouses are not allowed visitation. You know that."

"Oh, yes, I'm sorry. I forgot."

I realized he was telling me to be cautious. Even though he was probably one of the highest-ranking party members the locals had met, Uncle Ha was careful not to show any impropriety and had not requested to meet me privately without the proctor. These walls had ears. Perhaps he was afraid that I was foolish enough to blurt out something dangerous.

"Your wife asked me to explain to the local authority that you are a good citizen, and that you fled Saigon because you were afraid. You had no intention of leaving the country."

He was saying that I must stick to my original confession, harp along that line in every interrogation, and never deviate. I nodded and said, "Thank you, Uncle. Please tell my wife that the comrades here are treating me well and teaching me the importance of socialism. I am grateful for the opportunity to learn."

Uncle Ha wished me good luck and good health. Then without another word, he turned and left. I was touched because I knew he had a reputation of integrity and high morals. I wondered what made him decide to help me. My mother-in-law and I believe that Uncle

Ha, like many fighters of his generation who joined Viet Minh, was more a patriot than a Communist. Many high-ranking officials and party members of his age were not hardcore Communists. They had joined Ho's government to defeat a common enemy. They relinquished their political ideology until it was too late to do anything but become reluctant Communists.

When Uncle Ha went north, he left his mother and eldest daughter, Nga, behind in the care of my mother-in-law. Nga grew up and married a South Vietnamese lieutenant in the Special Forces. He was a decorated soldier who lost an eye in the war and was sent to a re-education camp after the fall of Saigon. Upon seeing Nga, who could not remember her long-absent father, Uncle Ha mobilized his considerable power and secured the release of his once-enemy son-in-law.

I thought of Aunt Thao's husband, my cousin Quyen, Uncle Ti, my adopted brother Vi, my best friend Hoi, and schoolmates from my village. Every person I knew had brothers, sons, cousins, or uncles on opposite sides of both wars: first the French, then the American. It was a conflict between brothers. No matter which side won, the family lost.

For several nights after Tin made his intention known, I stayed awake, eyes and ears trained on the dark spot where he lay ten feet from me. Night after night, he tossed and turned, but never left his sleeping mat. When I had thought his courage had surely deserted him, he vanished. I rose early one morning to go the latrine. Tin's place was vacant. Climbing up to the latrine set over the pond, I knew he was gone. I was the first one up, the only person at the latrine.

We never heard from Tin again. The guards made no announcements about their single escapee. They neither questioned nor punished us for his disappearance. From time to time, his name would come up in conversation, and someone would quip, "I bet Tin is in Thailand by now, drinking whisky and eating roast pork." It would stir up a round of chuckles and more speculations of marvelous things Tin could be doing at that very moment.

One by one, we fell victim to illness, accidents in the minefields, or the Viet Cong's trials. Some were pulled from our ranks without explanation. We never knew if they were released, sent to crueler camps, or executed. After they took Tung away, I often found myself looking to the creek. I could follow Tin to the Cambodian border, but I couldn't leave my family behind.

DURING one interrogation, I collapsed with a high fever. The inspector splashed water on my face, but couldn't revive me. Two prisoners carried me back to my quarters. Fellow cellmates nursed me with aspirin and penicillin from my stash of medicine. Three days and two nights I lay on the cold ground, wrapped in four layers of borrowed clothes, sweating, freezing, delirious. The body was ready, the spirit nearly there. Colleagues had fallen all around me, worthier men had perished, and I was learning to let go of my fears.

I thought of the Buddhist's third truth of existence: Death is a natural condition. There is no way to escape death.

In the long descent, I arrived finally at a place where what I had lost did not matter as much as what I had had, however briefly, in life. Here, I was free of bitterness and sorrow. Things, the essence of them, came to me, caressed me, entered and passed through me like familiar spirits.

Riding the border of sleep and wakefulness, I dreamt of the green fields of March, the yellow wind of summer harvests, the eternal gray of October rain, the blush of Hanoi winters, the gold foil on a champagne bottle buried in Tong Xuyen.

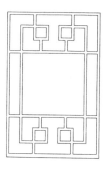

35 · FAREWELL, HANOI

When I first met him a year earlier, Lieutenant Gerard was a good-looking twenty-three-year-old. He strode into our inn, a tall, fair, and bespectacled young man, confident and full of promise. He struck me more as a scholar than a soldier. In fact, Gerard did enjoy reading and had borrowed many French volumes from our library during the dozen times he stayed here. But the war and his part in it had changed him. The longer he stayed in Vietnam, the less he read, and the more he smoked and drank. In the final days of the French occupation, he was wounded and discharged from service, a veteran and a wreck of a man at twenty-four.

"What will you do?" Gerard asked me in French, the morning he was due to be shipped back to France. He was slouching on a stool, his chest against the bar. He pushed his glass across to me.

"Go south," I said and poured him his fifth whisky of the morning. "We've lived under the Viet Minh once; we won't do it again."

"The inn?"

I shrugged. *"My relatives will take care of it."*

"After we're gone," he said, meaning the French, *"who are you going practice your French with?"*

I canted my head in that French manner of ambiguous acknowledgment without conceding a point. I didn't bother mentioning that I would probably no longer need a language that I had spent more than ten years learning.

"I'll miss our conversations," he said, looking into his half-empty glass. Gerard had expressive eyes, and I could tell he was referring to something else. The days of the empire were ending, and so with it the opportunities for French commoners to rise above their class by going to the colonies.

"Merci, monsieur."

"You should go to France. A man can not consider himself civilized until he has seen Paris," Gerard declared with a magnanimous wave of his hand. *"Come with me."*

He was joking. Playing along, I protested, *"Monsieur, what would I do for work?"*

"France is full of Annamites."

I smiled. Although "Annamites" meant "the people south of China," I somehow never got used to the tone in the way the French used the term. It sounded derogatory in my ears. They called our land "Indochine," but I had never heard a Frenchman used the proper term "Indochinoise."

He continued, *"There are plenty of jobs for your countrymen."*

Indeed, I aspired to go to college in order to be a servant in France. Surely he must have remembered that only recently did France repeal the law requiring the highest paid colonial subject to be paid less than the lowest paid French worker. A Vietnamese professor's salary had to be lower than a French janitor's wage at the same university. For a Vietnamese, France held little promise, certainly in my lifetime.

"Ah, Monsieur, but where would I find a girl?"

He jutted out his lower lip and shrugged. *"Whores are every-where. Some go with Annamites."*

For a French soldier, Gerard was not a bad sort. I liked him. One simply had to learn to be deaf when convenient. Gerard had come here directly from the hospital, hoping to convalesce in the arms of a woman. He was looking for Yen, one of the working girls he had seen regularly. I told him she went back to her village to find her family. Many refugees had left the city since the government de-clared a ceasefire. The last two nights, he was the inn's only guest. He was drunk the whole time, shouting to no one in particular: *"C'est la vie! They abandon you when you need them most."* It was impossible to tell if he was referring to the girl or the French army.

I took the good whisky bottle from beneath the bar and filled his glass to the rim. *"On the house, monsieur."*

"You're a good man, Thong."

"Merci, monsieur." I raised my glass of grenadine to avoid his eyes.

It was no easy task managing the halfway house to hell. The last few months had been particularly bad. The French knew they were losing the war. Both the French regulars and the legionnaires be-haved as though it was the end of the world. Those with orders to go to the front caroused as if they did not expect to return. The conva-lescing wounded on their way home to France poisoned themselves with alcohol binges. Soldiers spent money like barons. They drank, fought, and beat the girls with a vehemence I had not seen before. Then Dien Bien Phu fell, sending a palpable shudder through the French population in Hanoi. But it was more than that. It was the death knell of the French empire of Indochina.

Secretly, I was proud that the Resistance had defeated the French against horrendous odds. And I was also devastated that my family would lose our life of comfort and all our worldly belongings because of it.

Cung came into the lounge and said, *"Monsieur's taxi is ready."*

Cung took the suitcase. I held the stool for Gerard as he struggled onto his one good leg. The other had been recently amputated below the knee. His face reddened with the effort and his hands shook. We walked him slowly out the gate. On the shady sidewalk, old man Nghi was still in his kiosk selling his icy pickled lemonade. Gerard glanced at the tables where the girls and their pimps usually sat waiting for customers. All gone.

He sighed, then hobbled the rest of the way to the curb. We helped him into the cab. Gerard sank into the seat, head lolling backward against the cushion. *"Bon voyage, Lieutenant,"* I said. His eyes were closed. The young lieutenant neither looked at me nor said good-bye. Indochina had already faded for him.

I locked the gates, feeling more carefree than I had felt in a long time. Hoa Inn was closed. Its last French guest had checked out.

THAT evening Father took the family to La Maison, his favorite French restaurant. The Vietnamese owner was an old acquaintance. We dressed formally—the last time we wore our tailored suits, which would be left along with everything we owned in Hanoi when we went south. The restaurant's specialty was a superlative bouillabaisse. French expatriates and rich Vietnamese filled the tables. They drank and dined, laughing as though nothing had changed. Father called for champagne. Even Hung and Hong were allowed sips. Father raised his glass, and we raised ours. There was no toast. Father smiled. His hair was combed and slicked back, a dated style he had carried over from his younger years. Father was thin, but straight-backed. The opium's toll was not yet visible on him. He was a debonair and striking man just past his prime at thirty-six.

At home, we gathered in the lounge. Father announced that Uncle Chinh would manage the villa with the current staff. We were to pack one small valise each. Everything else must be left behind. Father had registered our family and his new in-law's family for airplane transport to Saigon the day after tomorrow. My mother's side of the family, Aunt Thuan's family, and nearly all of my relatives were due to follow us within weeks. My cousin Lang would go with Aunt Thuan's family, but his mother would stay behind to safeguard the clan's interests. It was the greatest of her many sacrifices for the greater good of the clan and harmony of her family, one with a terrible price that she would pay for the rest of her life. Father's younger sister, Aunt Thao, also chose to stay. Her husband, a former clerk, was now a ranking Communist party member.

I walked through the empty inn. There was nothing I wanted to take. The villa had been in our family as long as I could remember. As a toddler, I had played in these rooms; I knew their every nook. I remembered Father's famous parties, afternoon teas in the garden, my mother hosting dinners for relatives. But now these rooms also bore the markings of foreign soldiers and cheap sex. I went down to the bar and mixed myself a glass of grenadine. The villa was wonderfully silent. No music, no raucous games, no shouting. No drunken soldiers. At last, it was over.

A light was on in Father's room. I came to the door. He was sitting on his divan, a suitcase open next to him; inside a single change of clothes and stacks of loose photos. Father looked up and motioned for me to join him. He went to the cabinet and took out his opium apparatuses arranged on a tray inlaid with mother of pearl.

He picked up the pipe and handed it to me. It was the color of a dark plum. "It's *truc* bamboo."

"It looks like lacquered wood."

"It's a polishing treatment the old craftsmen used. *Truc* is lighter and never cracks like wood. See how perfectly the end ivory pieces flow into the bamboo? Slim and graceful." He handed me a thin brown bottle the hue of chicken liver. "Look at the opening on the bottle; it's all silver."

"Instead of nickel?"

"Instead of copper. This is a special type of clay from China. It's baked to be thin and very light so your arm won't get tired holding it. Clay won't crack like the enamel of ceramic. Over time, opium sap will creep into the cracks and make a ceramic bottle ugly. Can you tell that the lamp is also very expensive? Both the shade and the oil pot are crystal, and the base is silver."

I asked him if they were antiques. He said they were from my grandfather's generation. I glanced around his room at the other luxuries he could have taken: tailored suits, watches, imported hats, antique porcelain, paintings, and priceless poem scrolls. In the third drawer of his dresser were his silk mandarin robe and headdress, the official ensemble he had proudly worn at public functions in Tong Xuyen. I asked him how much his opium kit would fetch on the market. Father flinched and replied that people never parted with such items unless they were in very dire straits.

He was sharing with me his most treasured possessions—the things he would keep until the day he died.

It was our last day in Hanoi. Tan and I rented two Motobecane motorcycles—we could have bought them. Our pockets were stuffed with rolls and wads of French piasters, notes that would soon be worthless. We cruised around the city, looping through one district after another, visiting all our favorite haunts. The French were vacating their neighborhoods. The regal mansions looked desolate. The rest of the city was bustling, restaurants and shops thriving. Peasants streamed into Hanoi by the busload looking for missing family members separated by years of war.

At the new open-air market, prospective émigrés sold all their belongings. Normally secondhand stores handled such goods, but there was no time. Folks laid the entire contents of their homes on the ground: clothes, mirrors, combs, dishes, pots, pans, furniture, bedding, souvenirs, and knickknacks. One could almost read people's lives in the things they laid on the ground for sale at ridiculously low prices. It was a bizarre essay of desperation, these spoils of war.

I saw a spyglass and heaps of books I'd wanted to own. Tan wanted to buy a Japanese sword, but he knew he could never take it on the plane. We had more money than we could spend in months, but what was the point? It was like showing up at a feast where we weren't allowed to eat.

Bargains could be had throughout the city. Stores slashed prices to reduce their inventory. The wealthy liquidated their assets. Luxury items suddenly became very cheap. Those who weren't emigrating south were on shopping sprees. Even the poor did their share of window-shopping. Homes went for a third of their purchase prices. Mansions cost no more than an ordinary shop house, but there were few takers. The future was too uncertain for big investments.

Dealers went door-to-door, inquiring if the inhabitants were leaving, hoping to buy anything at a steep discount. Others came with offers to pack and ship émigrés' belongings south. Agents competed to be caretakers of homes and businesses. Hanoi took on a frenzied, almost festive atmosphere for those who stayed.

A week before, four village elders from Tong Xuyen had made the long trip to Hanoi to convince my father that his ancestral land still belonged to him. They urged him to stay; however, if Father were determined to leave, they would gladly, for a healthy percentage, be the leasing agents for his land. They had brought the same offer to Aunt Thuan in Hung Yen. She had also left the ancestral estate with her children to live with her relatives in the French-controlled area. Father treated them well and said that he was undecided. He knew the Communists had sent them and worried that they might try to stop him from going south.

Father had anticipated much of this. His foresight saved us from the madness and disaster awaiting those who evacuated later. The time would come when the Communists would rally the populace to physically halt the exodus of hundreds of thousands to the South.

OUR favorite restaurant on Umbrella Street was packed with a well-to-do lunch crowd. Tan and I waited for a table near the front so we could have a view of the pair of pretty sisters selling umbrellas just outside the restaurant. In the two years we had been coming here, neither of us had the courage to talk to them. It seemed silly to try now.

Instead of sharing as usual, we each had an order of *cha ca,* a northern delicacy we were unlikely to encounter in the South. A waiter brought us two platters of raw sea bass filleted paper-thin and heaps of fresh lettuce, vegetables, pickles, cucumbers, and herbs. The cook followed with a sizzling pan of turmeric and garlic oil. He cooked the fish by pouring the hot oil directly on it. The fragrance of garlic and fish was heady. We chopsticked pieces of fish onto sesame crackers and topped them with basil, cilantro, lettuce, purple herbs, and a dab of an ash-colored sauce made with fermented fish, fish sauce, chili, lime, and garlic. We quenched ourselves with liters of icy beer.

"I heard the weather in the South is much hotter than here. They might not have *cha ca* in Saigon," Tan muttered ruefully as he stacked another sesame cracker.

"Then there will be a lot of good ice cream," I reasoned.

"They say Saigon is like the Paris of Indochina. There should be plenty of good French restaurants."

"I don't know if we will have money for French restaurants."

Tan sighed. "We may have to quit school and work."

"Oh, don't say that! I want to go to college," I moaned. "Please, just enjoy your fish. We may never get to eat real *cha ca* again."

We never did.

WE rode down to West Lake and rented two boats. I lured Tan into a race. We sped up for a few lengths and then abandoned the game. Neither of us was in the mood. I sculled out to the middle of the lake and lay down at the bottom of my boat. It was hard to imagine that I would never see this place again.

Disheartened, we returned the boats. We went to Lake Nghi Tam, where we had swum every summer since we moved to Hanoi, but once there, we didn't feel like swimming. We sat on the shore and watched bathers splashing in the shallows. Somehow the view had changed completely. It was as if a silk screen had been drawn between it and us. The lake was no longer ours. We got back on the motorcycles and rode to the city stadium where we used to run and lift weights. The muscle boys were still sweating and grunting over the irons.

Tan declared to the bunch, "Please, boys, hold the tears! Just thought we'd come and tell you we're going south where the food is tastier and the girls are spicier."

"Fool, you've got it backward!" one guy retorted. The whole place hooted with laughter, and the banter started.

"Ah, Tan, you've been exercising that mouth of yours again."

"There's no smoke and you're already running from the fire."

"Deserters! You're leaving us here to clean up the mess?"

"That's fine, have your vacation," shouted another. "We'll see you in a few months."

"*Au revoir! Bon voyage*, cowards! See you in the next life." They all laughed.

Not one of our friends' families had planned to leave. It was the strangest farewell.

WE took the main road out of the city, the throaty single-cylinders hailing our passage. We needed to fly, to feel the planet pass beneath us. I glanced at Tan. He smiled, his eyes saying it all. We were losing our fortunes, our ancestral fiefdoms. First sons, we would be lords and barons no more. Side by side, we hammered down the impossibly straight highway, throttles wide open, engines howling at their limits.

The sun dipped low on the horizon. Miles from the city, we didn't want to turn around. For us at that moment, all the great avenues led away from Hanoi. In youth, motion was everything. We roared through the sunset, unimpeded. The flaming sky turned inky, but we pressed onward, it mattered not where. Behind us, the graves of our mothers, the homes of our forefathers, the fishponds of our childhood, the famine, the wars, the vulgar legionnaires, the soldiers and their whores, my dumpling-cheek peasant girl.

The farther we went, the easier it became. The twilight wind watered my eyes. Something within shattered. So much to lose, and yet before us, all the unlived years of our lives, a whole new world.

I was too young to understand the first taste of dignity and freedom.

36. THE RELEASE

The overloaded bus squeaked to a halt at the river-
bank. Exhausted passengers stumbled down onto the
copper-tinted dirt. The dockside clamor of vendors and
livestock was overwhelming. We were late. The rickety
ferry had eased into the wide creamy currents, leaving
a wake of coiling butterscotch and a streaming scarf of
black smoke. On the bank, the stench of the jungle and
shanty decay stewed under a wavering sky of pure heat.

This was my rebirth. I caught a glimpse of myself in a shop window and saw the image of my father
decades earlier looking back at me—that shadow of a
man the French had released, the emaciated body, the
sun-charred face, the cracked lips, the sunken red eyes,
wrinkles as deep as scars. Barefoot and penniless, we
were equally impoverished across a generation.

In the pocket of my pajamas was my release paper.
Last night, I went to sleep not knowing that today I
would feel the breeze of the Mekong on my skin.

I owed my life and freedom to Uncle Ha, who had

placed himself in considerable risk on my behalf. We met only once, when he visited me at Minh Luong Prison. He had called in favors to secure my parole. During his first visit with Anh at our house in Saigon, he had sat in my study, perused my bookshelves, and read the quotes I had taped to the walls. He had told Anh that even though he had never met me, he judged me worthy of his help. He had pointed to a line from Voltaire above my desk: *"The comfort of the rich rests upon an abundance of the poor."*

The assistant warden had asked me in the last interview if I had learned my lesson, if had I changed my behavior, if I had decided to become an honest person, if I had repented.

He knew nothing. What was my crime?

Seven months of psychological torture, brainwashing, brutal imprisonment, starvation, physical abuse, and hard labor had not changed my confession: I was a draft-exempted teacher who, in fear, had fled from Saigon without any intention of leaving the country. I had wanted to ask him for which part should I repent? That I was a teacher or that I had fled Saigon?

I wanted to dance, laugh, howl like a madman. I stood in the dirt under the full weight of the sun. I was ill, lice-ridden, shrunken, no better than a beggar, but I knew two things with certainty: First, absolute power did, indeed, corrupt absolutely, regardless of race or political ideology. Second, I would risk prison and death all over again to escape the Viet Cong's brand of communism.

I FOUND my benefactor, Mr. Tu Sanh, standing in the shade of a diner on the riverbank. Mr. Sanh was in his late sixties with salt-and-pepper hair and a weathered face that had known the sun for a lifetime. He wore clean peasant pajamas and sandals made of used car tires. Earlier this morning, he had overheard me pleading with an unsympathetic ticket agent for a fee waiver. I had just been released from jail and had no money. I was terrified of being caught sleeping on the street at night and imprisoned again. I needed to get home and report to the neighborhood constable the following day or I would be violating my parole.

"Mr. Sanh, I want to thank you again for buying me the ticket. I don't know what I would have done. I didn't know how I was going to get home," I gushed. I couldn't help myself. I had spent the whole time standing at the back of the bus. His seat was up front. I hadn't had a chance to thank him properly.

"It's nothing. We all need help sometime."

"May I have your daughter's address in Saigon? I would like to repay your kindness."

"Don't worry about that. Someday you will have a chance to help someone else."

"I will. Still, I'd like to repay you."

He steadfastly declined and invited me to lunch. I said I couldn't impose on him any further, but he was very sincere in his insistence. The smell of grilled pork was irresistible. We joined other passengers under the tin shade of the shack diner. A grinning woman with curly hair served us two beautiful plates of white rice heaped with stir-fried morning glories and grilled pork ribs marinated in fish sauce and garlic. I never prayed before a meal, but this time I thanked Buddha and my mother's spirit.

Mr. Sanh was a landowner, but his holdings were not large enough to be targeted by the Communists' land redistribution program. He was going into Saigon to see his daughter and grandchildren. Her husband was a former South Vietnam government official, which meant that they suffered discrimination and persecution under the Communist regime. Mr. Sanh asked about my background. I told him my family had also been landowners in the North, but we lost everything in the French War.

"Were you in the army?"

The food turned sour in my mouth. Was he a spy? Could I repay his generosity with a lie? I searched his eyes. It was a matter of decency. For the first time since I was captured, I said, "I was in the army."

For the kindness of a stranger, I surrendered the single secret that could cost me my life.

The old man nodded solemnly, picked up the tin pot, and refilled my cup. I nearly wept as I accepted the tea. I savored the meal he bought me. Grilled pork ribs had never tasted better.

"Mr. Sanh, do you have other children?"

"I had a son. He would have been forty-four this year—just a little older than you." He smiled. "He joined the Resistance in 1950. There was so much national pride at that time. After the Geneva Accord, my son went north with many young men from our village." The old man canted his head, looking out on the long expanse of the river. His eyes had gone watery with age. "He died early on in the American War."

The ferry horn sounded. We rose. He grasped my hand and said, "Take care of your family. There are hard times ahead. Beware. The best of luck to you, son."

My throat felt swollen. I could not find the words to thank him, to comfort him. I bowed deeply. I wanted to remember the gnarled contours of his bony farmer's fingers. The weight of our tragedy, its horrific immensity so vast I dared not peer into its depth.

It wasn't over; not for my people, not for me.

This river led to the sea. Could it take away all the poison, all the hate in this land?

There was no safe shelter left. Nothing here beneath the eaves of heaven remained untouched by war.

I could feel the pull of the ocean, violent and unforgiving—that dark expanse of wind and waves I must cross with my wife and children. For life, I must risk everything precious to me yet again. May the gods be merciful. May our ancestors watch over us.

The bitterness was but an aftertaste. Freedom, however precarious, remained very sweet. My final journey had just begun.

BIBLIOGRAPHY

Bates, Milton J. (compiler); Lawrence Lichty (compiler); Paul Miles
(compiler); Ronald H. Spector (compiler); Marilyn Young (compiler).
Reporting Vietnam: American Journalism 1959–1969 (Part One).
Library of America, 1984.

Jamieson, Neil L. *Understanding Vietnam.* University of California
Press, 1995.

Karnow, Stanley. *Vietnam: A History.* Penguin, 1997.

Oberdorfer, Don. *Tet!: The Turning Point in the Vietnam War.* Johns
Hopkins University Press, 2001.

Young, Marilyn B. *The Vietnam Wars 1945–1990.* HarperPerennial,
1991.

ACKNOWLEDGMENTS

This project began as a short story about the games my father had played in the countryside as a child. It only became a book through his generosity, dedication, and good intentions. I thank him for everything, for his trust, for this opportunity to know him.

For their invaluable contributions, I'd like to thank my readers, Mark Pomeroy, Elizabeth McKenzie, and Sue Lawton. Writing is a long, lonesome journey. It's a pleasure to be in the company of such fine writers.

My agent, Jandy Nelson, has been a dear friend, confidante, deft reader, and brilliant champion in every way. She is without equal. Many, many warm thanks.

Once again, it has been a privilege to work with my editor, John Glusman. I am very grateful for his confidence in my endeavors.

For being a friend to a stranger, my heartfelt gratitude to Dr. Ted Achacoso.

For their generous support, I'd like to thank QPB, OBA Literary Arts, Kiriyama Prize, and the Whiting Foundation.

ABOUT THE AUTHOR

ANDREW X. PHAM is the author of the memoir *Catfish and Mandala: A Two-Wheeled Voyage Through the Landscape and Memory of Vietnam,* which won the Kiriyama Pacific Rim Award, and the translator of *Last Night I Dreamed of Peace: The Diary of Dang Thuy Tram.* He is the recipient of a Whiting Award and lives in Hawaii.